My Life
LI NA

Li Na was born in Wuhan, China, and started playing tennis at seven years old. She joined the national team at fourteen and turned professional two years later. She left the national team in 2008 to pursue an independent career, becoming one of the first Chinese athletes to do so. In June 2011, Li Na won the French Open and became the first tennis player representing an Asian country to win a Grand Slam singles title. She continues to dominate professional women's tennis and consistently ranks within the top ten.

My Life
LI NA

Translated from the Chinese by
Shelly Bryant

VIKING
an imprint of
PENGUIN BOOKS

VIKING

Published by the Penguin Group
Penguin Group (Australia)
707 Collins Street, Melbourne, Victoria 3008, Australia
(a division of Penguin Australia Pty Ltd)
Penguin Group (USA) Inc.
375 Hudson Street, New York, New York 10014, USA
Penguin Group (Canada)
90 Eglinton Avenue East, Suite 700, Toronto, Canada ON M4P 2Y3
(a division of Penguin Canada Books Inc.)
Penguin Books Ltd
80 Strand, London WC2R 0RL, England
Penguin Ireland
25 St Stephen's Green, Dublin 2, Ireland
(a division of Penguin Books Ltd)
Penguin Books India Pvt Ltd
11 Community Centre, Panchsheel Park, New Delhi 110 017, India
Penguin Group (NZ)
67 Apollo Drive, Rosedale, Auckland 0632, New Zealand
(a division of Penguin New Zealand Pty Ltd)
Penguin Books (South Africa) (Pty) Ltd
Rosebank Office Park, Block D, 181 Jan Smuts Avenue, Parktown North, Johannesburg 2196, South Africa
Penguin (Beijing) Ltd
7F, Tower B, Jiaming Center, 27 East Third Ring Road North, Chaoyang District, Beijing 100020, China.
Penguin Books Ltd, Registered Offices: 80 Strand, London WC2R 0RL, England

First published in Chinese as *Du Zi Shang Chang* by Penguin (Beijing) Ltd in association with China Citic Press, 2012
This edition published by Penguin Group (Australia) in association with Penguin (Beijing) Ltd, 2014

10 9 8 7 6 5 4 3 2

Text copyright © Li Na, 2012
Translated from the Chinese by Shelly Bryant

The moral right of the author has been asserted

Cover design by Suo Di © Penguin Group (Australia)
Front and back cover images by Kubinska & Hofmann © Penguin Group (Australia)
Text design by Steffan Leyshon-Jones © Penguin Group (Australia)
Printed and bound in Australia by Griffin Press

National Library of Australia
Cataloguing-in-Publication data:
Li, Na, 1982- author.
Li Na: my life written by Li Na; translated by Shelly Bryant.
9780143800057 (paperback)
Li, Na, 1982-
Women tennis players -- China -- Biography.
Bryant, Shelly, translator.

796.34209252

penguin.com.au

To all my supporters

Contents

A Note on Chinese Usage and Names

In Chinese, a person's given name always follows their surname. Therefore, Li Na has the surname Li and the given name Na. Pinyin, the standard romanisation method for Chinese characters, has been used throughout the book.

My Life
LI NA

Preface

My Life in Tennis

My name is Li Na. I was born in Wuhan, a city that marks the seasons with a furnace-like summer and a freezing winter.

My name is an extraordinarily common one in China. (But it's very convenient when it comes to looking for your name in a tennis draw, because a name with only four letters is always the shortest.) Since my earliest memories, I've always felt that I was nobody special. If it weren't for winning the French Open and everything that it has brought me, I believe I would have gone to my grave feeling much the same.

I'm a professional tennis player. Of course, it was only in 2009 that I really entered the professional arena, so before that, it's more accurate to say I was a vocational athlete. A professional athlete and a vocational athlete must seem to most people to be practically the same thing, but to me they're completely different.

I have mixed feelings toward tennis. When I was young, it was my parents who wanted me to start training, and eventually I came to love it. I have fifteen years of experience, if you count my early training. In the first decade or more, I didn't enjoy tennis at all. It's only over the past few years that my understanding of the sport has steadily grown and deepened, and I've finally begun to enjoy the game and to really love the sport.

Tennis has brought me much more than just fame; it's brought me profound emotion. The joy I felt the first time I won a Women's Tennis Association championship; the nervousness of playing in a Grand Slam; the surreal feeling of being watched by more than ten thousand spectators as I walked nervously across centre court; the first time I spoke uncomfortably in English at an interview; the first time I saw an inaccurate report about me and suffered the hurt alone; the joy of hearing my coach say I could enter the ranks of the world's top twenty players; quietly applauding myself when I defeated a top ten player for the first time; the horror of undergoing surgery and the subsequent rehab, and wondering whether I would be able to continue my tennis career; the peace of mind I felt when I didn't have to worry about paying the team expenses; the pride I felt when I broke into the world's top ten; the first time I came close to a Grand Slam trophy and simultaneously felt the disappointment and the thirst for that top prize; the emotions I had when I held a Grand Slam trophy for the first time; the touching moment when I heard our national anthem in the middle of the court at the French Open; the first time I felt helpless to bear up under all of the pressure and stress . . .

All these and more are the most important treasures that tennis has brought to my life.

by Li Na, August 2012

Chapter 1

Morning in Paris

As a professional tennis player, I spend most of each year globetrotting. In January, I travel with my team to Australia to compete in the Sydney International and the Australian Open. The Australian Open, one of the world's four Grand Slams, boasts a long history, but it's still the youngest of the Grand Slams. It lasts for about two weeks and is the first Grand Slam of the year.

In February, I usually hang out in Dubai and Doha, where there are two relatively large tournaments. I can adapt to the time change within a week. Then I fly to the US to take part in a pair of events in Indian Wells and Miami. Once that's over, it's April. I take a couple of weeks at this juncture to get adjusted to clay courts. During the clay-court season, I travel to Stuttgart, Rome, Madrid and Paris. As soon as this season comes to a close, competition on grass begins, and you know what that means: the Wimbledon championships in late June. Wimbledon is the oldest and most prestigious Grand Slam, but also the only one that's played on grass. When Wimbledon winds up, I might take two or three weeks to regroup for a trip to the US where I compete in a few tournaments, culminating in the US Open in late August. When that's done, I finally have a couple of weeks to unwind. Afterward, I fly to

Japan, where I play in Tokyo, then travel on to Beijing. When Women's Tennis Association competition ends in Beijing, the world's top eight players will be determined. This is how I spend each year.

It sounds exciting, doesn't it? All of the world's well-known cities, and the world's top players. But in reality, I haven't even been to the most famous attractions in most of these cities. From the airport, I'm whisked to the hotel. I spend all of my time each day training and competing, only to be taken straight back to the hotel to rest. After the match, I usually take the earliest flight possible, returning to my base to train, or travelling on to the venue of the next competition. The hotel room's always the same, no matter how much the designer has tried to transform each one into something unique. Somehow, there's a sort of coldness built into the structure of a hotel room that leaves you feeling detached.

When I awake in the morning, I often spend several entranced moments wondering exactly where I am. Miami or Madrid? Or perhaps Paris?

I glance at various spots in the room – Jiang Shan is still asleep, my gown for the French Open is on a clothes rack, bags large and small are in a heap on the floor next to the TV. I rub my eyes. Yes, that is the Suzanne Lenglen Cup standing beside the television: the lifelong dream of all female professional tennis players.

So, today I'm in Paris, and my impressions of the previous night aren't just some fleeting fantasy. I close my eyes. The images are still fresh in my memory: the applause, cheering, the referee's face filled with an encouraging smile. My team, wearing custom-made yellow T-shirts, sits on the sideline. The women's faces are all covered in tears. In the locker room after I'd won, Francesca Schiavone smiled and told me, 'Enjoy your time.' Was it really more than just a dream?

Jiang Shan wakes up. He's always been faster to reach the fully awake state than me. I ask softly, 'It's not a dream?'

'Of course not!' He embraces me. 'You're the best!'

I'm a little embarrassed by his rare statement of direct praise. But his comment makes me feel warm all over.

Yes, this is Paris. Today is 5 June 2011, and yesterday at the Roland Garros Stadium I became the French Open women's singles champion.

To be honest, until this morning, I was more or less in a daze. I still couldn't take in that I'd really won the championship.

In 1998, when I was an idealistic sixteen-year-old girl, a television station in Beijing interviewed me and asked what my biggest dream was. Standing in front of the camera, I tilted my sun-darkened face to the lens and said, 'My biggest dream? I hope I can be a top ten tennis player. I know it's extremely difficult, but I'll work hard.' God knows how much courage it took for me to make that statement back then. But now, I wish I could say one thing to that little girl: 'Hey! We made it!'

I was told that I was the first Asian woman to win a Grand Slam singles title. My world ranking leapt from seventh to fourth, surpassing Japan's Kimiko Date-Krumm to become the highest seeded woman in Asia. As I smiled and received everyone's congratulations, my mind was a blank. I knew that I'd won, but winning a championship should have felt better than this. When I'd lain on that clay surface after winning, I did feel a huge sense of accomplishment, but when the reporters swarmed me, I had nothing to say. They all said my performance was too calm, but in fact, I had no clear idea of the glory and honour attached to a Grand Slam title. Up to this point, it didn't feel so different from any of the other four championship titles I'd previously won. It seemed to me that the only difference lay in the prize money and media attention.

There were so many emotions flooding over me. I cannot describe the joy, the great relief, or even the feeling that I'd finally bought myself some breathing space with the media. I knew I would no longer see articles in print that referred to me merely as a bad-tempered, stubborn girl from Wuhan. Now I would at least be called a bad-tempered, stubborn girl from Wuhan who was a damn good tennis player.

But this wasn't the most important thing. To me, the greatest gift that victory brought was peace of mind. After the match, I didn't need to cover my face with a towel or hide in the locker room or bathroom while I wept. I would no longer need to hate myself for every little mistake. I would not have to continue torturing myself. I knew that my performance was passable. My internal referee would let me off the hook, for once.

'Li Na, this time you've done all right,' I said quietly to myself.

To my team and my agent, however, my victory clearly meant something else entirely. Over the next few days, my travel schedule was packed. The day before, I'd accepted an invitation to be interviewed by CNN, and in addition, this morning at ten a.m. I was to be interviewed by Sina's reporters for all the viewers back home. I jumped up and began my first day as the French Open champion.

The Sina reporters told me that during my match with Schiavone, a record number of Chinese viewers had watched the live televised event – about 116 million of them. So many? It seemed that tennis was slowly creeping into the lives of the Chinese public.

After the interview, I returned to the hotel for a little downtime, then headed out to the Champs-Elysées to do some promotion for my sponsor, Nike. One of Nike's staff, who's also an old friend of mine, Shi Ling, sat in the car with me, chatting as we drove along the Champs-Elysées. When the car reached the Nike Store, I could see nothing but the forms of the four hulking bodyguards who surrounded the car. I felt this was a little excessive. I'm just a tennis player after all.

But when the car door opened, I understood. Shi Ling was afraid we'd be crushed in the throng waiting at the store's entrance. She told me to wait a moment, then take her hand and we'd walk into the store together.

I nodded and then followed her into the store. There was a huge poster on display in the most prominent position. It was large enough to command the attention of everyone who entered. The face on the poster was mine, and the slogan below the image read, 'Movement changes everything!'

Since I was a teenager, Nike had been my sponsor. I'd seen many posters in its stores that displayed the faces of great players like Roger Federer, Rafael Nadal and Maria Sharapova. This time, I finally saw my own face . . . and it was really quite embarrassing, even though I knew it wasn't unreasonable.

I was in a bit of a daze. The initial joy of winning slowly receding, my mind flew to the grass of Wimbledon, and I got sick of the endless promotion. Frankly, even at this point in time, I still didn't have a firm grasp of what it meant to be the French Open champion. It was nothing like the excitement I'd earlier imagined. The victory seemed to have not actually changed much. Everything remained in its original orbit. *There's really not much to it,* I thought.

After the event, I asked my friends from Nike to come shopping with me in the flagship store of a famous brand on the Champs-Elysées; a good friend of mine back in China had asked me to buy a bag for her.

One of the Nike employees asked, 'Do you need us to clear the store?'

Assuming it was a joke, I said, 'Don't exaggerate!'

The store we visited on the Champs-Elysées is known for luxury, famed as 'the fashion centre' of Paris. I'd been there a few times before. The store has seven levels and is the brand's largest store in France. Every day, visitors from all over the world line up at its entrance. Asian tourists turn up in especially large numbers. Inside, every visitor enjoys the services of a private shopping guide, but each shopper can only buy two bags per passport. How could such a store possibly consider clearing an area for my private use? I had a good laugh.

When we arrived, I was surprised to see that a smiling clerk stood waiting to greet me. He said that as soon as they'd heard I was coming, they had specially arranged a VIP room for my use.

My God! I was shocked. I knew I'd won the French Open, but this was the flagship store of a famous luxury brand. I'd gone there with the typical tourist's mindset that I was on a pilgrimage to the mecca of consumerism, but I'd ended up receiving a royal welcome. It was flattering, and I can't deny that at that moment, I felt fantastic. This was the first time I came to understand the weight of the title I'd won.

Paris. It had truly become the City of Love for me.

Chapter 2

City of Love

Paris is an elegant city. It's a world-renowned capital of art and fashion. The River Seine winds its way through the city, giving it a poetic flavour. The months of May and June are the best season in Paris, when the climate is pleasant and the flowers are in bloom. Beneath clear skies, the Roland Garros Stadium is particularly beautiful. This venue, on the edge of western Paris's Bois de Boulogne, commemorates one of the legendary heroes of the French people, the pilot Roland Garros, who sacrificed his life during World War I. This is sacred ground in the hearts of tennis players and fans and is the most iconic of all clay courts.

Clay courts were one of the earliest playing fields for competitive tennis. Even though clay courts today are now rarely true clay – they're usually made from layers of crushed brick or shale – the properties of the clay court remain unchanged. It has greater elasticity than hard or grass courts, and the ball bounces higher. The spin is also greater, meaning that the ball is slower, so when the player is running and has to make sudden stops or turns, there's greater latitude for sliding. This puts higher demands on the athlete's stamina and physical agility.

It's difficult to win a championship on clay courts because you not only need well-rounded skills, but you also need to be exceptionally fit, very patient and extremely tenacious.

At the 1989 French Open, the seventeen-year-old American-born Chinese, Michael Chang, defeated several star players and won the championship, becoming the youngest singles champion in French Open history. He was also the first person of Asian descent to capture this honour.

In 2011, I entered the French Open as the number six seed. To tell the truth, I didn't expect too much from this tournament. I'd never played well on clay courts, preferring hard courts and mostly training and competing on them. The French Open was the one Grand Slam in which I'd never made it to the quarterfinals. A local reporter had asked me in a one-on-one interview before the event, 'How would you feel if you won the French Open?' I replied, 'Incredible.' In fact, I believed that I could win at least one of the four Grand Slam titles, but the French Open might be the last.

The beginning of the tournament wasn't easy for me. It took some time to adapt to the clay court, and the first two rounds were very difficult. Every time I felt my mood swing, I would look at my team in the box. One look from them, or perhaps a gesture, could renew my confidence. The most important person in the box was my husband, Jiang Shan, and in the course of the entire French Open, he left the courtside a total of three times.

The first time was during the first round when I played the Czech Barbora Zahlavova Strycova. At first, I thought the match would be a walkover, since I'd defeated her without difficulty at the Australian Open earlier in the year. But in the three short months that had passed she'd made a huge change in her game, practically becoming a new person and playing a fabulous game. We'd played one another many times, and we knew each other's character quite well. I remembered that Strycova was a girl who was easily shaken up, but that day she was very composed, her mood remaining steady. Moreover, she was able to return practically every ball. Though I won the first set 6–3, I was in constant danger in the second set. When it was 5–2, with the set within reach, I suddenly lost my next two service games, and my opponent tied it up. It was at this point that Jiang Shan couldn't sit there any longer. He got up and left the courtside.

Without Jiang Shan present, my mind grew strangely calm. I won the next game to take it to a tie-break, but then I lost two match points. In the end, I let my opponent score four points, and I eventually lost the set. I was particularly upset. I felt I'd been running up and down the court, looking foolish and ridiculous.

At the beginning of the third set, I felt too tired to go on, and my legs wouldn't move. I looked courtside and saw Jiang Shan, an unusually helpless expression on his face. It ignited a fire inside me, and I thought, *I've worked so hard on the court, put in so much effort. No matter what the score is, you, Jiang Shan, should use your body language to give me some encouragement!* By the time I finally won that third set, I was so tired that my whole body was limp. I thought, *Finally, this can end.*

On the court, the athletes and coaches cannot communicate. Sometimes as I'm playing, I go near Jiang Shan's box and yell a couple of times as a way of adjusting my mindset. Everyone has different habits. When I play, I don't like to shout – although the high-decibel shrieking of players like Maria Sharapova or Victoria Azarenka is said to be a way of regulating breathing, and also of releasing pressure.

My opponent for the second round was a new face, Silvia Soler-Espinosa. She was Spanish, and had scored an upset in the first round, defeating Elena Vesnina. I didn't know Soler-Espinosa at all. I had no impression of her. Before the match, I asked a lot of other players about her, hoping to pick up a few clues, but I didn't come up with anything.

The beginning of the match was difficult. She had a very good forehand, with a lot of power, and was quite a difficult player to deal with.

In the first set, I started out falling behind 0–3. Jiang Shan left the courtside, so he didn't see when I began to turn the tables. When he returned to the stadium, I took a deep breath and relaxed.

When I'm on the court, I especially hate for other people to call the shots. Those watching tennis and those playing may have quite different ideas about what will work. When you're on the court, you know what you need to do, but others don't know what you have in mind. Under intense pressure, I interpreted Jiang Shan's gestures as his trying to convey messages such as, 'How could you do that? Why are you doing this?' He was clearly not satisfied with my performance. My temper immediately flared and I thought, *You should go back out and forget about it!* Then I shouted at him a couple of times: 'Don't say anything!' He didn't move or gesture for the rest of the match.

As soon as I'd finished yelling at him, I felt refreshed and less stressed. I was back in the right frame of mind and won the set and then the match.

It seems that God intended to test me. From the fourth round onward, I began to encounter the hot contenders for the title. In the fourth round, I faced Petra Kvitova, then the number nine seed. She'd recently defeated me in the semifinals at the Madrid Open. I remembered her powerful, deep serves. Almost every one of them hit over 180 kilometres per hour.

I couldn't break her serve at all. When I made just the slightest mistake, she broke mine. I quickly lost the first set 2–6. I decided that no matter what, I just had to get past her serve. I couldn't let her get comfortable with it. When I started to pay more attention to my serves and returns, my opponent's serve became less lethal. I clawed back the second set, sending the match to a deciding set.

In the third set, my first serve was broken, making me struggle again. And once more, Jiang Shan left the stadium, unable to watch. To be honest, I didn't expect to be able to come back from a 0–3 deficit. I just kept telling myself, *It's only one break point. I just need to break her back, then I'll have a chance.*

Armed with this belief, I won three games to tie the score. To boost my own morale, when it was deuce in the sixth game, I shouted at myself, 'Come on, Li Na!' This phrase was like a clarion call to victory. Then I started to get on a roll and even managed to achieve a huge reversal by winning six games in a row. I don't know what happened. Maybe I was able to win six consecutive games because Jiang Shan had left the courtside.

After the match I joked with Jiang Shan, saying, 'You should leave the courtside more often. As soon as you leave, I start to win!'

Jiang Shan understands my feelings better than anyone else, and I understand him. I knew he wouldn't take to heart what I'd yelled on the court, because that was essentially just a way to calm myself down, a way of venting. When a match in which you once had a big lead suddenly turns, with your opponent easily regaining ground, you begin to feel incompetent and powerless. At such times, you need to communicate, and you need connection and help. But according to tennis rules, once the match has started, the players are prohibited from talking to anyone. Tennis is a game in which the individual must compete on her own.

Tennis is a lonely sport. You can't experience the sense of belonging that comes from having fought alongside your teammates. You know that everyone's watching you, so when you get bogged down, you can only crawl along under their watchful eyes. You have to put all your effort into finding solutions, even as you constantly curse yourself in your mind and host a sort of internal debate, looking for a crack in your opponent's serve. Of course, this is all on your shoulders alone. You can't even have any physical contact with your opponent. Your field comprises of the small boxes within those few white lines, a racket, and your own lonely and highly irritable mind. This sort of lingering, clinging solitude combined with waves of overwhelming pressure is enough to really drive a person mad.

When your opponent's attack is raging like a storm, and your own internal debate is raging without any answers, all you can do is vent your anger on yourself. Many tennis players find odd ways to give vent to their inner pressures – throwing rackets, screaming or raging at the line judges nearest to them.

Yelling at Jiang Shan is my catharsis. Courtside he will appear uncharacteristically gentle, understanding of all my crude, childish ways. Afterward, I offer neither explanation nor apology, because I know he understands why I did it.

Some of my friends tease him, saying he is my 'punching bag', and they ask if this makes him angry. He says very frankly, 'Not at all. I also play tennis, so I know what she's going through. When the match isn't going well, she feels helpless. When she feels helpless and alone, right there under the watchful eye of all her loved ones, she gets nervous. This is something that anyone would feel. She's not the only one: at moments like that, all athletes in the presence of their parents, children, friends, sponsors, coaches, or anyone else related to them – none of whom can help at that moment, even though they have high hopes – feel especially anxious. When Li Na feels this sort of anxiety, she projects it onto me, seeing me as equally nervous, and she earnestly wishes that I and all her other friends and relatives would leave the court. She isn't really directing those barbs at me. It's just that I'm the most suitable target. She knows I understand her. She knows I won't blame her. Actually, I can take all those emotions from the court. If she weren't stuck in that kind of extreme situation, I could sit beside the court, open a bottle of wine, drink, chat and even sing karaoke and it wouldn't affect her. So I just get up and leave. When I do, she's able to gradually calm down.

'Because tennis is confrontational, the mindsets of everyone involved in the match will fluctuate. When you're happy and every-thing is smooth sailing, you hope a lot of people are watching you, seeing you put your best foot forward. Everyone likes to put their best on display and to hide their weak points. When things go against Li Na on the court, she doesn't want her loved ones to see it all, and she shows it. Everyone's way of expressing these things is different, but the psychological aspects are fundamentally the same. Furthermore, some-times when you're going through a period of bad luck, you're desperate for something to change the present circumstances. To break out of the situation, you need a time-out – just like basketball.'

His friends asked him if he worries about me when he leaves, and whether he finds some spot to watch the action live. He replied, 'Of course I worry after I leave, but once I'm gone, I don't look for a big screen or television to watch her compete. It's not that I don't dare to watch, but that I'm confident she has the ability to turn things around. This sort of situation has come up many times, and she's not a kid. She's able to maintain control. I believe in her, and I know that she's excep-tional. She won't have any problems.'

Everything he said was what I wanted to say. Jiang Shan gets me. A reporter once flatteringly said, 'Fortunately, Chinese tennis has Li Na.' I thought, *That's not the whole picture. Fortunately, Li Na has Jiang Shan.*

Having played my way into the quarterfinals at the French Open, I be-gan to feel I'd slowly built up a sort of rapport with the clay court. I was able to get into the zone more quickly, and Jiang Shan no longer needed to hide off the court to allow me to play at my normal level.

I met the number four seed Victoria Azarenka in the quarterfinals. Azarenka is a really good player. Along with her powerful serve, she likes to shriek, as if giving some encouragement to the ball. After each shot she utters a sharp cry, her voice piercing through the stadium. Many players like to yell like this. Perhaps this is a spirited performance typical of the Western personality. I'm a little too reserved to cry out like that.

I was very cautious at the beginning of the match with Azarenka. We were both very careful to hold our serves. Right up until the tenth game, the score was tied 5–5, but in the eleventh game, I produced a beautiful backhand to break through to 6–5. Azarenka was clearly nervous, and she failed to hold her next service game. I won the first set 7–5.

Young as she was, Azarenka was an emotionally volatile player. During the second set she was very tenacious, even saving match point twice, but it wasn't enough. As we played, my confidence grew and I knew this match was mine. The clay court seemed like a haven to me. With each attack, the result was just what I wanted, and I felt like I was back in my childhood athletic stadium. The dazzling light of the midday sun glowed on the surface of the old school court, and the heat burned the thin soles of my Warrior-brand shoes.

I won the second set! I won in straight sets! I was going straight to the semifinals! I'd defeated Azarenka!

Jiang Shan's heart seemed to resonate with the joy in my own. He didn't need to seek refuge outside of the arena but sat in the box, smiling, as he watched the whole game.

I finally reached the semifinals, and my opponent was Maria Sharapova. We'd played each other many times before, so for me this match was mundane and not something to make a fuss about. But reporters, as they are prone to do, circled us like sharks smelling blood. They asked, 'Now that you're facing Sharapova, how do you feel?'

There was one thing getting them hot under the collar: Sharapova's current coach, Thomas Hogstedt, had been my coach not long before. Did the reporters want us to face off like boxers? If I followed Mike Tyson's example and bit my opponent's ear off, would they like me more?

Although it was just the semifinals, the media had already dubbed this a 'revenge match between Li Na and her coach'. I'd seen headlines in more than one newspaper that read, 'The Revenge of Li Na's Coach'. I thought this was quite funny.

Still, I must admit that Thomas was a good coach for Sharapova. Though Sharapova had never played well on clay courts before, she was very good this time. On clay, like all players who were used to competing on hard courts, Sharapova's power stroke was diminished. This self-effacing girl had once joked, 'When I get onto a clay court, I feel like a cow on ice skates.' But this time was different. Earlier, she'd easily defeated Germany's Andrea Petkovic 6–0, 6–3. Thomas had helped Sharapova discover a better serving style, and she was now able to offer high-speed serves without having to worry about her old shoulder injury. This, of course, made Sharapova's already powerful game even stronger, as if a tiger had sprouted wings.

Everyone knew that Sharapova yearned for a victory at the French Open. If she won the title, she would not only be champion here, but would have won titles at all four Grand Slams. She would be one of the legendary 'career Grand Slam winners'. Many in the media believed that Sharapova was the strongest contender for this year's French Open title.

We'd played one another seven times before this, and Sharapova had won five of those contests. Added to that, my former coach – who knew my strengths and weaknesses like the back of his hand – was in Sharapova's camp, giving her a distinct advantage. Everyone had broken out in a sweat on my behalf. I told one reporter that I had enough confidence in myself, as did Jiang Shan. No matter how strategic the coach's plan, once we got on the court, it was all in the hands of the players. I believed I had the ability to respond to the challenge.

To tell the truth, I never imagined I would reach the French Open semifinals. I told myself, *You've already surpassed your previous performances. This is the best you've ever done at the French Open. Now what you need to do is put all of your effort into enjoying the competition.*

But the warrior-like Li Na inside me was stirring, stoking the fire. Like a barren land thirsting for a timely rainfall, I experienced an unprecedented hankering for victory. On this same court, Michael Chang, a fellow 'descendant of the dragon' and my senior in tennis, had already created a spectacle. Would Lady Luck now favour me in the same way?

I won the first set 6–4. Sharapova fought back in the second set. She won three break points in the first game, winning it easily. But I made every effort to keep my own serve and tie the score up at 4–4.

In the crucial twelfth game, Sharapova seemed to lose some confidence when she double-faulted twice. I finally took the second set 7–5. This had been an unusually tough competition, but I prevailed. As with Azarenka, Sharapova tended to shriek encouragement to herself, but the previous match had already allowed me to adapt to such shouting. And anyway, I had my own special means of handling stress: I could yell at Jiang Shan.

Chapter 3

Showdown

Going into the finals, my opponent was Francesca Schiavone. This Italian player, the previous year's French Open women's singles champion, was invincible on clay. We'd faced each other four times before, the last time being the previous year's French Open when Schiavone defeated me. After that loss I'd been pretty depressed, and with no way to vent my disappointment I went crazy on a shopping spree, buying an expensive luxury-brand ring. I rarely wear it.

The champion of the French Open wins the Suzanne Lenglen Cup, named after one of the greatest female tennis players in history. Lenglen is my idol, a true heroine in my mind, and 2011 was the first time I'd been so close to her. My heart sang and my spirit cried out. The Li Na in the depths of my being was roaring. I knew that she and I both wanted this victory very badly.

I was a different player to the one who'd made it to the finals of the Australian Open in January that year. That was my first time to get within one step of a Grand Slam title, and I'd been very excited. I'd had little experience, but now I knew what to do. I needed to stay calm.

Schiavone was a respectable opponent, a veteran with excellent technique, superior defence and a tenacious style, and she was very flexible in her strategies. She was tough. Off the court, we were actually quite friendly, having much in common. We were both considered 'late bloomers' in tennis. I was twenty-nine years old, and Schiavone would soon be thirty-one. Before the tournament, as fifth and sixth seeds respectively, we hadn't been favourites to win. Our campaigns had been similar, and, for each of us, this was our second time in the final of a Grand Slam. The difference was that my Italian opponent already had one Grand Slam trophy in hand.

It was sunny on the day of the final. I took a proactive approach to the first set, trying to restrain Schiavone's momentum, and took it 6–4. But during the second set, she put up a fierce counterattack, causing me no small trouble. We drew all the way, going to a tie-breaker.

Victory was right in front of me! I felt my heart pounding. The 'hey!' that Schiavone uttered as she served couldn't mask the booming of my heart. This was the moment!

I scored well in the tie-break. Schiavone's pace was a little chaotic. We eventually ended with a score of 7–0, and I'd won the French Open. My heart was pounding as if it would break out of my chest. I couldn't do anything but lie on my back on the court. With the French sun pouring over my body, I covered my face with my hands. I really wanted to cry, but the tears wouldn't come.

Before the match, I'd thought privately about what sort of pose I might strike if I won, but when the moment of victory really came, I forgot all my ideas. At the end of the one hour and forty-eight minutes of play, I'd won the Suzanne Lenglen Cup.

I only lay on the clay for a second or so, then scrambled up. The most important thing was not to make Schiavone wait too long. A loss in the finals is hard to take. I'd lost before, and I knew how it felt. I got up from the ground and went to hug her. When I released her, I looked to the sidelines and saw them – all my team members, wearing yellow T-shirts, embracing each other excitedly. Jiang Shan, coach

Michael Mortensen, Shi Ling and Susan (Susan was responsible for managing all the women's tennis players) – they were all there, along with many others, and those fifty yellow Nike T-shirts were really quite eye-catching.

I didn't see their expressions clearly at the time. It was only when we had dinner together later that I had an opportunity to ask them about their reactions, since I'd not seen them myself. Their answers were all the same. They said, 'Li Na, you got up too fast!'

When I received the cup after the match, there was a small hiccup. The guest of honour, in some confusion, gave the mini replica of my trophy to Schiavone. There were two Suzanne Lenglen Cups on the court at the time, a big one for the courtside photos, and a small one that the champion takes home. The guest of honour mistook the smaller cup for the runner-up prize and so gave it to Schiavone. She whispered to me, 'That's wrong!' I was so happy that I said, 'It doesn't matter. Just take the photos – it's fine.'

After the awards ceremony, five teams of CCTV reporters interviewed me. They were especially excited and were choked up when they spoke, but I was all right. The initial excitement had passed, and now this was a game just like any other. But the people around me could hardly contain their elation. An online video shows a ball boy high-fiving me as I walked back to the locker room. While I was having a conversation with the referee there, I noticed a huge pile of fan mail on the sofa. I came out from the locker room and on the right, I saw my coach Michael Mortensen giving an interview. I went to hug him. He said, 'I'm so proud of you!' After I hugged Mortensen, I hugged Jiang Shan, and everyone around us kept encouraging us to kiss. After that, I hugged the Chinese women's team coach, Lu Lin, and Shi Ling. When I hugged Shi Ling, the tears began to flow, mostly because her face was already streaked with tears. In my acceptance speech, I'd spoken in Wuhan dialect to wish Shi Ling a happy birthday, and she'd been crying since then.

Back in the locker room, Susan came with me to help me dress and do my make-up for the post-match proceedings. I wasn't hungry at all, but she insisted that I eat something, because there would be a long press conference, followed by a urine test and then the photo session. Susan had brought a sandwich for me, but I had no appetite and couldn't eat.

After such a long contest, I was extremely tired. As I was changing my shoes, my legs began to cramp. But oddly, I felt neither exhausted nor hungry. I was still revelling in the thrill of victory.

I changed into my skirt and boots, then looked at the empty locker room in front of me. As I thought of the sea of people who had filled the room at the start of the French Open, I couldn't help but have mixed feelings. It was in this room that I saw the glory and dreams of so many players, as well as the laughter and tears. The longer we played, the smaller the numbers grew. When we reached the finals, only Schiavone and I were left, and now I was in the locker room, all alone.

Moments later, I had a magical experience. While I was in the lounge waiting for the press conference, Martina Navratilova (God! It was really her!) came to tell me, 'I've been there before, and I can tell you that this is the time you need to learn to say no, because everyone wants you. You need to choose for yourself, to create a protective barrier for yourself.'

I was stunned. Navratilova was one of the greatest players in tennis history. Her longevity in tennis was legendary. During her career she won eighteen (*eighteen!*) Grand Slam singles titles, and she was known as the 'Golden Woman' of tennis. She was fifty-four years old now, wearing a short-sleeved shirt and casual trousers, and looking elegant and refined. Her voice and appearance were impressive: she was very intelligent, without the least hint of aggressiveness, and she was trustworthy and willing to share her knowledge.

A few years earlier, before she retired in 2006, I'd seen her on the court. She ran over and asked me whether my surname was Li or Na.

Such a great woman asking an unknown player like me how to read my name was a little flattering. To my mind, someone like Navratilova was beyond reach – but here she was, speaking to me. It felt like we were old friends, without barriers of nationality or age. As well as the respect I already had for Navratilova, I felt a sense of intimacy with her.

Right before the press conference, Nike staff from China came running into the lounge and gave me a newly designed T-shirt to wear. Their flight from Beijing to Paris had just landed, and they'd been racing to get to the venue on time. I wore the T-shirt for the press conference, which lasted an incredible two hours. The reporters wore excited expressions. With a new champion from China, this could mean the opening of a new chapter for tennis in China, and even for all of Asia.

At first, all of the reporters asked questions at once. As I answered, I kept catching glimpses from the corner of my eye of the big trophy nearby. I'd just missed the championship trophy at the Australian Open in January. Today, on the Court Philippe Chatrier, I finally fulfilled my dream. When I eventually got to hold it, I nursed it as carefully as if it were an infant. A hard-earned infant.

After the conference, we went to the Eiffel Tower for a photo session. Outside the stadium there were many people carrying Chinese flags, waiting for me as I left. They wanted to take pictures with me, but I had to apologise – since I was rushing, I could only pose for a single photo with the whole group. When we got to the Eiffel Tower, another large group of reporters was there. The days are long in the European summer, and it was still bright at eight p.m. As I got ready to pose for photos, I noticed a newly married Chinese couple nearby. I heard the bride ask her new husband, 'Is that Li Na?'

Later, a friend told me that during the finals, the CCTV sports channel altered its live broadcast for two days straight to cover my matches. This news pleased me even more than my victory over Sharapova because it signalled that tennis was generating a greater interest among the Chinese public. The sport that I loved was gaining more attention and respect in the country that I loved, and it wasn't unrelated to my own effort.

I have strong feelings for tennis. I started playing at the age of eight, and right now almost all of my life is somehow tied up with tennis. I devoted a lot of effort and emotion to tennis, just like my father had devoted much of his hope and love to me. Unfortunately, when I was a child, my father left me too soon. Today, I finally reached the pinnacle of tennis.

And all I wanted to say was . . . *Dad, I made it.*

Chapter 4

Father

When I think of my father, I recall my childhood. My father is the warmest ray of sunlight in my childhood memories, the most refreshing consolation. Over the years, my father has been my source of strength. His death and the fact that I didn't get to see him one last time are the most painful scars buried deep in my heart.

When my father passed away, I was in Shenzhen playing in a youth tournament. No one told me that my father was dying, and no one told me the news of his death. My father's wish was that it be kept a secret from me because he was afraid it would affect my play.

After the tournament I took the train from Shenzhen to the city of Hankou in Wuhan where I lived. The sound of the train stopping was like a long sigh. Surprisingly, my mother didn't come to pick me up. Instead, it was my uncle, my father's younger brother. My uncle took me to eat, then took me back to my grandparents' house. The whole time he acted very naturally, as if nothing were out of the ordinary. When we arrived downstairs at my grandparents' house, I saw a wreath with my father's name on it.

I was fourteen at the time.

I don't have any idea how I reached the sixth floor of the house. I only remember that when I got there, I saw my father. He was lying flat, stomach bloated, face pale. Before his death, he was a very handsome man.

His portrait hung in the most prominent place in the room. The man in the photo looked at me, eyes kind and full of affection. Yet the black drape hanging heavily next to the picture was a shocking reminder that the person in the picture had passed on.

Seeing my father's body, I didn't dare reach out and touch him. Touching that cold body was like admitting that he was gone. In fact, for the next few years, I continued to fool myself into thinking that my father was just away travelling, and that he would eventually be back. I couldn't admit that he was really gone.

My mother didn't say anything when she saw me, but just sat there crying. My father had always managed every major event that happened at home. Now he was gone, and I felt like the sky had fallen in on me. I felt beaten, weighed down, but there was no pain, and I didn't cry. I stood there, numb, for a long time, until the uncle I'd been closest to since I was small came over to comfort me. That was when I began to cry. And once the tears started, they wouldn't stop.

Before, I'd always thought that growing up was a gradual process. But that day, I learned that people can grow up in a single moment. I thought, *From now on, I'll have to take responsibility for the family.*

My father was the first person to lead me on the road to sports. When he was young, he'd played for the Hubei provincial badminton team. Many years later, he would still occasionally talk about his days playing for the team. Every time he mentioned it, he became like a spirited boy all over again.

People of his generation went through a period of great social turmoil, and it was especially difficult to have the opportunity to play sports. Despite this, we were considered a sports family. My grandfather was a PE teacher for the Baoshan Street Elementary School. My father used to be a badminton player. We had several generations of sports lovers in our family.

My father was the oldest in his family and was not only tall and handsome, but also very smart. He was known as a happy man by everyone around him and was a pillar of the family. My father was the oldest son, and so bore the daily burden of family duties. The conditions of his home life were typical of any working-class family, but my father never refused anyone help.

He worked in sales at the Yangtze River Metal Products Factory. He travelled all year round, and the time he could spend with the family was limited, but when he was home, the atmosphere was cheerful and warm. He was an excellent conversationalist and had a huge store of riotous jokes. When I asked him to tell me a story, he would roll his eyes and come up with one on the spot, making me laugh so hard my stomach would hurt.

My father was not only eloquent but well versed in the art of living. He cooked competently, using the kitchen utensils deftly to create wonderful flavours. Before each business trip, he would steam a fish or stew a pot of meat so that when my mother got home from work, she need only cook some vegetables and dinner would be ready. There was always enough for my mother and me to eat for several days. On the rare occasions when my father had free time, he always wanted to play badminton. All of the appliances in the house and the clothes my mother and I wore were things my father brought back from his travels. They were pretty though not expensive. Even though his salary wasn't high, we lived a comfortable life.

When I was a baby I lived with my grandparents in nearby Wuchang. Both of my parents worked, so couldn't be my full-time caregivers. Many households leave the care of the children to the grandparents, fostering the children out in this way. After I turned four, I went back to Jianghan District to live with my parents.

At this age I had some baby fat, and my father wanted me to grow up healthy, so he took me running and taught me to play badminton. When we would take a break during our run, he would talk in a low voice about his days playing for the provincial team.

He'd been especially dedicated to badminton. At the time he'd fought his way onto the team, slogans about the educated youth being 'sent down' to the countryside to work were being shouted all over the country. My father's own family was very poor, and he had a younger brother to take care of, so he opted to be 'sent down' to Hanyang, thus losing his spot on the team. He figured the sooner he went, the sooner he could come home, work and earn money to support the family. After coming back, my father first went to work for the Second Light-Industry Board, then was transferred to the Yangtze River Metal Products Factory.

I've often asked myself whether my father's input into my training was motivated by his own thwarted boyhood sporting aspirations. I suspect he might have harboured a dream that I would be on the national badminton team.

I hated winter most. Our house in Wuhan didn't have central heating, and as soon as winter arrived, even the bedding felt cold and damp, and it was hard to get warm. Crawling out from the bed, I would be covered with goosebumps. It took a lot of determination to get up each morning.

Summer was also a trial. Wuhan has always been known as 'the oven city', and the difference between day and night temperatures isn't significant. Unfortunately, even in the morning it's boiling. I would stumble after my father through the streets, enjoying seeing the street vendors selling beancurd skins, sesame balls and dumplings. For a moment after the baskets of dumplings were opened, white steam would cover the face of the old stall vendor. I was also like a dumpling, my face covered in sweat, bright red and steaming.

Running in autumn, the plane trees would drop their seeds, and I would come home covered in a veil of them. My mother would scream and pull me outdoors to wipe them off. The seeds would slide down my collar and make me very itchy. My skin was so irritated by them that I would develop small pimples there.

Spring was the only time it was really comfortable to run. The grass beside the road was bright with dew, and the road was wet with a white mist. As my father and I ran, we would gradually awaken, our whole bodies covered with sweat by the time we got home, where my mother had a breakfast of milk and cake waiting for us. After that sweet treat, my father would take me to kindergarten.

Taking me to and from school was my father's job. The perch on the crossbar of his bicycle was my throne. But by the time I was five, I'd grown tall and could no longer fit there, so I had to move to a seat behind my father.

This height was what helped me start in the world of sport. A representative from the local amateur sports school visited the school where my grandfather worked, hoping to recruit students for the badminton team. My grandfather told him that his granddaughter was tall, so why not give her a try. My father took me to the interview, and soon I was training at the school. Students who are accepted into sports schools in China continue to attend classes at a normal school, but train and often live at the sports school. I would train at the amateur sports school while living with my parents and attending my normal primary school.

My memories of playing badminton are somewhat vague. I don't remember ever taking the court. Instead, I stood beside the court and practised my stroke. It was a very boring way to spend a day, but because I was small, I didn't take it too seriously. Anyway, I was a compliant child, and if the coach wanted me to practise my swing, then I obediently practised my swing.

The older students on the team weren't so obedient. The students here were more playful than students at ordinary schools, and often caused a lot of trouble. Fortunately, there were a dozen or so students in my class and my results were average, so I didn't attract the attention of the older players.

It seems that I wasn't fated to be a badminton player. To be good at badminton, you need a lot of wrist action, but I used the brute force of my arm, leaving the wrist action a little lacking. When children play, they just muddle along, not really caring about how well they do. My coach would sometimes look at me and say, 'Oh! Your wrist . . . What are we going to do with you?'

I didn't care. Sending me to school to learn to play badminton was my parents' idea. The only reason I played was because my father wanted me to.

At a time when people were deprived of material wealth, my father seemed willing to do anything at any cost for me. When I was four years old, my father asked a friend from Nanjing to help him buy a piano. That was because someone had praised the length of my fingers, saying they would be good for playing the piano. My father was very happy when he came home one day and found someone had delivered a piano to our house. When I was in a good mood, I would play for a while. When I was in a bad mood, I would refuse. Children are more interested in playing with their friends, so I would often stop practising in the middle of a piece and run outside to play games with the other kids.

From time to time, my mother urged me to play the piano. My father, on the other hand, left me alone, never forcing me to do anything. 'As long as you like it, that's fine,' he would say.

When I started playing badminton, I didn't practise the piano any more, so my father sold it. He never looked back or made any complaints. He quietly continued looking out for me and making sure I had the best.

I did well in class, especially in maths class. Maybe it was because I inherited my clerk mother's genes that I breezed through maths classes. I even attended the Maths Olympics class on my teacher's recommendation. I like maths because it's a logical, coherent curriculum. In the world of mathematics, everything operates according to fixed laws. It's like playing tennis. When you hit the ball, as long as you keep the point of contact back, it will result in a beautiful, flat stroke. A tennis ball never decides to change trajectory as it's flying over the net. It won't just turn around and fly back. Maths and tennis are no different. As long as you master the laws governing them and learn to work within those laws, you can use them to your advantage.

I didn't like language class. Writing a composition or summarising a central idea was boring. All of our essays had to somehow culminate with 'My name is red scarf' or 'This is such a meaningful day'. I didn't like these teaching methods – I didn't want to lie, even for the sake of a composition. Children lead simple lives, play every day, jumping about and being noisy. How much 'meaning' could there be in our lives? I couldn't find any. Every time I wrote on the green-lined paper of my composition book, 'This is such a meaningful day', I would feel like a liar. I usually only scored seventy or eighty per cent on language exams, much worse than my results in maths. Fortunately, my parents were fairly relaxed about my results in school. When I had to bring my exam papers home for my parents to sign, they just looked them over and signed them. I don't remember them ever saying things like, 'Other people's children scored this or that.' On this point I was very lucky compared to my peers.

Neither my appearance nor my results were particularly outstanding. Aside from my maths teacher, no one took me seriously. Both in the classroom and on the badminton court, I was dispensable.

If the tennis coach Xia Xiyao hadn't seen me soon after that, everything that's a part of my world today wouldn't have happened.

Sometimes I think, *If I'd not turned to tennis, where would I be today?* It's a question without an answer. The only thing I do know for sure is that my life would have been completely different.

The summer of my second year at the amateur sports school, the tennis coach Xia Xiyao came to scout, and she zoomed in on me as I practised my badminton swing. She thought I had good velocity and force, and Coach Xia suggested I stop training for badminton and join her for tennis instead. My badminton coach, Lin Shuhui, the one who'd said my wrist was dead, was delighted with this suggestion.

I was caught a little off guard. I'd been practising badminton for two years and hadn't expected this sudden diversion. What sort of sport was tennis? I hadn't heard of it. But I knew that students selected by the school coaches would enter specially focused classes. It was only by going to these more focused classes that you'd have a chance to be on the national team, so this should have been good news.

But changing from badminton to tennis was a big deal. Coach Xia asked me to bring my parents by to talk with her. At the same time, she wanted to see how tall my parents were. There were certain height requirements for tennis, and the most direct way to predict the height of younger players was to look at the height of their parents.

The next day, my parents and I stood before Coach Xia. We met at the Zhongshan Park tennis courts, and Coach Xia had quite a pleasant talk with my parents. To my surprise, they were very accepting of my moving from badminton to tennis, saying, 'Okay, no problem.'

My mother later admitted that she had always worried that the older kids on the badminton team would bully me. At the time, the badminton team wasn't strictly disciplined, and when the coaches weren't around, the older team members would make fun of the younger children. We younger ones had to do whatever the bigger kids said. My parents were thus very happy to let me go to the tennis team.

Coach Xia was satisfied with my parents' height. My father was 175 centimetres tall and my mother 166, both a little on the tall side for people from Hubei. When my bones were measured, the results suggested that I might grow to 172 centimetres, and the coach was very pleased with this.

In China in the 1980s, very few people had heard of tennis. At that time, the idols of the nation were the members of the women's volleyball team, Lang Ping, Sun Jinfang and Zhou Xiaolan. Table tennis was another popular sport, and the concrete ping-pong table at school was always surrounded by a crowd. We could hear the crisp drumming of the little white ball on the table all the time we were in class.

But tennis? Who knew what tennis was? When my family first started following tennis, they called it 'fuzz ball' because of the yellow-green fuzz on the tennis ball. The first time we went to Zhongshan Park to meet Coach Xia at the tennis court, we saw a lot of people playing 'fuzz ball', and it was totally unfamiliar. At that time, finding a court to play tennis on was very difficult, and there was rarely any tennis shown on television. Even in a large city like Wuhan, the number of people who knew anything about tennis was extremely small.

Coach Xia asked me, 'Are you afraid of spending time in the sun?' I said I wasn't, but also wondered why I should be afraid, since the sun was so far away. I suspect she was asking if I was afraid of getting too tanned. But she only said, 'That's good. The court is outdoors.'

And that's how I left the badminton team to start playing tennis. On the tennis court, I met many of my future teammates. They all had short hair and were tanned in a way that's now very popular, what we would call 'bronzed'.

Coach Xia said, 'If you want to get onto the school's team, you must first defeat one of my players.' My father clearly wanted me to make it onto the tennis team, so I knew I needed to defeat one of the bronzed players.

I began the arduous attempt; it didn't happen overnight. When I first started playing, I used to swing the racket vigorously, hoping to land the ball where my opponent least expected it. But no matter how much force I used or how fiercely I served, the return from the other side of the net was faster and more ferocious. The yellow-green ball flew as fast as a meteor, and I had to keep running just to receive it.

Many years later, I still often dream of the tennis courts where we practised and of that first day I set foot on the tennis court. I remember the way the serve roared down from a height, sometimes rushing to a far away place, and sometimes right into my own body. I had to swing the racket early, stopping the ball before it could show its power, changing its course, keeping it under my control and letting it know that on this court, I was the winner.

I appreciated the strict training of Coach Xia. Competing with players older and more experienced than me might have been very difficult, but it pushed me to fully concentrate, and this was good mental exercise for me. It also improved my play rapidly. A couple of months after I started training, Coach Xia said to my father, 'This kid is pretty good. Let her board at school so we can make sure that things proceed smoothly.'

The meaning behind her words was that I was quite valuable. She was afraid I would be snatched away by other schools. Qualified players would sometimes be 'closed in on' by other coaches.

My parents were not the least bit reluctant. The coach valued me, and that was a good thing. My father put my luggage on his bicycle rack, and I followed him in a daze to the dorms at the sports school. I was eight years old, the amateur sports school's youngest boarder.

My dorm was on the second floor of a simple building near the tennis court. You could see the stadium from our room. A dozen or so children all lived in a big room, everyone sleeping on bunk beds. We weren't all chosen for the same sport. Besides tennis players, there were others who practised fencing or track and field. I happily looked around my new, large home, thinking how wonderful it was that there were so many other children to play with.

My parents got me settled in and then left. I went to the court alone to see the teammates I'd made friends with. I happily told them about moving into my new home, and this sense of pleasure lasted until just before I went to bed. As I lay there, I was suddenly terrified. How was I going to sleep alone? Where had my mother and father gone?

It was only then that I realised that I'd left home to live on my own.

At the sports school, we were under very strict supervision. Each day, as soon as I finished my studies at my normal school nearby, I had to go to training. Only my evenings were free. Even though my parents lived only four bus stops away, I could only go home once a week, and for just one night at a time. The weekend system hadn't yet been implemented in China, so my parents would pick me up after training on Saturday afternoon, and then I had to rejoin the team by nine o'clock Sunday evening. The highlight of my week was when my father picked me up on Saturday; I knew that he missed me a lot. He would collect me on his bicycle after my training, and I could tell him about how difficult my day had been.

My only comfort during the week was that my mother took the bus (about a twenty-minute ride) to the sports school every evening, rain or shine, to help me with my schoolwork. Those were the happiest moments of each day. Sometimes, if she arrived late, I would stand on the balcony, resolutely watching the front gate. I wouldn't leave until my mother arrived.

She always brought me a few of my favourite snacks. While I ate, she would wash my lunchbox and make my bed. When I finished eating, she would tutor me and then wash my clothes. We would chat about irrelevant things as any mother and daughter would. Only when I went to bed at ten o'clock would she finally go home.

Those parting moments were not easy for my mother and me. I remember how disappointed I was as night approached, but I refused to cling to my mother to prevent her from leaving. I was already eight years old, a big girl. I knew that if I cried, it would make my mother sad. And anyway, crying wasn't going to change anything.

The only decent farewell seemed to be to shut my eyes and pretend to sleep. When my mother left, I would huddle alone under the blanket and cry quietly. I absolutely refused to cry out loud. I would have been ashamed to let my roommates hear me. My mother wondered how I could plop down and fall asleep so quickly. Once, after she left the room, she stood at the window for a few minutes, only to see me get out from under the quilt and turn to the wall. My shoulders were shaking gently with my sobbing. Many years later, she told me that this had almost broken her heart, and she'd very much wanted to take me home. But in the end, she could only steel herself and leave, thinking about the weekend and asking my father to cook a few more wonderful dishes for me.

It took some time, but I gradually adapted to life at the sports school. All of my classmates were older than me, and they took very good care of me. My life turned toward tennis, and I no longer cried myself to sleep. I got up every morning at six to exercise and then went to the canteen for breakfast. At seven-thirty, I went to class, followed by training after school. To me, the worst part was climbing out from under the quilt in winter for morning exercises: we had to run four laps around the tennis court. In winter it was still dark when we ran, and one morning we took a short cut around the net, thinking the coach wouldn't know. But after the sun came up, she saw our footprints in the dew. We didn't quite know what to do when we were found out. We were a little foolish to think that such a strategy would succeed.

Every morning after breakfast, I walked alone to my school, which took about fifteen minutes (the other students at the sports school weren't at the same school as me). There were plane trees along both sides of the road, which I remembered from my runs – the furry seeds used to fall into my face in the autumn. After school, I rushed back to the sports school for training.

When others had holidays, we trained. At the time, Wuhan gave primary school students every Thursday afternoon off. But for us, Thursday afternoon was an important block of time. It was when we had round-robin matches with the team.

In my first two years boarding at the sports school, I was very enthusiastic about tennis. Every day after school, I couldn't wait to run back to train. The conditions for those of us playing tennis in the early 1990s were relatively simple. We trained in the open air, there were no hard courts, and of course it was even more difficult to find clay or grass courts. We just practised on patches of hard dirt, and all the players had to help prepare the court. This was actually quite fun.

We first scraped the lines on the court with our feet, then used the field chalkers to go over the lines with lime. In Wuhan, it's common for summer temperatures to reach forty degrees Celsius, and as we drew lines on the ground with the thin soles of our Warrior-brand shoes, our feet became blazing hot. At the time no one could afford Nikes, and we thought Warrior was the best brand.

Rackets were also a problem. There were no rackets tailor-made for children, so we used adult-sized wooden rackets. They were heavy and very hard on the hands. The wood generated a lot of friction, and before we'd played for long, our hands had blisters. When the blisters burst, calluses would finally form, and only then could we play without pain.

I've always had a fairly high tolerance for pain. The blisters on my hands didn't bother me – I was more worried about my knees. When we first started playing against one another, we were just kids, and our sense of balance wasn't very good. Also, on the sandy surface we played on, it was easy to fall. Almost every day we had scrapes on our knees. We didn't have a team trainer, so the coach would take us to the faucet to wash the sand from the wound. When we'd wiped up the sticky red mess and applied a little antiseptic, we'd continue to play. Crying children were not a common sight at the sports school. Everyone got hurt, and everyone had to endure pain. Who could stand the humiliation of being the only one to cry? When we first got hurt, we'd use the red antiseptic, and then the next time we'd choose the purple one. Changing the colours made it more interesting. It's adorable how simple a child's life is.

As for injuries, the worst was falling on an old wound. The scar would reopen, and it really hurt. Often, the old wound hadn't completely healed. I remember one time I had a scab above the knee that was twelve millimetres thick. When it cracked, I could see pus, blood and remnants of sand in the wound, and I could tell that it hadn't been properly cleaned. Now I look at that scar above my knee, and I take my hat off to the child I was.

We trained at Zhongshan Park and because it was a public park, there would be a crowd of people watching while we trained. Yes, a crowd. Maybe everyone thought it strange, seeing a bunch of children running around, not sure whether they were boys or girls, all with short hair and tanned skin. When one of us little ones would fall, some people felt sorry for us, though many others would stand there, mouths agape as they laughed at us, enjoying the spectacle. But in retrospect, I think of that as a happy time, with so many children playing together.

Occasionally, my parents would come to watch after they got off work. But most of the time, they would give it a miss. Watching made them feel too distressed. When my parents saw the scabs and scars on my legs, their faces grew solemn. I had no idea why. Children have little concept of what is 'good-looking' or 'ugly'. It wasn't until adulthood that I realised my legs were covered in unsightly scars.

It was hard to tell the gender of most of the girls on the tennis team. Because it was more convenient for playing tennis, we cut our hair very short, and we wore the style of sportswear that nearly every child born in the cities at that time wore. It was easy to be mistaken for boys. Just outside the courts was a playground. We sometimes played on the slide or seesaw after training. One time, a little boy and girl looked on enviously. They came to me and said, 'Big Brother, let us play.' I could only reply, 'I'm Big Sister.'

Now that I think back, the cost of training was quite a big deal at the time. My rackets and shoes had to be replaced often, and I was growing very rapidly and would quickly outgrow my sports clothes. All of this cost money, and there were also my tuition fees and the cost of food at the canteen to consider. My parents spent a lot of money on me. We were an ordinary working-class family, and these expenses weren't minor. But every time I needed to replace my equipment, my parents acted like it was easy. They never wanted me to bear this mental burden. They preferred to live frugally so I could live without the worry. Many of my classmates were from families that owned their own businesses, and they were much better off than my family. But I never felt there was a gap.

When I'd been playing tennis for two years, the novelty started to wear off. I began dawdling on my way home from school. Between my school and the tennis courts at Zhongshan Park, there was a shopping centre, and sometimes there was a performing monkey there. I would stand and watch until the show finished, and by the time I checked the clock, it was almost the end of training. I rushed to the field in time to hit a few balls before practice ended.

I was losing interest in tennis, but it had already become an integral part of my life. This became obvious when it was suddenly snatched away from me. That summer, while playing hide-and-seek with the other kids, I hid on the balcony of the second floor. I accidentally fell off the balcony and onto a rock, suffering several bruises. The doctor told me to rest and to stop training for a while.

This was just the result I was hoping for. Finally, I didn't have to train under the hot sun! I could sit comfortably at home, watching television and drinking iced water.

The first day I rested, happy and relaxed. Comfortable, I slept during the day. On the second day, the emptiness closed in on me. I started to go to pieces. I didn't know what to do. On the third day of my 'recuperation' at home, I begged for my father's compassion, asking him to take me to see the team. When my teammates saw me back at school, they were very happy. I didn't want to leave; I wanted to stay for practice.

My father laughed. 'And how would I explain this to your mother?'

In the end, I stayed with the team. I began training again that day.

Even when I went home on Sunday, my father would take me to play tennis. It wasn't training, but 'family time' at the Wuhan Youth Palace tennis courts. The three of us brought boiled water and fruit for snacks. It was all adults training there, mostly young men in their twenties. There were also training partners for hire. It cost five yuan per hour to hire a training partner, which was quite a high price at the time. Still, my father said without hesitation, 'Play!'

The first time I played with a training partner it was extremely hard, playing a grown man. It was difficult, but as I played, I was able to adapt and find a way to get by. Eventually, I developed a bit of a reputation at the Youth Palace, and every time I went, someone would ask me to play. Maybe it was because of my professional demeanour, but I didn't seem like a little girl who was just a beginner.

I really liked my coach, Xia Xiyao: her warm personality and the way she would joke with us. She wasn't like other coaches, who were so serious. She was my favourite person when I was small. In consideration of the fact that we were still just primary school students, Coach Xia made our training schedule a bit flexible. When we had a lot of homework, she would let us leave early to finish our schoolwork. When we had less homework, she would extend training time.

As I grew older, the conflict between training and schooling became more pronounced. It wasn't as simple as just backing out of the Maths Olympics class. A person's energy is always limited. Before the primary school leaving exam, I reviewed my lessons at school, keeping me from training for a whole month. I was studying at the Wuhan Dandong Xincun Primary School, and my form teacher, Ms Huang, had high expectations for me. She tried to persuade my parents to make me give up tennis and concentrate on my studies. She said that unless I was outstanding in tennis, it would be hard for me to amount to anything in the future. She advised my parents to let me concentrate on the exams so I could get into a good school. Coach Xia, on the other hand, thought my tennis prospects were good and that, if things went well, I could play my way to something great one day.

My teacher really wanted me to give up tennis, and my coach wanted me to put all my effort into training. Both sides were thinking of my well-being, and they had the best intentions. My parents were stuck in the middle. In the early 1990s, everything was worthless except performing at a high level academically. This was the overriding value of mainstream society. The stereotype of those who played sports was that they were especially stupid. There was much uncertainty in sports, and who could really guarantee you'd be a 'breakout'?

At the time, the Hubei provincial tennis team coach, Yu Liqiao, was the Asian tennis champion, and in my eyes, she was amazing. When my classmate and I were taking the bus home, I asked him, 'Do you know Yu Liqiao? She's the Asian champion!' My classmate said, 'Never heard of her.' This shocked me. Tennis was such an unknown! Being the Asian champion was quite impressive, but when I mentioned her name, no one knew who she was.

Many of my training friends dropped out of tennis at that time, one after another, but my father eventually decided on my behalf that I should continue down the sports path. When I went home on Sunday, he didn't mention the complaints my teachers had raised at the parent-teacher conference, but just encouraged me to continue focusing on tennis. Nevertheless, I could feel the conflict between my coach and my teacher, all the disdain they felt for one another.

To be honest, I often wonder whether I should have continued on the path to tennis. But at the time I had no choice. In my generation, most of us did things that didn't interest us at all. Many in the Maths Olympics class didn't enjoy it, but their parents liked to say, 'My child is in the Maths Olympics class', so they sat in the classroom, concentrating on figuring out how many chickens and rabbits were in the cage if there were fifteen animals and a total of forty legs. I can't say I loved tennis (and sometimes I hated it), but I still continued practising. The only reason I went on was because everyone thought I should.

While I would sit in the classroom faced with some boring text, thinking of how to write a paragraph summarising its meaning, I sometimes missed the bright sunshine of the tennis court and the sound of tennis balls hitting the rackets. But when my classmates were enjoying summer or winter holidays, or when they sat about discussing the programme they'd watched on TV the night before, I could only walk away with a wooden expression. I had no summer or winter holidays, and I had no time to watch TV.

When I was eleven, I was chosen with several of my classmates from the amateur sports school to train with the provincial team. Our instructor was Yu Liqiao, the former Asian champion, and she became my coach. She remained with me for nine years, until I retired for the first time. Yu told us that there was only one spot in the provincial team, and that if we wanted to make it in, we needed to work very hard.

This was the first time in my life that I really understood the meaning of the word 'competition'. We all stayed in a dorm together. We ate together, and we trained together. We were as close as a hand and a foot. 'Competing' with these good friends, I was a little conflicted. On top of that, I was the youngest in the group, and came from a humble background. Though my results were relatively good, I didn't have the confidence I needed.

While I was disappointed when I failed to make the team, a new opportunity came my way. I occasionally got to represent the Hubei team in amateur tournaments, and at one particular competition, the coach of the locomotive tennis team spotted my talent. He contacted my father, expressing his wish for me to play for his team.

My father was quite indecisive because although he didn't know whether I'd end up making the Hubei team, he was reluctant for me to join the Locomotives. At the time, Hubei had the strongest of all provincial teams, and had won several national tennis championships in a row. Though the Beijing team was also very strong, it wasn't quite as good.

After thinking about it for some time, my father finally declined the coach's offer. He always hoped that I would become the national champion, and Hubei's team was traditionally stronger than any other province's, so he had no doubt that this would be the best soil in which to nurture a champion. At the time, my father and I hadn't given much thought to Grand Slams or such events. It was our dream to be the national champion. If I could become the number one in China, that would be a great honour.

In refusing the Locomotives' offer, my father also had more practical concerns. The Hubei team trained a mere three bus stops from my home. If I joined the Locomotives, it would be very difficult for him to see me often. I didn't know anything about these matters at the time. It was only after my father passed away that my mother told me how anxious he had been. I also didn't realise how serious my father's illness had been for many years.

It started in a small blood vessel. He first felt a pain in his stomach, but didn't think it was serious, assuming it was a common stomach ailment due to stress from work, and that it would improve over time. In 1992, he suddenly got a high fever that wouldn't go down, so he went to have an ultrasound. The results showed that he had congenital stenosis in the blood vessel between the heart and the liver, which was blocked because it was too narrow. The blockage caused the high fever. The doctor said this sort of illness was quite rare.

The only form of treatment was a vascular resection, replacing this blood vessel with an artificial one made of plastic. The treatment wasn't very advanced at the time, and the artificial blood vessel was made locally. It would only last for four years, at most. This vessel was like an evil curse, a time bomb ready to explode, deep inside his abdominal cavity.

The surgery was successful, but from beginning to end, I was kept in the dark. My father didn't allow anyone to discuss his illness with me.

In 1996, the artificial blood vessel began to shrink. The blood couldn't pass through, and fluid began accumulating in the peritoneal cavity. When it was very serious, my father couldn't even breathe. At the time, I was training in Beijing, preparing for the upcoming youth tournament in Shenzhen. My father repeatedly instructed everyone not to distract me, so my mother didn't dare tell me the truth about his condition.

My father had good days and bad days. When he was alert, on one of his good days, he wrote a letter to my coach, Yu Liqiao. With sincerity, he thanked her for nurturing and guiding me. He said he was seriously ill and might not have long to live. He could only entrust my future to my coach, and he hoped she would continue to help me. He didn't want her to be constrained by courtesy – if I needed criticism, she should criticise, and if I needed correction, she should correct.

My coach kept this letter for a long time, and she also told her colleagues, 'Be prepared. If something happens to Li Na's family and she needs to be away for a while, approve her leave immediately.' By this time, my father's health was quite bad. I had no idea of any of this.

The last time I saw my father was at the Wuhan train station. There were many children training in Beijing, and I was travelling with a group of them from Beijing to Shenzhen. My father told me to alight when the train passed through Wuhan, and the two of us met on the platform. We were together for less than five minutes. I hadn't seen him for three months, and when I saw him dragging his bloated body along, walking with such difficulty, I was shocked. My father was so haggard now, like a different person. But he kept telling me not to worry, that he was starting to get better and would be completely well before long. He would come to watch me play soon. This was a wonderful lie. I still deceive myself even now, saying that one day this will come true.

If I'd been smarter, I would have guessed the truth about my father's illness. I wouldn't have gone to Shenzhen, and I wouldn't feel the horrible pain every time I think of him now.

Every day that I was in Shenzhen, I phoned my mother. She said my father was recovering quickly and was out with his friends. I wondered how my father was able to recover so quickly if he'd been sick for a few years, but I took what my mother said at face value. I asked her to take good care of my father and said that since he'd just recovered from a major illness, she shouldn't let him move around too much. I later learned that when my mother was talking to me on the phone, my father was in the operating room undergoing emergency surgery.

My family's financial situation had never been very good, but after my father got sick there were even more constraints. My father's work unit hadn't performed well, and even though he had health insurance, we had to find a way to cover most of the medical expenses ourselves. During that time, it was my mother who suffered most. Before, she'd been in the habit of letting my father take care of everything. Now that he was sick and bedridden, her only recourse was to visit various friends and relatives to borrow money. Initially she was able to raise some funds, but later it became much harder. All of the creditors had their own concerns. And a woman with a child – how were they ever going to get that money back? My mother was too worried to even cry. She hadn't had to worry about food and clothing since she was young, and she'd never had to go around borrowing money before.

Leading up to his death, my father kept regularly losing consciousness. When this happened, my mother would rush him to the emergency room. The first time, he was revived and was okay for more than a month. After the second rescue, he was conscious and coherent for twenty days, and after the third, for only ten. Subsequently he was incoherent and confused. The hospital sent us several letters warning us of his critical condition, but we couldn't afford to take him to a better hospital.

The third time my father was admitted to hospital, he apparently decided it would be the last time. He went to the subsidiary branch of the Number Five Hospital, got a shot of amino acids and then rested at my mother's work unit, which was nearby. She took care of him while working the night shift. The next day, my father attempted suicide. He sent my mother out to buy a steamed bun for him, and when she came back carrying buns and vegetables, she heard her neighbour, Zhu Shifu, lean out the window and call, 'Xiao Li! Xiao Li! Come up quick! Something's happened in your house!'

My mother went inside and saw the floor covered in blood. She and my uncle rushed my father to the Number Six Hospital, saving him.

My mother was stuck with no way out. It's said that relatives forget poor family members, even if they live nearby, but they never forget the rich ones, even if they live far away in the mountains. Only when you're in such a situation will you realise the truth of this.

What was most chilling to my mother was that my paternal grandmother indicated early on that she'd given up. When my father was sick, my grandmother said to my face, 'Don't treat a dead horse like it's alive.' This hurt me deeply. My grandparents had five sons, and they weren't able to take care of all of them. Even if they lost one, they still had four more. But I only had one father.

Later, when my mother tried to borrow money from my grandmother for medical expenses, my grandmother said bluntly, 'I can't loan it to you.' But the next day, she took her family out to buy them new clothes. My youngest uncle was only seven years older than me, and he was studying at university at the time. Without hesitation, my grandmother paid for his school fees.

Since my father passed away, I've seen my paternal grandparents no more than three times. I know they have their own position, and their own difficulties, but I can't forget, and I can't forgive – at least not yet. I don't want to see them. It only makes me recall all those painful memories.

My father died on 14 November 1996. He wasn't even forty years old when he died. Not long after, I registered with the Hubei provincial team, officially becoming one of their regular players. My friends all congratulated me, but I didn't feel any joy. Joining the provincial team and becoming a national champion was what my father had hoped for, but he didn't get a chance to witness it.

Later, I saw the letter my father had written to Coach Yu. It pierced my heart. In it he'd written, 'A child must not wait to take care of his parents.' How true these words are, and how cruel.

Chapter 5

The Little Breadwinner

After my father passed away, my mother went to pieces even more than I did. My father's illness had left us in debt, and we couldn't even afford the funeral. My mother wasn't sure what to do. She discussed everything with me. I suddenly felt very grown up, and that I was strong enough to support the family and protect my mother.

When I was small, I had no concept of money. If I needed a new racket or new shoes, I just mentioned it to my parents. When I started playing competitively, whatever winnings the team gave me I handed over to my parents to manage. I only really began to understand the importance of money after my father died. In order to pay the debts we owed for my father's medical treatment, my mother rented out our house and moved back in with her parents in Wuchang. She haltingly asked me when my winnings would come in, as her own salary wasn't enough to pay our debts.

I really wanted to play matches. The more I played, the higher my bonus would be, and the quicker we could pay off our debts at home. I was fifteen years old.

I was still training with Coach Yu. She continued to guide me until 2002. This nine-year stretch was the longest I've spent under anyone's tutelage, and her influence on my game has been the greatest. Coach Yu was a very good, dedicated coach, with a bit of a hot temper and a tough approach. She was demanding with her players, and was famed for her strict discipline. If she'd said the same thing to you several times and you didn't modify your play, frustrated words would rush out of her mouth: 'If I were teaching a pig, it would have learned by now. How can you be so stupid? How come you haven't learned yet?'

Such talk often brings out a rebellious attitude in kids. Every time I heard something like that I would think, *If you could teach a pig, then why don't you do it now and let me see?*

Many of the girls who'd been accosted in this way would cry a little. Coach Yu really hated seeing others cry. 'What are you crying about? Aren't you ashamed of yourself for crying?' But then, if the child didn't cry, Coach Yu would say, 'Do you have a brain? Does nothing I say get through to you?' At first, when I was a victim of such comments, I would feel angry and resentful, letting it affect my mood while I practised. Later, when she would say such things, they didn't hurt me any more. I grew immune to it.

But I always felt that I could do nothing right. Back then, another student called Li Ting and I were both coached by Yu. Li Ting was a little older than me. When Coach Yu would feed us the ball, we'd both try to hit it. If either of us made a mistake with our forehand, she would grumble at us furiously. If we made a series of mistakes, she would push us impatiently, shouting in our faces, 'Get out! Get out! Get out!'

During the nine years I was with Coach Yu, I almost never received any praise, nor did I have any chance to express myself. Perhaps as a result, I've never thought myself clever. In fact, I've always considered myself quite silly. Later, someone told me that I had 'inner strength'. I couldn't help but smile. Anyone who'd grown up with this sort of coaching would have to have inner strength, wouldn't they?

This is not to say that Coach Yu was a bad person. She was both a very dedicated coach and an upright person. She was born in 1957 and was widowed young, leaving her to raise a two-year-old daughter alone. It couldn't have been easy for a young woman, raising a child and shouldering such a heavy workload. Every time she took us out to a tournament, she'd have to ask her daughter's uncle to look after the child. Despite the precarious state of my family situation, especially compared to the other players, she chose me for the provincial team. Sometimes, she would even spend her own money for us to go to competitions.

However, Coach Yu was indeed hot-tempered. To the best of my recollection, she never spoke softly or gently. Those of us who trained together never thought, *I'm glad the weather is so nice today*, or anything so carefree. Instead, every day when we got out of bed, we could only think, *It's time to start training now, and to get yelled at*. We would gingerly awake, as if walking on thin ice, not knowing when we might make a wrong step nor when the coach would make us run laps as a punishment. All of the players lived in fear. We didn't know when punishment might come, but we knew for sure that it would come.

When I was an adult, I realised that this wasn't Coach Yu's fault. In China, it's said that 'a strict teacher makes for an excellent student', and so coaches tend to be very severe. After students grow up in such a repressive environment, they become coaches themselves, and they unconsciously visit their own repressed anger in intensified form on their students. This is something like the meaning of the saying, 'A daughter-in-law of many years eventually becomes a matriarch'. But it's also because the coaches don't know any other way to teach. They were taught under pressure, and when they grow up and become coaches, they put the same pressure on their students. In this way, it's passed from generation to generation, and each player grows up under this accumulated pressure. It's inhumane . . . but it's also very effective. Under the shining banner of achievement, any means were quietly permitted.

In 1997, in the National Tennis League finals held in Qingdao, I won the first singles national title, becoming the youngest champion ever in the adult division. My one regret was that my father wasn't there to see the fulfilment of his dream. Sometimes I would imagine what his expression would be. Would he hug me, smiling happily? How proud would he feel? From the day my father passed away, I tried not to use the word 'father', or even to think of it. I hid it in my heart, hoping that through my hard work I could protect it and keep it from harm. Sometimes I couldn't help but think, *If my father had not passed away so early, would I be very different?* I could be irrational and act like a baby in front of my father, a little naughty and weak-willed at times. If he were alive I wouldn't have borne the family obligations at such a young age, and that would have made me completely different.

Shortly after joining the provincial team, I gained the opportunity to compete abroad. I was sent to Beijing to train with young people from across the country, those considered to have a promising future in tennis. The activities were organised by the National Tennis Centre with Nike as the corporate sponsor, and after careful consideration, Nike selected six men and six women to attend the Nike tennis academy. The final winner would have the chance to go to the US to study and train for ten months. I was very lucky to receive this opportunity.

In 1997, getting a visa to go overseas was still very troublesome, involving a lot of red tape. Before I went to the US I would need all of my energy for the National Games, which were held every four years. Once they were over, I would be travelling directly to the US, and my mother was worried about me. She came alone to Shanghai, where the games were held, and the two of us spent a little time together, treasuring every second. When she took me to the airport, she started to cry. Partly, she was sad to see her young daughter travelling so far away, and without anyone to accompany her. But partly her tears were also for the recent death of my father. Even though she couldn't say so, I knew those tears expressed the sorrow in her heart.

The Nike tennis academy was in Texas. From Shanghai, the only direct flight was to Los Angeles so I had to transfer there. I had a student visa, and needed an I-20 form to enter the country, but the organisers forgot to give it to me before I left. At customs in LA, the immigration officer treated me like a criminal and repeatedly asked me the whereabouts of this form, but I couldn't speak any English. We could only stare at one another, at a stalemate. Finally he found someone who could speak Chinese to translate as he asked me about it. I told him I hadn't ever heard of or seen this form. He didn't believe me, saying it wasn't possible. He asked again where I planned to go in the US, and how long I was staying. I told him the name of the tennis academy I was going to, and then he opened both pieces of my luggage and checked them carefully. Other than the daily necessities, everything in my bags was sportswear sponsored by Nike.

The result of this troublesome situation was that I was put in a dark room as he went to contact the tennis academy. I didn't know why I was locked in that dark little room. I only knew that my connecting flight was departing soon. I was frightened, and I didn't know what I'd done wrong. I sat there, helpless and alone, and cried a little. Before, I'd been to several other countries while playing in youth tournaments, but I'd always been accompanied by a coach and a translator. I'd never encountered a situation like this.

When I'd been in that dark room for about twenty minutes, the customs officer let me out. He'd contacted the people at the tennis academy, and now said I could go, but that I needed to get someone from the academy to take me to the immigration department and submit the missing form within two months.

By this time, I'd missed my connecting flight. I began asking people around me for help. I'm not sure where this courage came from, but since I didn't understand English, I looked for Asian faces. One man was very kind, telling me that the next flight to Texas was the following morning at six a.m. He helped me change my ticket to that flight.

It was four o'clock in the afternoon, so I had to wait fourteen hours at the airport. All alone, I pushed my luggage cart, piled with bags, and went to sit in front of the great glass windows in the departure lounge, looking at the vast sky.

When it got dark, I watched a plane take off. I recognised the aircraft from my earlier flight. It was on its way back to China. At that moment, I very much wished I was aboard, and that it would take me home. But I wasn't.

I sat there, watching the sky outside turn little by little from blue to black, letting the tears drop in silence. During the night, I felt very helpless and lost. I thought of calling the tennis academy, but eventually gave up on the idea when I thought about the language barrier. As the night wore on, there were fewer people at the airport. I just sat there the whole night, pushing my luggage cart with me even to go to the bathroom.

Sometimes I really want to go back in time and tell that helpless little Chinese girl in the midst of a crowd of strangers to cheer up, that everything will be fine. But other times I know it's not necessary. At the end of the day, those hardships and obstacles proved to be fate's way of teaching me bravery and fortitude.

The next morning, when I boarded the flight and finally made my way to Texas, the coach from the tennis academy was waiting for me at the airport. He'd been there waiting a very long time.

During my first two weeks at the tennis academy, I couldn't understand any English. A Chinese boy who'd arrived at the academy before me had left to attend a tournament, and the only other person with whom I could communicate, a Taiwanese player, stayed far away from me. In order to familiarise us with an English-language environment more quickly, the tennis academy had arranged for us Chinese speakers to be separated. My American roommate was two years older than me and was very different from the Chinese girls I had always been in contact with. She was very outgoing and talkative, and even though I couldn't understand her, she chattered on to me every day in a flow of English. At times when we really couldn't make ourselves understood at all, we relied on sign language, gesturing to tell each other it was time for dinner, training or bed. She played an important role in my English language learning.

At the tennis academy, we split our time between studying and training. In the morning, a big yellow school bus took us to a school ten minutes away, where we had classes. At noon, the bus picked us up and took us back to the academy, where we all had lunch together in the canteen. At one-thirty, we trained or played a friendly match, or sometimes did exercises with a fitness trainer. Around six-thirty we had dinner, followed by free time. The tennis academy was near an airport, and I could always see airplanes flying overhead while I was training. I couldn't help but imagine myself on a plane flying home.

The tennis academy was like a mini United Nations, bringing together languages and people of all nationalities from all over the world. You could encounter eight- or nine-year-old children who already played tennis like model players. There were also professional players in their early twenties who came to train for a few weeks at the end of the season. The morning school curriculum focused on language and maths. For those of us from China, the maths lessons were easy, so we focused on language learning and playing friendly matches.

Later I saw news reports saying, 'Advanced training in the US significantly improved Li Na's game'. To be honest, the training programme was nothing special. What made the biggest difference was that I had more opportunities to engage in competition. You can gain a wealth of knowledge from this kind of practical experience.

There are many tennis academies in the US, and there are often friendly matches between them. There would be weekly friendly tournaments with other academies in addition to the games within our own academy that took place practically every other day. The results of each competition affected the ranking of the academy overall, and the students were ranked within their own academies too. Winning a match today would add points to your name, perhaps raising your ranking. A loss tomorrow would mean your ranking would drop. Boys and girls were ranked together. It was all very interesting, and very challenging.

I played at the tennis academy for ten months, and my rank floated between numbers three and four. The best-known player at the camp at that time was a Hungarian girl a year older than me. She was highly ranked, having already played her way to a number three or four ranking in world junior tournaments. The tennis academy held high hopes for her and had specifically engaged a very experienced coach to give her private lessons. After we'd grown up and entered professional competition, I met her on the court from time to time. Each time we met, we'd smile and greet one another. We lived together at the tennis academy for ten months, and sometimes we'd even ride on the same bus to play matches outside the academy. Even though we couldn't communicate well enough to become good friends, seeing a familiar face many years later gave me a feeling of intimacy each time we met.

The last time I met this Hungarian girl was in 2007. I haven't seen her since then. Just about all of my friends from the tennis academy have retired now. The boy from mainland China who'd gone to the Nike training camp the same year as me has retired. The Taiwanese boy, who played a very powerful game and was highly ranked as a junior player, dropped from sight. He's probably not playing any more either.

Language and East-West cultural differences created barriers to communication between players. Added to that, I've always been fairly quiet, and so I never really got close to others at the academy. Everyone was busy with studies and training, though, so it didn't get too desolate and lonely. When I felt most lonely was Christmas time, when my classmates all went home to see their families and the huge campus was suddenly empty, leaving only me and the other two Chinese students. It was winter and everyone fell into a reticent mood. This sort of loneliness is really indescribable. It didn't matter that the streets off campus were filled with the sweet sound of Christmas songs. This wasn't our holiday.

When I was really homesick, I wrote letters. Many years later, my mother told me that she'd kept videos of all my matches on hard disks so that when she missed me, she could stick them into the computer and watch whichever match she wanted, hearing what I'd said while playing, and seeing what I wore. She knew it all. At the time, I didn't even have money to call, so writing was the most important tool I had to fight loneliness.

After my father passed away, I sent my earnings to my mother, hoping to clear our debts as soon as possible so that my mother could live a more comfortable life. Sometimes when I played a match, the organisers would give me a little bonus. That was my pocket money.

While I was abroad, my mother worried, thinking I needed money. She asked in every letter whether I had any money. I always wrote back to tell her I was fine. The irony was that we were both extremely poor, but we were both quick to assure each other, 'I'm fine. I have money.'

Now that I read these long-ago letters, they reveal a very immature ego. A lot of them were written like a book on determination. There wasn't much variation in content. *Mother, I played against so-and-so today. The game went like this. I will continue to work hard at such-and-such.* My mother's replies, apart from giving me encouragement and support, mostly contained questions about my living conditions. She missed me, but didn't dare to burden me with family matters.

The competition funds for the athletes at the tennis academy were set, and Nike wouldn't give us additional subsidies. I improved quickly at the tennis academy, and my results at school were also fairly good, so the coaches wanted me to play in as many tournaments as possible. But I didn't have the funds. I called my mother, and she quickly went to discuss the matter with Coach Yu. Yu immediately went with my mother to the sports association, telling them that my performance was good and, employing both soft and hard tactics, she finally persuaded them to invest US$1000 so that I could have the opportunity to play more matches.

It's said that what happens in one's youth will greatly affect a person because that time in their life is important for shaping values. When I was young, I was easily satisfied. If I needed something, I just had to ask my parents and everything would be fine. After my father died, my whole world changed. When I think back on my girlhood memories, everything is grey, unlike those of other girls, which are full of youthful ease, beauty or romance. I was stubborn, depressed and hard as stone. This memory of being underprivileged seeped deeply into my bones and may stay with me for the rest of my life. No matter what wealth or life of ease comes my way, the memory of being a young girl struggling to pay off debts is always entrenched, lingering in my mind. It affects everything I do, and perhaps its influence runs even deeper than I realise.

Chapter 6

Mother

When the ten months of training in the US ended, I went to Japan to play a match. And when the match was over, I could go home at last!

By this time, I had no problem in daily communication with Americans. Foreigners liked my name because it was simple and easy to pronounce. My trainer had an Italian girlfriend and had learned a lot about Italian culture. He asked me if I was of Italian descent. When I told him I was an authentic Chinese, he said he felt my character was a bit Italian, because I could talk with someone amicably for the first five minutes and suddenly turn antagonistic. Being simple, straightforward and temperamental was typical of the Italian character. When I heard this I wanted to laugh. From his description, Italians sounded a lot like people from Wuhan.

The diet at the academy was very nutritious and balanced, and very scientific. But the flavours of one's home soil are forever the ones that will most satisfy. Having been born and raised in Wuhan, my favourite foods included Hubei-style cooking and the similarly spicy flavours from Sichuan. At the thought of my hometown cuisine, my appetite couldn't help but be stimulated, and my mouth would start watering.

And it wasn't just the heavy meals but the simple, light breakfasts that I missed.

In Wuhan, we call breakfast 'starting the day'. When outsiders come to Wuhan, those with means make their way to Hu Bugang, a street full of roadside stalls, to 'start the day'. But to us, starting the day doesn't mean going to elaborate lengths. It's enough to buy a bowl of fried noodles at a roadside stall. The flavour is equal to that of the old restaurants opened decades ago. Wuhanese people have many options for starting the day: the overwhelmingly fragrant sesame-paste noodles; a 'noodle nest' fried golden-brown; glutinous rice glittering on beancurd skins; a bed of soft, freshly scented mushrooms covered in egg; fresh bamboo shoots with diced meat; or rice noodles in soup with fritters, with the thickness of the noodles complementing the crispness of the dough sticks. Besides all of this, there are plenty more options, such as sticky rice in lotus leaves, dumplings, rice balls in rice wine, beef brisket noodles . . .

My mother told me she had homemade sausages hanging on the balcony, waiting for me to come home. Even though I was far from eating the sausages, I could taste the flavours of home in my dreams. I was homesick.

When I was in Japan for the tournament, I unexpectedly received a call from my mother, saying that someone had introduced her to a man whom she liked very much. My parents had been middle-school classmates, and they'd married very early and loved one another deeply. During those lonely months when I was in the US, my mother suffered the double grief of her husband's death and her daughter's departure. My uncle and maternal grandmother were afraid the shadow in her heart would consume her and so, wanting to pull her out of her grief, kept asking people to introduce her to a new man. My mother was very pretty (my father was handsome too, but somehow I managed to be only a combination of my parents' shortcomings), and she was also still young, so remarrying was a very natural thing.

I asked my mother, 'How do you feel about him?'

She replied, 'He's not as handsome as your father, but he's a good person.'

I told her, 'As long as you like him, it's fine.'

When I hung up, I fell into a despondent mood. It suddenly struck me: was I losing my mother too? I didn't know whether, at the end of the day, I was too simplistic or too mature, but my only thought was, *I don't care whether this man is good or bad to me. As long as he's good to my mother and takes care of her, I'll accept him.* I would be spending most of the year travelling around for competitions, and it was impossible for me to keep my mother company throughout her life. If she could find someone dependable to spend the rest of her life with, then of course that was for the best. I had my own life, and I knew I shouldn't interfere with her happiness. If my mother spent all her energy on me, I'd feel sorry for her. It would be selfish of me to let that happen.

Deep down, though, I was sad. It felt a bit as though I'd been deserted.

We'd rented out our house in order to repay our debts, and now my mother wanted to marry someone I didn't know and start a new family. The perfect, beautiful home that I'd known had disappeared without a trace. The bliss that I'd experienced had faded like a mist, not leaving behind even an imprint of happiness. My mother would never belong to me again.

I'd known that sooner or later, this day was bound to come. But I hadn't expected it would come so soon. My father had been gone for not much more than a year, and now a stranger was coming to take his place.

When I got back from Japan, my mother brought Uncle's son (I've always referred to my stepfather as 'Uncle') to the airport when she came to pick me up. I looked at her blankly, and her expression was unnatural. She took me back to stay at Uncle's house.

On 14 November 1996, my father had passed away. In December, I made the provincial team. In October 1997, I went to the US, and when I returned in June 1998, barely a year and a half after my father's death, I found that my mother had been fully integrated into a new family. I was a superfluous person, a wandering bystander outside this happy family.

Objectively speaking, Uncle was an honest person. He was very good to my mother, and also treated me well enough. What made me feel awkward was my mother. She always hoped Uncle and I would be a bit closer, even asking me to take the initiative to call him or make more of a connection with him so that we could form a closer bond. Perhaps she was hoping, on a subconscious level, to rebuild the happy life she'd once known, and that we could all be a real family. Perhaps she hoped to erase all traces of my father, forgetting her sadness completely. But I couldn't. I couldn't forget my father, and I couldn't forget the sweet, happy times we'd had together. I couldn't pretend he'd never existed. Those memories were my most treasured possession.

Initially, I had to bite the bullet and try to please my mother, occasionally phoning Uncle. But what was there to say? Every time our conversation was stilted. He was good to my mother, and good to me too. I could see that, but he could never be a substitute for my father.

I had a serious talk with my mother. I said, 'Mum, I'm your daughter, and we two are bound by blood. I know that Uncle is a good man, but he's your husband. He can't take the place of my father. You have your way of looking at life, and I have mine. You can't impose your ideas on me.'

From then on, my mother never forced me to be closer to Uncle. But she always said that I didn't want to spend time with her. It seemed her life and mine were moving further apart, and she was taking to her new life like a fish to water. As soon as she opened her mouth, all she could talk about was Uncle.

On one occasion, I'd gone to Paris for a competition. My mother had distant relatives in Paris, so I suggested she come with me, taking it both as a holiday and a chance to visit family. She said she couldn't. Uncle had to work, and if she was going, she wanted the whole family to go together. Inwardly, I sighed and thought, *Okay, it's up to you.*

My mother's life was already inextricably bound to Uncle's. Their new household was lovely and stable, but I felt more and more distinctly that I was an outsider. Several years later, I finally acknowledged that this matter caused me a lot of pain. In fairytales, love is wonderful. Maybe I was still living in my own ideal world.

In order to safeguard my mother's hard-earned happiness, I suppressed my own feelings, working hard to take a rational approach to my mother's relationship with Uncle. My mother had made the right choice. I knew this very well. But I was still an adolescent girl with a heart full of hurt and grief, and I had no one with whom I could talk about the situation.

I was deliberately indifferent toward my mother. Even though I knew I had no reason to resent her, I still couldn't forgive her. I was obsessed with the notion that she'd betrayed my father and me, and that she was responsible for making a virtual orphan of me. Although I knew this idea was wrong, I couldn't help hating her a little. Selfishly, I took my own feelings of loss, the agitation of being made 'homeless' and the discrimination I'd felt as a child from a single-parent family and turned them all into hatred, projecting them all onto my mother. Anger is stronger than sorrow, and anger can keep you from collapsing.

But inside, I felt an emptiness deeper than I'd ever experienced before. Underneath the hard shell, I was lonely, and I felt neglected.

I wanted a new home. I wanted someone I could love and trust.

Chapter 7

Behind the Tough Exterior

Not every girl is fated to be a princess. After my father died, I forced myself to be strong so that I could protect my mother and myself. Later, anyone who saw me thought that I was a capable, fierce woman who didn't need any protection. I was the only one who knew that throughout those long teenage years the tough exterior hid a weak, helpless girl, who was very envious of other children with two parents. The only problem was, I knew I could never go back.

I met my future husband Jiang Shan after I joined the provincial team. When I was still a budding novice, he already had an outstanding career. He was so handsome! All the girls whispered about him behind his back. At the time, Korea fever was sweeping China. The boy band H.O.T. was extremely popular, and everyone said that Jiang Shan had Korean style.

Hearing others praise him, I, too, decided he was quite attractive. In the early days we only regarded each other as teammates.

In a sports team, two years can be huge. Jiang Shan was two years older than me, in the wave of players ahead of me. While my group was still considered the newcomers in the provincial team, travelling all over, playing qualifying matches, Jiang Shan was the team's golden boy. Once, a few years earlier, when I'd gone to a tournament, I'd run out of pocket money, so I called my father and asked him to have someone bring me a little extra cash. When we played in the preliminaries, the younger teammates would play first. The older players who had better results could advance directly, and so would arrive at the tournament a couple of days later. My father knew the older team members hadn't yet left for the tournament, so he went to the Hubei team dorms and knocked on the door. All four of the senior players were there playing cards. My father went directly to Jiang Shan, a fellow Wuhanese, and said, 'Jiang Shan, will you help me by taking a few hundred yuan to Li Na?'

Many years later, I asked Jiang Shan, 'Why did my father pick you, when there were four of you in the room?'

Jiang Shan immediately seized the opportunity for self-praise, saying, 'Oh, your father must have taken a shine to me then.'

'Ugh. Don't make me laugh!'

'Then it must be because your father trusted me.'

Actually, Jiang Shan was the youngest of the four, but whenever anyone needed help, he was the first to come to mind. Even though he was an only child, he didn't have the sort of arrogance typical of an only child. He took care of his teammates and gave the impression he was dependable. He was very popular in the men's team, with a whole group of younger boys following him around all day as though he were the natural leader of the pack.

Jiang Shan was less popular with the girls, despite his looks. The other boys liked to laugh and chat with the girls but Jiang Shan was more reserved, sometimes with an air of contempt that suggested, *I really don't have time to talk to girls.* We were all still children at the time, and he seemed to find girls troublesome and irrational, so he seldom bothered to talk much with us. He didn't seem to feel contempt for me, though, and we talked more than he did with the other female players. Perhaps he felt that I was independent enough, and less prone to drama.

I didn't like boys who were too chatty, and Jiang Shan's muted, cool behaviour actually drew me to him. We were in the same team, and so were often in each other's company. During normal training hours, we had regular contact. As we played, we began to form an attachment to each other. But at the time, we never thought of ourselves as a couple. We were just teenagers, good friends who often ate together and played together, but nowhere near 'dating'.

People say that there are two kinds of love. One is passionate, the other lasting. I think this makes a lot of sense. Jiang Shan and I share the more lasting type of love. We've been together since we were teenagers, and we're practically an old married couple. If what we felt for each other were just passion, it would have burned itself out by now.

Having been influenced by my father, my expectations of my partner were that he be mature, tolerant and calm. A man should be like the sea, and this is exactly what Jiang Shan is. I'm not sure why, but I feel like I can be a child in front of him. After my father passed away, I had to pretend to be hard and strong, and no one knew how difficult it was for me to keep up this pretence. Jiang Shan gave me a chance to be a child again, and he gave me the sense of security I'd longed for. What's more, Jiang Shan reminded me of my father. With him, I felt steady and sure of myself. When I played tennis with him beside me, I felt more confident.

When we really started dating, everyone was very surprised. Jiang Shan is a very chauvinistic guy, and everyone thought a macho man like him would want a timid, lovable, girly girlfriend. I was an independent woman, and no one had suspected we'd get together. Everyone said, 'You want to know what it's like when a macho guy and an independent woman get together? Just look at Jiang Shan and Li Na and you'll know.'

When both partners have strong characters, there are bound to be quarrels. Jiang Shan and I were both born and raised in Wuhan, but Jiang Shan's parents were from Shandong. People sometimes asked him, 'Jiang Shan, where are you from?'

He would always answer, 'Wuhan!'

But then when the two of us argued he would say, 'You Wuhanese...'

I didn't know whether to laugh or be angry, so I would retort, 'Aren't you Wuhanese?'

He would immediately answer, 'No, I'm from Shandong.'

When I heard that, I really wanted to laugh, and I couldn't keep arguing.

When we got together, he even teased me in the Wuhan dialect. 'I'd rather marry a Wuhanese lad, not a Wuhanese woman! You matrons from Wuhan are too strong!'

Ha! Wasn't it marrying him that turned me into a matron?

Jiang Shan met with more setbacks in his sports career than I did in mine. People on the outside can't imagine how bleak life in sports circles can be. Jiang Shan is very stubborn, and when he sets himself on a certain path, a team of oxen can't pull him back. This is what I love about him.

Many people see me yell at him on the court and often feel he's too good to me, that he's to be pitied. But in fact that's not true. Not. True! When he yells at me, no one sees it. When I play tennis, I'm easily distracted. Having difficulty concentrating is a bad habit for professional players. Andre Agassi once said that when he was focused on playing, he wouldn't even hear a gunfight that happened outside the court because all of his focus was on his opponent. I really envy people who can be so focused. Jiang Shan is very good in this area. When he's playing a video game, if I stand beside him talking, he will answer, 'Sure, yes, fine.' But if I ask him afterward what was said, he just waves it off and says, 'I didn't hear.'

I don't remember where I heard it, but apparently scientists have proven that it's innate for the male brain to be more focused on a single thing, while the female brain is more adept at handling several things at a time. I don't know if that's true, but when I'm playing tennis, if a spectator on the sidelines gets up to go to the bathroom, I'll notice. I'm just as easily distracted as anyone else. Sometimes when my play isn't smooth, Jiang Shan will be nagging annoyingly on the sidelines: 'You changed your approach. Hit it straight.' He's not good at encouragement. The words that come out of his mouth all seem impatient and critical, and they make my head want to burst. When he says something the first time, I resist the urge to respond, but by the third time, I roar my heart out. 'Hit it straight! Hit it straight! Yesterday didn't you say our strategy should be to slash?'

I've always had a temper like a firecracker. If someone sets it off it explodes, and as soon as it does, I'm filled with remorse. With outsiders, I can usually endure all sorts of unpleasant behaviour. It's only with Jiang Shan that I pull this sort of ill-behaved nonsense. From what psychologists say, most people are only bad-tempered with those who make them feel secure, because you know that the person won't leave you. So losing your temper is in fact a form of dependency.

After being together for so many years Jiang Shan knows very well that my temper will flare up quickly, but recede just as fast. We quarrel often, but our arguments are never big. We usually get it over with in a few words. Arguing is normal – how can any two people live together without butting heads?

Jiang Shan really hates shopping with me. He claims, 'You can even spend two hours in a supermarket!' We talked about this a lot, and in the end it was me who gave in. Whenever I went shopping, I used to hate missing even a single store. Now my approach is simpler. Now, I know what I want to buy, so I find it, pay for it and leave. I don't take more than a minute, because he's waiting impatiently outside. Jiang Shan would rather spend time reading or watching television. He has a very rich inner world. I think this has much to do with his upbringing.

Jiang Shan's parents are ordinary working-class people, very simple, and especially kind to me. I like his family very much. My relationship with his mother is both close and natural. She's very thoughtful. When Jiang Shan and I bought our house, people asked her, 'Will you live with your son, or live separately?'

She answered jokingly in a way that pleased me no end. 'Why would old fools like us want to live with young people?' Then she added that she didn't want to burden us, and that when she got old she'd rather live in a nursing home, where there would be lots of people to entertain her. Since ancient times, the thinking in China has always been that you raise children to care for you in your old age. For a person to joke the way my mother-in-law did shows a good attitude and a strong character. Of course, we would never let Jiang Shan's parents live in a nursing home, just as we would never see them as 'old fools'. But their relaxed attitude makes us feel that there's no pressure on us.

Jiang Shan loves his mother very much. With our year-long travel schedule, he buys something for her in each country. Sometimes he'll buy her clothes, asking me to try them on for her. She's about the same height as me, only a little plumper and with a fuller bust. If the clothes suit me, we get a size larger and it's bound to be just right for his mother. When I walk out of the fitting room in an elderly woman's clothes, he looks at me for a moment, then says, 'Okay, let me see the white one now.' I obediently put on the white one. The shop attendants standing nearby must be thinking, 'These two are so out of touch, choosing such old-person clothes!'

The atmosphere in Jiang Shan's home is particularly pleasant, and very democratic. When we have dinner together, everyone talks excitedly, each presenting his or her views. Even if there's a disagreement, there's no anxiety or anger. Sometimes Jiang Shan's mother says, 'Who would ever guess that you're more insightful than your father?' When he hears this, Jiang Shan's ego inflates, and we all have a good laugh at his exaggerated expression.

This is what a family feels like. I had lost that feeling, and I searched for it again for many years. I find the experience both indulgent and fascinating.

Many of our close friends say that I'm very clingy with Jiang Shan. When we get back to Wuhan, if he and his old friends get together to play cards, I go with him. I watch while he plays, and then if I don't feel like watching any more, I'll lie on the sofa and read. I usually read until I doze off. Occasionally he plays all night, and I'll keep him company the whole time. Our friends laugh at me, calling me his cat. Whether it's shopping, watching a movie or eating out, I like to have him with me.

When I first joined the national team, a famous psychologist was hired to help us athletes strengthen our mindsets. Her name was Xu Haoyuan, and she wore her hair like the cartoon character Chibi Maruko. She once asked if I cried in front of Jiang Shan. I said I used to, but didn't any more.

'Why?'

'I don't feel the need to cry.'

'Why do you feel this way?'

'Crying is a childish thing to do. Now that I'm strong enough, I'm more in control of my emotions.'

She said, 'This shows that you trust Jiang Shan less and less, that you don't want to show him your vulnerable side.'

I don't think this is quite true. Interacting with others is not governed by set rules. When two people have been together for a long time, they naturally create a dynamic of their own. I feel that crying doesn't solve anything. One thing that Jiang Shan has taught me is that for a marriage to work, the two people must have a bit of independence and space. Sometimes when he has something on his mind, he suddenly becomes very quiet. At those times, I don't nag him about it, but just leave him to think it over, knowing that if I give him time, he'll share it with me when he's ready. Jiang Shan doesn't hide anything from me.

Marriage is like sand running through your fingers. If you hold it too tightly, it will slip away. There should be a basic level of trust and respect between a husband and wife.

Jiang Shan is the most important person in the world to me. He plays many roles in my life: on the court he's my coach and training partner, during practice he's my trainer, in life he's my husband and nanny, and in times of difficulty he counsels me sometimes like a guardian, sometimes like an older brother. Occasionally he even has to play the role of chef or health practitioner. He's smarter than me, more savvy, and when I need a shoulder to cry on, he's the only person to whom I can unload all my cares without reservation. He's the one person in my life that I cannot do without.

When he's with me, it's not intense or special, but when we're apart, we both feel very empty, as if something is missing. This runs very deep in me. Once when I was asleep, I dreamt that Jiang Shan and I were walking on the road, and suddenly he didn't recognise me. No matter how much I called him, he didn't respond, and I was very anxious. When I awoke, I turned to Jiang Shan and gave him a series of fierce pinches. He looked at me innocently and asked what was going on. When he heard the reason, he sighed and bore the abuse like an obedient boy.

I once told Jiang Shan, 'You always remind me of my father.' He seemed to find this hard to believe, so I explained, 'It's not your age, but your character and your way of thinking. And the way you make me feel . . .'

Sometimes when Jiang Shan is with me, I suddenly feel a sort of presence, as if my father were still living and watching over me. As I remember it, my father never told me off, but always guided me gently, and always played with me or told me stories. Jiang Shan's personality is like my father's in many ways. My father's early death was a turning point in my life. Not being able to watch his daughter grow into an adult would have been a deep source of regret for him. I think if my father could see Jiang Shan and me together, it would give him peace of mind.

Chapter 8

Official Retirement

In 1998, not long after I came back from the US, things started to develop at a very good pace. Nike was optimistic about me. It was at this time that I was interviewed in Beijing about what my biggest dream was. Nike used it in an advertisement after 2011, and it's become a well-known campaign in the advertising industry. Every time I see that ad, I'm overcome with emotion. I look at my sixteen-year-old self – green, but with no stage fright – saying to the camera, 'My biggest dream? I want to play my way into the top ten. I know this is very difficult to do, but I'll work hard.'

I was actually apprehensive about uttering the words 'top ten' in front of so many people. I didn't really have the courage to utter my dream out loud, but at that moment, I went with it. Making it public was like making a commitment, formally announcing my intentions to the world.

At that time, it was a distant dream. Of all the Asian players up to that point, the highest any had ever ranked was Kimiko Date-Krumm, who'd entered the semifinals in WTA play. That was at the time when Andre Agassi, Pete Sampras and Steffi Graf dominated the tennis world. A little later, it was the era of Martina Hingis. The inferiority of Asian players was obvious, and we didn't have enough experience in big competitions. We had no opportunity to pit ourselves against the best in the world.

Nike has been good to me over the years; at every Grand Slam event, the company sends someone to bring me clothing and to stay throughout, watching the competition. I've become very good friends with the Nike staff. Even when there's no professional reason, we'll get together for dinner. Staff have even dropped what they were working on to keep me company, just to help me get back into the right frame of mind. I'm very grateful for such loyal partners. They've never forsaken me, and I consider them as another layer of my own team.

After I came back from the US, my relationship with Coach Yu improved, and she also felt I'd grown up. I was no longer corrected at every turn. I tried to share my own ideas with the coach, and over time, we learned how to communicate.

Soon, I set out to compete in earnest. I'd got into the International Tennis Federation challenge in Shenzhen and won my first career singles championship. My third career championship was in Westende, Belgium, and this was my first time to win in an overseas tournament. Even though it was just an ITF event, it was encouraging. (ITF events rank below WTA events internationally.) In women's doubles, I teamed with my old teammate Li Ting and we won a WTA doubles event, my first WTA tournament championship.

In late August 2000, I got my first Grand Slam opportunity when I was offered the chance to participate in the US Open qualifiers. Unfortunately, my lack of experience meant I was knocked out in the third set of the first round. I didn't even make it to the real competition. As I was a novice, this wasn't so unusual. I had no expectations of myself in the US Open, but took it as a sort of boot camp, allowing me to get a feel for what Grand Slam events were like. In tennis circles, the Grand Slam is the ultimate dream of every player, a temple for all tennis fans and the big media drawcard. Even though I didn't play well, actually being at a Grand Slam left a deep impression on me. Perhaps it was then that the Grand Slam seed was planted in my mind. I couldn't imagine how effective it would be in taking root and eventually flowering.

In national competition, I fared quite well. In the 21st Universiade in Beijing in 2001, I won the singles, doubles and mixed doubles titles. That same year in the National Games, I won the gold medal for women's singles and doubles.

By 2002, my world ranking had jumped to 296. In February, I took part in the US$75 000 Challenge held in Midland, in the US. This isn't considered a big tournament, but I was in good shape, and from the qualifiers, I won eight straight matches, defeating seven players ranked higher than me to win. This was a good result, and I'd been making progress. But I found myself growing frustrated and struggled to keep fighting. The most important, and most direct, cause of this was my health.

Before the 2002 Asian Games, in May, I suddenly developed a disorder associated with my menstrual cycle. The team doctor said it was an endocrine disorder caused by stress and depression. I've read some articles that say that psychological pressures and problems can manifest in the body in real symptoms, sometimes leading to illness.

There was a simple solution: taking hormone medication in the form of regular injections. But I was allergic to the medicine, and the doctor failed to find any other solution. With this sort of disorder, I couldn't train much, nor could I compete. The tennis centre asked an external doctor to come see me, and he told us the truth: 'Her physical situation is not ideal.'

By this stage it had been two or three months since I'd trained. I was in such a serious condition that if I trained in the morning, I'd experience symptoms in the afternoon. If I immediately stopped what I was doing, resting all the way through the night, then I would be fine. My mother was strongly against me continuing to train. The shadow of my father's illness and death had not fully disappeared, and here I was with an uncertain future. She was scared. We didn't know how my allergic reaction would develop if I were to take the medication, and we weren't going to let my whole life be ruined for a match!

There were a lot of media reports at the time saying that I'd retired. Many reporters said it was because I wasn't allowed to enter the mixed doubles competition with Jiang Shan. This wasn't fair: I had health issues, and couldn't continue training.

That said, the idea that I was upset because I wasn't allowed to play mixed doubles with Jiang Shan wasn't groundless. This matter had already given me no small amount of stress. Jiang Shan and I had been mixed doubles partners for four years, and everyone could see we were a good team, so they didn't try to separate us. Before the 2001 National Games, there were the National Tennis Finals, in which Jiang Shan and I routinely played mixed doubles together. Before this, there had never been any objections to our pairing, but when we got to the venue for the draw, we found our names separated.

I was paired with another boy, while Jiang Shan was assigned to another girl. These two players had been a team before. They told us that the coaches had decided to split the teams temporarily and try this combination for the tournament. The other two players were also very uncomfortable with this arrangement.

We were completely unaware that the coaches had intended to do this. Jiang Shan was furious, and I was also very angry. The other pair didn't quite know what to do. We discussed the matter with the coaches for a long time, and finally they changed the names back. The draw was delayed by an hour and a half.

Afterward, we went back to the relevant coaches to ask, 'Can you inform us in advance when you want to make this sort of decision?' The result of the discussion was that the coaches said, 'This time we'll let it be. Wait until the National Games organising committee gives consent for your pairing. We'll let them decide.'

And when the National Games started, we were separated again.

We were very unhappy. We were human beings, not pawns on a chessboard. Jiang Shan and I were partners because we'd practised together, and we'd been doing so for four years. We had an in-depth understanding of each other's technique and strategy, and we were fully aware of each other's strengths and weaknesses.

It was reported that the provincial team was considering how it might maximise its power in the mixed doubles pairings, with the decision to break up the combination of Li Na and Jiang Shan. The newspaper claimed that I had an ulterior motive in pairing with him: I hoped to stand together with my boyfriend on the champion's podium as a way of commemorating our affection. This was a totally ridiculous hypothesis. Jiang Shan and I had been together several years, and we had long ago stood together on the winner's podium. Our affection didn't need to be commemorated in this way.

We found it difficult to accept the team's strong desire to break up our pairing, especially since the coaches couldn't offer any reason for it. In order to get us to accept the situation, they finally called a meeting and promised that if we both got into the finals, then the runner-up would get an equal champion's treatment at the National Games. They miscalculated one very important fact. We didn't want the champion's treatment. We wanted respect.

We both left that meeting without saying anything, but our hearts were cold.

At the National Games, Jiang Shan and his partner won the championship. My partner and I got third place, but none of us were remotely happy.

In China each national team has a leader or leaders in addition to the coaches, who are officials of the government. To make sure that I could play in the upcoming Asian Games, the leader of the team said, 'You just need to make sure she has the injections.' Hearing this froze the blood in my veins. I was only twenty years old. No matter how much I loved tennis, I wasn't going to let it ruin my health and happiness. My first reaction was to call my mother and ask for help. She was anxious for me. As soon as she heard the situation, she said, 'Let's not play. This body is yours for life.'

Many years later, I still remember my mother's blazing, firm words. At the time, I felt as if an extremely heavy burden had been lifted. I was filled with the urge to go home. It's said that people who aren't close to you care how high you can fly, but those who love you care about whether you get tired while flying. Having been an athlete practically since birth, I can attest to the truth of this statement. My insomnia and anxiety suddenly went away. The haze dispersed from my mind, and I slept normally that night.

The next day, when the rest of my teammates went to train, I call-ed and booked a plane ticket from the tennis camp in Beijing to Wuhan. That afternoon, the tickets were delivered to me. Two days later, I took the bag I'd packed earlier and left, taking a taxi straight to the airport.

I'd filled out an 'Application for Retirement' form and left it on the desk in my dorm room. To show my determination, I didn't even take my racket with me, leaving it on the writing desk as a paperweight on top of the form. Fearing that someone would see me with my luggage and realise something was amiss, I packed light, putting a few changes of clothes and daily necessities into a carry-on bag, and left in a hurry. As soon as I got home, I turned off my phone. I didn't accept any calls.

The taste of freedom was so sweet!

Jiang Shan was already back in Wuhan. A month after the 2001 National Games had ended, he'd talked to the coaches of the national team. They'd agreed to allow him to retire, and he'd returned to Wuhan. He retired six months before I did.

Jiang Shan's experiences had been much worse than mine. He had been through hell and back on the team, and being forced to split up with me was the straw that broke the camel's back. He had suffered much worse.

In September 2002, we started our next chapter together at university. At first, we'd planned to study at Wuhan University, but the new head of the Hubei provincial team helped us get into Huazhong University of Science and Technology.

I didn't know I would make a comeback after bidding tennis farewell, just like I can't judge now whether the two years in retirement were ultimately good or bad for me. I recently read in the biography of Steve Jobs something that resonated with me: 'You can't see the future from here. It's only when you look back that you'll find the relationship between these points of time. So you just have to believe that those points will somehow connect in your future.'

Those words describe where I was at in 2002. Maybe it'll only be when I'm older, when I've completely left the tennis world, that I'll be able to really evaluate the choices I made in my youth. But at the time I didn't think what effect my retirement might have. I only wanted to pursue a free, full life. I wanted to do as I pleased.

I watched a lot of movies during my retirement. One of them starred Zhou Xun, who wasn't yet well known, playing a blind girl. Her whole family was killed, and she said to the killer, 'Kill me. If you don't kill me now, I'll have to beg for food for the rest of my life, and there's no dignity in that.' This line was like a tennis ball flying full speed right at me. I felt as if I'd found a kindred spirit. I wanted to live with dignity. And I realised that I wasn't alone in feeling this way.

I was a silly, ignorant little girl when I embarked on the path of tennis, but the sport had come to occupy an unrivalled place in my life. It had brought me too many ups and downs, too many sorrows and joys, and I had many contradictory feelings about it. Now, the chance to make a change was right in front of me, and I grabbed it without hesitation. I needed to change my way of life, to live quietly, with dignity, like an ordinary person.

I'd always moved in athletic circles. Now I was suddenly entering university, and I felt a sort of transfiguring joy. It was as if my life could start afresh. This new beginning filled me with both awe and pleasure.

Chapter 9

University

I knew I was walking a narrow path that not many had travelled before me. Most of my peers had gone to university to improve themselves, and ultimately to put their degrees and knowledge to work to land them a job, but my future was destined to take another route.

After constant training, matches and rankings, an athlete's retirement usually means becoming a coach or working in some other profession related to sports. This is the professional athlete's life trajectory. I would likely follow the same path. But something had happened: my mindset had changed. I didn't know if it was good or bad. I only knew that I couldn't let this time be wasted. I was serious about learning, and I wanted to apply what I learned in a way that made me realise my own sense of self-worth.

I didn't have the pressures of playing matches, nor did I have anxieties about my finances, and I was still young. I suddenly felt a sense of joy and nervousness about facing a new life, and a delayed feeling of solemnity.

Many people rely on crude stereotypes of athletes, assuming that they're merely simple minds with well-developed limbs. Even though athletes such as Yao Ming, Deng Yaping and Li Ning are recognised as studious, smart people, everyone still seems to think of athletes as ignorant. I was used to this. For many of our classmates at uni, when they heard that Jiang Shan and I were athletes, it was almost automatic for them to say, 'Oh, you didn't have the chance to study then?'

I felt that this way of looking at things was a bit one-dimensional. There are many types of education, and formal classroom study is just one of them. A professional athlete, especially one who's reached a certain level of achievement, must have very high expectations of him or herself. Without a strong sense of self-discipline and physical stamina, and a character built on self-respect, it would be hard to accomplish anything at all in professional sports. And not all contests can be won by physical prowess; we also have to keep our minds open and rigorous if we're to stand out from other players. It seems to me that many of the athletes who've gone on to find success in their sport are very talented people. When they work in other fields, these outstanding qualities help them succeed there too.

Furthermore, a sports team is not an uncivilised, primeval forest. During our cultural studies class at sports school, we had to learn certain manners, how to manage the media and how to handle our relationships with our coaches and leaders. (Though I've obviously not yet mastered this one, I do think it an important life lesson.) In tournaments where the prize money is substantial, there will always be public attention. This inevitably produces some grey areas in the lives of athletes, but also makes us more open-minded. We have a better understanding than most of our peers of the weight of the word 'unfair', and we have a better understanding of how we should regard such unfairness. Honestly, when I started at university, I was often amazed at the innocence and idealism of my peers – how could they be so simple?

A foot can be very short, and an inch very long. It all depends on what you are measuring. In the same way, everyone's own experiences have value. I ignored what others said and focused on making the most of my time at university.

In fact, my priority was to choose a new profession for myself. Science and technology fields required a lot of solid background knowledge, and I was afraid it was too late for me to enter these programmes. Jiang Shan and I both opted for the liberal arts, where we felt we could be more easily integrated.

We both quickly went for a journalism major. We knew the difficulties and ideals of athletes and felt that if we became sports reporters, we could speak from the point of view of athletes. I hoped to be a sports reporter with real ethics. I wouldn't resort to scurrilous headlines or misrepresent athletes for the sake of front-page coverage. Never.

The uni had a separate dorm for what was termed the 'sports class', and there were over thirty of us living there, comprising two groups. One was the average sports student, having studied at a normal primary school, middle school and high school. I didn't go to high school, but I could guess that the pressure experienced there was enormous, because these sports students complained that they'd been in school long enough.

Jiang Shan and I belonged to a different category: the former professional athletes. We'd gone into sports academies very young and started professional training, so we hadn't had much formal education. We hadn't had the opportunity to carry out a systematic study of anything aside from our sport, so our thirst for knowledge was strong, and we approached our studies with an almost pious attitude. We were sponges, trying to soak up all the things we hadn't been able to learn on the court. There were several other retired athletes taking journalism besides Jiang Shan and me, including former track and field stars and basketball players. Here we were all free from the stress of competition, and we enjoyed uni life, far away from the daily pressures of success and failure faced by athletes.

The teachers usually used a projector or PowerPoint during the classes. Jiang Shan and I would rapidly jot down notes, trying to keep up. I told Jiang Shan, 'I'll write down the first point, then you write the second, and if we continue on like that, we'll have a complete set of notes between us.'

We were never late and we never left early, and we went about our studies very seriously. Once during exams, the former professional athletes were pulled out and tested separately. Jiang Shan and I arrived early for the exam, and the teacher, who'd also come early, was very surprised to see us sitting there looking at our notes. 'You mean you two are in the sports class? I thought you were in the ordinary class.'

To hear those words meant a lot to me. It was the first time I'd ever had anyone show me respect for a reason other than the 'women's tennis champion' tacked onto my name. I was drawing closer to my goal of achieving a sense of self-worth.

This time away from competitive sports was the easiest, most stress-free period of my life. University helped me learn how to think in another way, to view life's problems from a different perspective. I liked sitting in the classroom hearing the students express conflicting views and listening to them argue over one point until they were red in the face. I liked walking through the calm campus. This was utterly different from my previous life. Everything at university was so fresh.

Huazhong was very big. It took fifteen minutes to ride a bike from our dorm to the classrooms on the east side of the campus and at least twenty-five minutes to those on the west. The first day on our way to class, Jiang Shan and I got lost. Adding to the problem was the rain, making us almost miss the class altogether. Class started at eight o'clock, but we entered the classroom at five minutes past eight, a string of students trailing in behind us. The teacher was very unhappy and made us write a self-criticism. After that, we were careful to avoid being late again.

The students were very friendly. Our journalism class was big, with two hundred students, but if there were any exam review materials, whoever had them made copies for everyone. It was like a large extended family.

Suffice to say the atmosphere was a little different from that of a sports team. With the team, I had to face many things on my own. The sort of pressure felt when a friend was named as your opponent wasn't matched in school – in sports, you compete with everyone, and you can't relax for a moment. That was the kind of atmosphere I'd been immersed in since I was eleven years old, without respite. Naturally, it had many negative effects.

Chinese sports culture is largely based on competition. All of our results are motivated by competition. Very few people can enjoy sport in that environment. We were used to establishing an imaginary opponent, then finding a way to defeat that opponent's advances. To fight this imaginary opponent in our minds, we expended gigantic efforts of will, to the point where no one really cared whether we took any pleasure in the actual game. When I was playing tennis, I accumulated so much pressure inside me that it would finally burst out. I'd feel momentarily better, and then it would start accumulating again, increasing and growing . . . finally transforming into a time bomb. If you live with a time bomb, how can you ever be happy? How can you relax and enjoy things? This is a huge departure from the original intent behind sports.

Sometimes, I'm really glad that I made the choice to go to university. It allowed me to see things I'd never seen before. My life is richer for it.

At uni, I didn't talk about tennis, so the people around me didn't know I was a tennis player. I took a lot of foundation courses, which were held in an amphitheatre that could accommodate more than two hundred people. The sports students and ordinary students all sat together and, unless you asked, you couldn't tell who was who. A female classmate who sat next to me often exchanged notes with me, and through this we became close. Not long after, the school started a tennis class for second-year students. This female classmate immediately decided to sign up, and encouraged me to enrol too.

'I don't know how to play tennis,' I said.

Later, when one of our classmates graduated and became a reporter on Beijing TV, she interviewed Zheng Jie and Yan Zi, the famous doubles players. She told them that she knew that I played tennis, but hadn't realised I played so well. She was shocked that after only four years I was playing at such a high level, believing that it was only after university that I took up the sport.

I liked it this way. I wanted to pass through my university years without any excitement and then, like everyone else, find a nine-to-five job, get married, have children and live the life of an ordinary woman.

During the two years I spent at university, I came into contact with much I hadn't had time to experience before. The university had automatically given all sports students five credits for physical education, which exempted us from PE class and gave us a bit more free time. Jiang Shan knew I wanted a new life, so in that free time he took me to play badminton, learn taekwondo, go dancing and generally have a lot of fun. Our taekwondo teacher liked tennis, and he was one of the few people at school who knew our background, so sometimes when he was bored, he would poke fun at Jiang Shan. During training, when we were doing stretches, the instructor would say to Jiang Shan, 'Open up! Wider! Do the splits! Come on!'

Jiang Shan's whole face would turn red and he'd be covered with sweat. 'I can't!'

But the teacher wouldn't give up. 'Come on! Try!'

We were a bunch of young people having fun. I was always happy, even if it was an especially hot summer day and we still had practice at the taekwondo hall. I even planned to try for a belt, but I didn't end up taking the test. I found that it wasn't difficult to learn after adapting to the rhythms of school life. There was a lot of free time at the university in the evenings, and I'd drag Jiang Shan out to stroll around.

I liked to go to the small shops at the night market and buy fruit, duck necks or other snacks. Jiang Shan found a small shop next to the market where he could hire DVDs. He would always pick some up, and we would go home and watch DVDs. At the time, I liked American television dramas. *CSI: Las Vegas* was one of my favourites, and I watched it over and over. Jiang Shan liked movies like *Young and Dangerous*. We watched a lot of movies and television series at that time.

Never had I lived such a life of leisure! I no longer had to get up early to run, nor did I have to knock myself out in training. The only downside was that I had to have braces, which meant I needed to take a bus to the orthodontic clinic once every two weeks. Braces were very painful. Just putting slight pressure on my teeth hurt, and I didn't dare eat hard foods. Instead, with a sullen face, I would eat plain porridge or rice noodles. But fortunately I had Jiang Shan around to take care of me.

Once, I sneezed and cut my upper lip on my lower teeth. It hurt so badly it brought tears to my eyes. I wanted to eat, but it hurt too much, and I lost my appetite. Jiang Shan went to the canteen and bought rice noodles for me to eat slowly. Because Huazhong was a big campus, there were twenty or more canteens. Every day, we could eat someplace different, sampling lots of good food. But because of the braces I missed out on a lot of the good things.

At Huazhong's main gate there was a statue of Chairman Mao, standing with one hand raised. Old people called the statue 'Mao Waves Us Onward'. Jiang Shan said it looked more like 'Mao Hails a Taxi'. In order to cheer me up, whenever we passed by the statue, Jiang Shan would shout, 'Look! Mao is helping us get a taxi!'

Although our background as professional athletes was relatively unknown, sometimes we had to represent the university in competitions.

Although we didn't put in as much effort as we had when we were professional, we still had to go to practice sometimes, or else when we went out to compete we wouldn't be up to standard and the university would lose face. During these practice sessions, there wasn't the time pressure or expectation that we'd had with the team, so we played more if we were in a good mood, and went home early if we weren't. It was for the sake of exercise, and there was no strong sense of purpose to it. Occasionally, when I played a little, I didn't mind it.

In our first year, Jiang Shan and I represented the school at the National Undergraduate Tournament. The school encouraged us to compete by giving us three academic credits. During our summer vacation in July 2003, we went back to train with the Hubei provincial team for a while, preparing for the university tournament. Stepping onto the court at Hubei, our mentality was completely different. Because we'd been focused on our studies, the training was enjoyable. But a few weeks into real training, I had blisters on my feet. The return after a long period away was good for the mind, but bad for the feet.

The finals of the National Undergraduate Tournament were held in Qingdao. While I was there, I ran into many of my old friends who'd remained in tennis circles. Before, everyone had been a friend and also an adversary. Off the court, we would eat together, but on the court, we would face off desperately. It was a little strange. Now it was more relaxing, and it felt like competing for the sake of meeting old friends.

After the tournament, I went back to university to continue my studies. But however much the trees prefer to remain still, the wind won't stop blowing. I wouldn't be left alone for long. Even though I'd left the Hubei provincial team, I maintained good relationships with the younger players. My teammates began to visit me often. As time wore on, they began to bring word to me: 'The team wants you back.'

Chapter 10

Negotiations

The National Games, Held every four years, were in Jiangsu in 2005. From late 2003 players from Hubei kept visiting me at university, all trying to persuade me to come out of retirement and play in the National Games.

I snapped at one of them, 'Are you crazy?'

The girl stuck out her tongue and left. It would be another girl the next time, but the words were the same.

When I left the team, it wasn't with entirely fond memories. Some of the players had secretly told me that the coach at that time had said, 'Let her go! Within two years, I'll train more good players to take her place!' Well, if she was such a good coach, let her train them then. There was really no need for me to get entangled in it all again.

Even with so many of my teammates coming to me and asking me to return, I continued to refuse. Finally, the coach came, and then the leader came. They all said the same thing. They hoped I would come back and compete in the National Games.

There are many behind-the-scenes facts about the sports community that remain unspoken. There are conflicts between players, coaches and leaders, and it's not something that can be explained easily. Before the previous National Games in 2001, the coaches basically had final say in everything, and the athletes essentially had no right to speak. Some of the leaders believed that eighty per cent or more of the credit for any success went to the coach, without taking into consideration the personal effort on the part of each athlete, so they continued to issue high-handed policies that would elevate the position of the coaches. When I went solo years later, I found that coaches in the West had a more service-oriented approach, as opposed to the domineering style I was used to. So in the West, the athlete's hard work is valued more.

At the 2001 National Games, eight of us from the provincial team participated: four men and four women. When the Games finished, there was only one man and one woman left on the team, while the rest had quit. We were all heartbroken, which showed in the flood of early retirements that followed. For athletes at their peak to lay down their hard-earned careers and retire, you know there's something wrong. We had striven through injury in order to gain honour for the team, but we really couldn't endure any more. If we didn't get along with our coaches, the leaders only listened to one side of the story. As the old saying goes, if you listen to both sides, things will become clear, but if you listen to only one side, you'll be left in the dark. How was it that the leaders didn't care about the athletes' feelings?

Now I told the team leader, 'You seem to believe the coaches can do no wrong and you never think about the athletes. Why come looking for me now? This really isn't very appropriate. Why do you think I left the team? Have you ever considered the reasons for that?'

So many unpleasant things had happened when I was on the team, and my decision to leave hadn't been an easy one. Why would I go back just because of a few words of persuasion?

The leader and I weren't on the same wavelength, and our discussion was deadlocked for a long time. It was only when the director of the

National Tennis Centre, Sun Jinfang, came to talk to me in late 2003 that we reached a turning point.

Sun Jinfang, the former captain of the national volleyball team, had been an acclaimed athlete. Before taking office, Sun had spoken privately to the Hubei coach and got a general idea of the strength of the team leading up to the National Games. She'd asked, 'I heard you have someone called Li Na. Where's she gone?'

'She's studying,' the coach replied.

Sun said, 'I'll get together with her and discuss a return to the team.'

We really did get together.

We met in Wuhan, at the provincial team's offices. It was just the two of us in the room. For Sun Jinfang, trying to keep a low profile, the meeting must have felt a bit clandestine. At the time, she'd just transferred from the National Sports Department to the National Tennis Centre. I'd known who she was since I was young. She'd led the national volleyball team to five consecutive championships.

Meeting her now, she didn't feel distant at all. She was thin and very tall, about 170 centimetres at a guess. She didn't put on official airs, but was very warm and enthusiastic. We got on well. Despite this, I figured it would be more of the same old tricks, that she would try to convince me to return to tennis. I thought, *I'm going to stick to my guns. If the leaders want to come, let them come. It's got nothing to do with me. I'm just here to finish my studies.*

But the conversation with Sun was very different than what I'd imagined. She started by asking me what I'd been doing recently, and I said I was going to uni. Then she asked what I planned to do next, and we continued chatting pleasantly. And then she cut straight to the chase. 'I heard many people say that there used to be a great player called Li Na who suddenly retired, so I decided to look into the matter. A lot of people say that you're very talented and that playing is your way of proving yourself. Why don't you play for yourself?'

I was a little surprised. I hadn't talked to any of the leaders a lot before, and I'd had the impression they were just full of hot air. Very rarely did they look at things from the athlete's perspective and act for our benefit. It was the first time a leader had been so open with me, and the first time anyone ever told me it was possible to 'play for yourself'. She said, 'If you want to come back, I can give you the opportunity.'

Sun didn't push her point too hard, but she re-established my relationship with tennis. Although her words had struck a chord, they still didn't completely shake my resolve to complete my studies. I was a little hesitant, and didn't give her an answer. The meeting was a brief interlude in my studies, and I eventually forgot it. But the visits from my old teammates increased. They'd been coming twice a week, and now it increased to three times a week. Eventually, they came every day, saying 'We really need you.'

From my point of view, their visits were affecting my life. What had been a comfortable, leisurely paced life had suddenly become interrupted by nonstop daily pestering. But I felt their sincerity. I was an outspoken and impatient woman, and very impressionable. If others bullied me, I wouldn't stand for it, but if others helped me, I would never forget it. A gentleman will die for his closest friend, and a lady will preen herself for her admirers. I'd played tennis since I was small, and had basically been raised by the Hubei provincial team. You could say it was a desire to return this kindness that made me decide to help the Hubei team compete in one more National Games.

During this period, I had a number of concerns weighing on me. Coming out of retirement was a big deal. When I retired, I was ranked number one in the country. What if I didn't play well when I came back? What would people say? And I didn't want to interrupt my studies, nor did I want to put my degree in jeopardy. If I came out of retirement, what would happen to my degree?

After much thought, I still couldn't come to a conclusion. I discussed it with Jiang Shan, and he said, 'I'm not going to stop you. You need to consider everything carefully. No matter what you decide, I'll support you.'

I asked my mother, 'Mum, what do you think of my going back into tennis?'

She was shocked. 'What? Are you serious? Don't joke with me!' Of course my mother knew the real reason I'd retired: my hormone imbalance. She'd taken me to a Chinese physician, and after two years of traditional Chinese medicine, I'd finally recovered.

I said, 'I'm serious.'

After a brief silence, she said, 'Then I won't ask anything of you except this. If you get worn out, come home again.'

In January 2004, I returned to the provincial team. The next tournament was in April, so I decided to start training again after the Chinese New Year in late January.

It hadn't been easy to make the choice to retire in the first place because it meant leaving my familiar circle, leaving a world that I'd devoted myself to heart and soul and trying to start a new life. The decision to come back was even more difficult because I had the dual stresses of facing an unknown future and feeling as though I were backtracking.

Sun played a crucial role in my comeback. She spoke to me very honestly. Perhaps it was because she was new in the role and we didn't have any history of conflict between us. Or perhaps it was because she too had been an athlete. In fact, she'd been one of the best athletes, and so she had a better understanding of how other athletes thought. She made me feel that she was a person who dared to speak up, who dared to act and who wasn't overly concerned with what others had to say. She sincerely wanted to do something good for tennis.

I've always remained grateful to her in my heart, but I never had the nerve to tell her how appreciative I was. We didn't have many opportunities to communicate directly, because I didn't report to her. When I went back to Beijing to handle official matters a couple of years ago, I looked her up to say hello and ask how she was. She knows I have knee problems, as she does, and we talked about that. Later, when I was back in Wuhan, we talked again, and Sun listened carefully.

When I came home after winning the French Open, CCTV celebrated with 'Li Na Night'. Sun was there in the studio too.

Chapter 11

Comeback

Before 2004, I didn't really have any goals. I'd blindly followed the crowd, and other than making the decision to be with Jiang Shan, I was pretty much doing things to conform to others' expectations. Especially between 1999 and 2002, the first time I played for the national team, I was in a bad state. I had a strong desire for independence, but the national team had so many rules. Everyone was very submissive and obedient with Coach Yu. No one dared to resist anything she said. In fact, we didn't even dare to *think* of resisting. Of course, these problems were not personal, but cultural and institutional.

During the two years I was at university, I'd straightened out my own mindset. My knowledge and experience in playing tennis also changed. Tennis in this new state of mind felt very different. When I first made my comeback, people would often say, 'That's Li Na,' then keep quiet. Sometimes they would add, 'Oh, she's come out of retirement.' Actually, it wasn't that significant. Retiring or making a comeback is a big decision to the one making it, but to everyone else, it's not a big deal. This made me relax and think, *Don't put too much pressure on yourself. No one's really paying attention to what you do. Just do your best.*

The first tournament after my comeback was a US$25 000 ITF

competition, a small event. Coming back to the scene after two years away, I had conflicting feelings. Everything seemed familiar yet strange. At the time, the courts we played on in ITF competition were at Yuting Qiao, where there were four or five courts side by side. Outside the stadium, there were two glass-walled lounges we could use to rest and watch the matches, or we could go upstairs and watch from there. The stadium didn't have a locker room, so we had to take our clothes into the bathroom to change, then wait for the matches to start.

When I started attending WTA tournaments, I realised how different they were. They're held at courts with much better conditions. The lounges are usually big, able to hold at least a hundred people. In the locker room, everyone has her own locker. The organising committee has a trainer on hand, and you can ask them for treatment.

The locker rooms are usually only open to the athletes. Almost everyone in this circle knows each other. If the person you're facing the next day is a friend, then you might greet her in the locker room with, 'See you on the court tomorrow.' Sometimes you might not know your opponent at all before you play her. Nowadays, there are many newcomers, and I might not know anything about them. A few days before I play a new opponent, I read up about her online, taking note of her style of play. Before the match, you can also observe your opponent in the locker room. Many of the outstanding players have unique personalities. For instance, Sharapova's general aura is very tough. Her proud demeanour can give her momentum to really dominate an opponent. But when you get to know her better, you find that her pride is not directed at any one person. It's just the way she is.

When I first made my comeback, I had to start in the qualifiers of every tournament because I had no points. Each tennis player earns points as they play in the tournaments throughout the year, and the final world rankings are based on your annual performance. On the first day of training at the competition, I saw the tournament's number one seed in the locker room. Her world ranking was 180 at the time. If I remember correctly, she was Portuguese, and a little younger than me. Jiang Shan always accompanied me to events, and unable to hold it in, I kept saying things to him like, 'Why is she ranked so high?' and 'She looks pretty good.' Jiang Shan didn't say anything, but just sat watching the people training. When we got home after watching, he said very calmly, 'She's not in the same league as you.'

I said, 'How can that be?'

Coming back after two years of retirement, I didn't have a very good understanding of the overall tennis scene in China or the world, and I wasn't sure of my own standing in that situation; I felt a little off kilter. In my mind, 180 was a high rank. My confidence was fragile, especially since there were so many new, young players. Some of the young players I was closer to on the Hubei team told me that this or that person was really good. But I adopted a tolerant attitude toward myself, just wanting to do my best and play to whatever level I could.

I played a total of three matches in the qualifiers, all of which were unusually smooth. But then something happened.

I'm not very good at handling stress, and the first three matches had gone smoothly only because I had no expectations. I was uncertain and thought of the matches as training rather than real matches to win. But as soon as I made it into the actual competition, I suddenly realised that I wanted to win, and that I *had* to win. It was like the plot in *Journey to the West*: the monkey king went to steal the celestial peaches, intending at first just to eat one, but then ended up deceiving himself into believing that the whole tree belonged to him. This desire built up tremendous pressure inside me, and I suffered a lot of self-inflicted psychological torture. In the last match of the preliminaries, I sustained a slight injury to my back. For a professional athlete, these sorts of injuries are no big deal, but in this instance, my chest started to burn and my breathing became laboured. My whole back hurt very badly.

When I saw that the draw was about to begin, I felt like a hammer was pounding on my back. It hurt so much that I couldn't sleep that night. My blood flow was disrupted, and the old hormonal problem was aggravated again. I hurried to find the Beijing team doctor.

All women know what this type of hormonal disorder feels like. The bloating, oppressive soreness coupled with a backache made me very anxious about whether I would be in a state to compete. During the first round of matches that day, I felt very nauseous, which kept the doctor busy. After I arrived at the court, the umpire kept looking in my direction. He clearly thought I would choose to withdraw, and had even filled out the necessary forms for me.

I told him I would not withdraw. I could still play. And I played the match quite well.

Perhaps an illness caused by tennis could only be cured by tennis. Perhaps it was because the match had gone so well, but the tightness was released, and my mind was unburdened. The doctor considered this an acute incident, one that came quickly and then receded just as fast. By the time I got to the semifinals, I felt almost no pain in my back.

Jiang Shan was with me until the semifinals. After that, his leave had been used up and he had to go back to Wuhan for class. By this time, I'd developed a better understanding of myself and my opponents, and I returned to the more relaxed state of mind I'd been in during the qualifiers. In the semifinals, I met the number one-seeded player from Portugal, the one Jiang Shan had said was 'not in my league'. I won that match without trouble. After the match, I called Jiang Shan and said, 'I won in straight sets, 6–4, 6–0.'

He said very calmly, 'Oh, 6–4, 6–0. You won. Good.'

I tend not to believe Jiang Shan's every word. We often joke with each other that I have to assess the context to distinguish whether or not he's joking. I thought that he'd said the number one seed was not in my league just to comfort me, and so hadn't taken it seriously.

Only when I'd defeated her did I begin to believe what he'd said.

Winning the first battle after my comeback really helped restore my peace of mind, preparing me for the series of four tournaments that followed. These tournaments were tightly scheduled: the first in Beijing, the second in Tongliao, the third in Ulanhot and the fourth back in Beijing. When I was competing in the first tournament, there were three heats, which included eight matches. According to competition regulations, since I didn't have a world ranking, I had to play in the qualifiers. However, because I'd won the championship in my first tournament back, according to ITF rules, I was given a pass, allowing me to go straight into the draw. I went on to win in both Beijing and Tongliao.

The first two tournaments had been on hard courts. For the third tournament in Ulanhot, Mongolia, the organisers sent out a fax telling us that it would be on clay courts, but when we arrived, we discovered that it was dirt. This made many of the foreign competitors very angry, feeling they had been deceived. Their managers went to the umpires asking for a change of venue, threatening to withdraw from the tournament if the venue weren't changed. They also approached me and suggested I withdraw from the tournament. Since I'd won the championships in the two previous tournaments, and since I was a local Chinese player, they felt the name Li Na would carry some weight. In fact, I was in a more embarrassing situation than anyone. I was never an eloquent speaker. Whatever words came out of my mouth, however reasonable, would sound unreasonable. And the tradition in our country has always been 'don't cause the people at the top any trouble'. Feeling very awkward, I could only tell the foreign players that I needed to train, and that it was best for them to solve the problem themselves.

Aside from the fact that using dirt courts as a stand-in for clay was disappointing, the backward conditions at the hotel were also a headache. The local hotel wouldn't accept credit cards or charge to players' rooms, so even a cup of coffee had to be paid for in cash. The waiters stood there staring at the players, expecting payment. This made the foreign players feel that the whole situation was ridiculous. On top of that, it was very windy in Ulanhot, with sand flying everywhere, making training and competition difficult. We asked the hotel staff how often they encountered such scathing winds in a year, and they said, 'Twice: the first for six months, and the second for another six months.' Upon hearing this, everyone just laughed. We could only assume that as soon as one wind died down another started up.

In these harsh conditions, many of the players dropped out of the competition, and others just played the matches half-heartedly. The organisers became concerned, so they started searching for an indoor venue.

What really touched me was that the day before the third match, my coach said, 'Li Na, you've already played two matches. It's exhausting. The fourth will be even harder than the previous three, so let's make some arrangements to help.'

The result was that we took a day trip to the nearby grasslands. Our tour group included the leader, the coach, the team doctor and two other young members of the Hubei team. We all rode horses to the grasslands, which took about an hour. I didn't know how to ride a horse, and after a day on horseback, I was extremely sore. But the scenery at the grasslands was beautiful and very relaxing. The local people were very friendly, and we got to watch some traditional Mongolian dances in the yurts, then went riding again, tried our hand at archery, and had a really enjoyable time. At night, we were entertained with a feast of a whole roasted lamb. It was the first time I'd ever seen a whole lamb roasted, tail and all. Even its head stood at a stiff angle, giving me a bit of a shock. The people kept asking us to eat more as we sat feasting in a big yurt. They even brought out *manai* wine to serve us. It had a slightly fishy smell that I wasn't quite used to, but I appreciated the kindness, and we all at least gave it a try.

After a while, another group of local people led us all in song and dance. A person told us the history of Mongolia, singing the praises of their heroic ancestor Genghis Khan. By the time we left the grasslands and returned to the hotel, it was already after eleven at night.

I was very happy that day, and I sang a lot. When I had emerged from the yurt, I saw the empty space between earth and sky, the vast expanse of the grassland, and the sky full of bright stars hanging so low you felt you could reach out and touch them. At that moment, I felt a sudden awakening and thought, *What is winning or losing a couple of matches, really? They won't be obstacles on the path in front of me.*

And with that in mind, I was very relaxed as I went through the final two matches. I won the championship in four matches. The media dubbed it 'a strong comeback for Li Na', but really that was a bit of an exaggeration. It wasn't difficult to win in four straight matches because a lot of players had dropped out. Although there were some who didn't drop out, most didn't go at full tilt, fearing injury. Still, it did help restore my confidence, and that was very important.

I ended up winning all four tournaments, and less than a month after, I was ranked number 182 in the world. Now I began to get nervous again, wondering whether I should continue my studies or stick with tennis. The original intent of my comeback had been simply to help the Hubei team in the National Games, but my form had surprised me. On the one hand, I was eager to complete my bachelor's degree and lead an ordinary life, letting my volatile moods settle. On the other, the prospects for my playing career looked very promising, and I started to think I might be able to really achieve something big.

Chapter 12

Matches

In August 2004, during summer holidays at uni, I had the opportunity to go to the US to play in a tournament. The US$50 000 competition was in the Bronx, in New York City. The tournament itself wasn't that important, but being held just before the US Open qualifying matches, it was a good chance for practice.

Usually when I went overseas, it was with my teammates, a group of a dozen or so people travelling together. At the very least there would usually be a coach travelling with me. This time I was alone, stumbling along by myself, and I ran into trouble. While I was checking into my hotel, the staff couldn't find my booking. When I called home, the staff who took care of the reservations for the team said they'd reserved the room, but the hotel still couldn't find any record of it. The hotel staff said I could use a credit card to check in, but I didn't have one. Athletes like us, travelling at the public's expense to compete, usually only carried cash. That day, it was already very late, and I was alone and dragging a huge suitcase around on the streets of a foreign city, trying to find a place to rest. I was almost ready to just sleep on the street. Fortunately, at that moment I ran into a woman from Tianjin who had also come to play in the tournament, and she let me stay in her room that night.

The next day I went to the organising committee to sort the problem out. They contacted the hotel and made a new reservation for me. This was how my first overseas tournament after my comeback started.

I once again had to play in the qualifiers. But with the four championships I'd just won as a foundation, I had plenty of confidence. I was relaxed and I played quite smoothly, eventually making my way into the semifinals. My doubles results were also very good. The player from Tianjin was my partner, and we won the championship. After the tournament, I packed up and got ready to play in the next tournament, the qualifier for the US Open. But here I encountered another mishap – the team had failed to register me!

To be more precise, at the end of the online registration, there was a confirmation procedure, and they'd failed to complete that. The registration process is handled by individual professional athletes all over the world, but for us, it was done by the team staff. Due to my retirement, I was out of touch with these things. I'd assumed that the team staff had prepared everything for me. The final result was that, after muddling my way through discussions with the American organisers, it was not to be. This was my first chance at a Grand Slam qualifier after my comeback, but because my registration wasn't confirmed all I could do was pick up my bags and go to the airport, alone. I thought to myself, *This opportunity wasn't easy to come by, and I have to miss out because of a minor error. I don't know when I'll get another chance. Maybe there won't be another.* I was full of regret and resentment.

After returning home, I began to prepare for the China Open. In late September 2004, after establishing myself with a winning streak in the three qualifiers, I got a pass to the inaugural China Open. The opponent I encountered in the first round was the Australian veteran Nicole Pratt. She was ranked forty-ninth in the world.

Before this, I'd never played against any of the world's top fifty, so I was very stressed and kept wondering about Pratt's standard. She was older, already thirty-two, while I was still very young at twenty-two. I joked with my teammates saying, 'I'll fight with all my strength, because I can't win against her any other way.'

I won 6–3, 6–2, and after my victory, I went to shake hands with Pratt and the umpire. I was in a daze. Was it really that simple? Did I really just defeat one of the fifty best players in the world? Before my retirement, I played my heart out and never won. Now after two years away, it was all coming more easily. How come I was so relaxed as I played, and yet still won? It really was like a dream.

In the press conference that followed, many reporters asked me questions, but my mind was elsewhere. Jiang Shan reminded me that my opponent in the second round would be Svetlana Kuznetsova. She was from Russia, nicknamed the 'St Petersburg Powerhouse', and had just won the championship title at the US Open; she was really hot at the time.

This would be my first time playing against a Grand Slam champion, and I was excited, as if I were close to a master. While I was training, I told Jiang Shan, 'I've only seen her on TV before. Tomorrow we can really play each other.'

In the warm-up before the match the following day, I was practising my serve and joking with Jiang Shan, saying, 'My opponent is too strong. Will I even be able to return her serve?' But when I actually got onto the court, I found that I could. I realised that I might have overestimated Grand Slam champions; Kuznetsova wasn't quite as invincible as I expected.

The first two sets of that game were back and forth affairs, and the score was tight. Although my confidence had certainly received a big boost in my victory over Pratt, it was wavering a little as I faced an opponent ranked in the top ten, who also held the US Open title. Kuznetsova was the most formidable opponent I'd faced since my debut, and I couldn't compete with her imposing experience. I talked a good game, but I really wasn't that confident.

The result of this was that I was under pressure the whole game and was a bit too passive. In the third set, I got to match point twice. I should have moved steadily ahead and put the match away, but my heart started pounding rapidly and the thought was in the back of my mind, *I might defeat a US Open champion! One of the top ten players in the world!* This sort of awareness in the mind of a player who had only just returned to competition was too sudden, and it led to heart palpitations and shortness of breath. With all my concerns, I lost my edge.

Kuznetsova was, after all, a Grand Slam champion. She was more experienced, and she at once noticed my loss of concentration. Seizing the opportunity, she pulled the score even several times. After that, she regained control of the momentum, and I lost the match.

Later, Jiang Shan said that even though I lost the match, he firmly believed that I was close to being on par with the world's best players. I wasn't far from the top ten, or the Grand Slam champions. He reminded me that I'd just come back and that my training was still not very systematic, and that if I could play at this level now, he had a lot of faith in me for the future.

I had a similar feeling. Prior to that match, a Grand Slam championship was something sacred and out of reach. Now it appeared closer than I could have imagined. I just had to reach out for it, and I could pluck the fruits of victory. This tournament left a deep impression on me. Losing two match points, and allowing Kuznetsova to regain control, was a little disappointing, but I knew what to do next time. And the media clearly thought I had something: from this match on, the media attention on me increased greatly.

After losing to Kuznetsova, I rushed to Guangzhou to play in the inaugural Guangzhou International Women's Open, which was part of the WTA competition. Younger competitors who have impressed at earlier tournaments receive a wildcard, eliminating the need for three rounds of qualifiers to get into the tournament. After playing in the China Open, I assumed I would get a wildcard, but when I arrived in Guangzhou, my hopes were disappointed. The qualifiers started the day after I arrived, so with no time to rest, I went directly into competition.

In the three qualifying rounds, my play was steady, so it was smooth sailing to the main draw. In my fifth round, which was the second round of the official draw, I met Jelena Jankovic from Serbia. She was one of the world's top-thirty players and was the number two seed at the tournament.

When we played the first set, I lost 0–6, and then I won the second set. In the third, I had two match points, but failed to close it out, and I grew impatient. Coming just after the Kuznetsova game, where I also failed to take two match points in the third set . . . My impatience and nerves lasted right up until I finally won the match. I breathed a sigh of relief and thought, *At last, the result goes my way.*

From then on, the tournament went well. Including the qualifiers, I won eight straight matches, defeating a world top-thirty player in Jankovic and a top-fifty player in Vera Dushevina. I entered the finals, where my opponent was Slovakia's Martina Sucha. This was the first time I'd played in the finals at a WTA tournament. I hadn't even made it to the semifinals before. I went online and read up on Sucha. A few years earlier, she'd been the world champion. She was very good.

Before the match, my mind was relatively calm. I paid careful attention to my opponent's strengths and weaknesses, very patiently preparing before the match. This hard work paid off. When I was on the court, I felt good, and ultimately won 6–3, 6–4.

The match was played on 1 October. When it ended, a reporter from *Sports Illustrated* came to congratulate me, saying, 'You're the first Chinese to win a WTA singles championship.' It was only then that

I realised I'd set a record. I was utterly clueless – if no one had said anything, I wouldn't even have known.

Being the first Chinese WTA singles champion seemed like a good omen, and for a period of time after that, I was in pretty good shape. On 3 October 2004, with the help of the win at the Guangzhou International Women's Open, my world ranking jumped in a week from 145 to ninety-two. This was the first time I'd been ranked in the top one hundred. By the end of the year, my ranking was locked in at eighty.

For me, 2004 was a memorable year. After my comeback I was like a blank page, wiped clean of all previous results. The rebuilding process wasn't easy. I was like a child lost in the woods, slowly feeling my way along, trying to make my way through the trees – Jiang Shan helped me find the right path. He recognised my potential and encouraged me to keep going. There were honours I never dared to think of, so he thought of them on my behalf. His boldness and certainty gave me great confidence. I was full of hope for my future. Gradually, I broke through the barriers within myself and came to believe that I too could become one of the world's top players.

Chapter 13

Approaching the Grand Slam

For the 2004 Olympics, I was sent as a practising partner for the Olympic team players. Afterward, the national team gave me and another female player the chance to go to Uzbekistan to take part in the Asian Games. There, I sailed my way through to win the championship. I didn't think too much of winning the title, and when the ceremony was over, I hurried to call Jiang Shan and tell him, 'Tomorrow I can come home!' There was a two-hour time difference between Uzbekistan and China, and when I called, it was three o'clock in the afternoon and Jiang Shan was still in class. He went into the corridor to answer the call and hurriedly said, 'Okay, okay. I'm in class.' The implication was clear: 'Don't interfere with my studies.' At that time he was always busy at university.

When the team had failed to register me and I missed the qualifier for the US Open, I was quite depressed, and I hadn't considered that this could be a blessing in disguise. Thanks to my Asian Games title, I snagged a wildcard for the 2005 Australian Open in January. Without a wildcard, I would have to go through the qualifiers. The Open was still several months away, and to Jiang Shan and me, it was still just an abstract concept.

Thinking of it several years later, I said to Jiang Shan, 'Remember how calm I was back then?'

He dismissed my recollection. 'You mean you were so dazed you were slow to react?'

It was true. I remember feeling a sort of vague surprise at the news of my wildcard, but I wasn't quite sure what was waiting for me. Only when the wildcard was actually sent to me did I realise that I was going to the Australian Open.

My first Grand Slam: it really was a milestone. What's the goal of all professional athletes? It's to compete. And what's the most important competition in tennis? The Grand Slam! I was energised.

In late January 2005, I took my wildcard and went directly into the Australian Open draw. After the opening rounds, I was in good shape, on a two-match winning streak. Defeating the twenty-eighth-seeded Shinobu Asagoe from Japan, I made it into the third round.

I learnt that my next opponent would be the famous Maria Sharapova. She'd just won the Wimbledon title and was enjoying the limelight. Our match was at Rod Laver Arena – centre court. According to the regulations, before the start of the match we had to wait for someone to take us in to play. I was extremely nervous. The corridor leading to the stadium had pictures of previous Australian Open champions displayed on both sides, but I was in no state to enjoy them. My mind was a blank as I strode mechanically onto the court. Later, my teammate Li Ting told me that my posture as I walked was a dead giveaway of my nerves.

I heard the announcer saying, 'Now we warmly welcome the Chinese player, Li Na.' Aside from nerves, I felt nothing. Rod Laver Arena stood proudly in front of me, grand, magnificent and unfathomable. This stadium has outstanding features, including a retractable roof, and it made a deep impression on me. It seemed huge, like the *Titanic* of tennis courts. Its size was overwhelming, so much larger than any place I'd played before. I stood on the court and suddenly felt like I was standing in the Roman Colosseum. Cries from the spectators roared like a tornado overhead. They were calling out for their invincible queen, and I stood there as the unlucky gladiator holding a racket like a wooden shield. But I'd forgotten my spear.

How can there be such a big stadium? As I stood on the court, this was the only question I could conjure.

Sharapova ranked higher than me, so she came to the court after me. When she entered the arena, the applause was thunderous. Sharapova was already tremendously popular, and the stadium was filled with her fans. There was hardly an empty seat as far as the eye could see. A dense mass of humanity reached almost up to the roof. Later I learned that Rod Laver Arena was very popular with locals and could seat 15 000 people. But if you'd told me at the time that it seated ten million, I would have believed it.

I could feel my own nervousness, but didn't know how to relieve the tension. I remember trying to act fearless, playing it cool as I put my bag down, then I took my racket and went to the umpire and listened to the rules of the game. During that time, Sharapova's supporters were shouting her name nonstop. Cameras flashed from time to time in the stands.

We separated and hit the ball back and forth to warm up. Then the match began.

I only won two games in that entire match, losing very quickly. It was the fastest I'd lost a match since I started playing tennis.

I didn't feel sad. I was only nervous; extremely nervous. When the match was over, I took my racket and things and went down the corridor to the lounge. I noticed that my hands were still shaking. That sort of anxiety gets right down into the marrow.

At the post-match press conference the reporters flocked to me as usual, asking how I felt. I said I just felt that the stadium was huge and that I hadn't been able to adjust to it. It was the first time I'd seen such a big court, and I had no idea what to do. I think several of the experienced reporters must have been suppressing a chuckle. They continued asking, 'How do you plan to adapt?'

I said, 'I can only adjust slowly. As I play more games and gain more experience, I will naturally adjust.'

And so my Australian Open odyssey came to an end. I comforted myself with the thought that, no matter what, I'd got close to a Grand Slam and had seen the gap between myself and the world's top players.

In 2011, when I again played in the Australian Open, I'd gained a lot of experience playing on centre court. I even practised often on centre court. I was surprised to see that the arena wasn't so big after all. How could it have felt so huge back then? Maybe the change wasn't in the place, but in my mind. Perhaps this was the outcome I'd been fighting for over the years I spent on the circuit.

When the Australian Open finished, I took part in a series of international tournaments. I'd previously played in smaller ITF tournaments, but since my comeback, I'd found my rhythm and begun playing in WTA tournaments, steadily accumulating points toward my world ranking. It was perhaps my most brilliant period, as if a desire had suddenly awakened within me after two years of silence. Although I hadn't really broken into the core of international tennis competition, everything was pointing that way.

I improved quickly. At the Estoril Open in Portugal, I defeated world number forty-four Dinara Safina to get into the finals. In the Fed Cup World Group II playoffs, I played well in two separate singles events, including a defeat of Katarina Srebotnik, world number eighty-seven. In Toronto's top event, I defeated world number eighteen Jelena Jankovic. This was the first time I'd beaten a player in the top twenty. I found that I could take on some of the world's best players, and my confidence correspondingly increased.

In late August 2005, I got into my first US Open. This time I wasn't an unknown, and I was no longer intimidated by centre court. Unfortunately, luck wasn't with me. In the first round, I faced the top seed Lindsay Davenport. The American veteran was fighting in her hometown with exceptional courage, and to match her I had to fight my heart out. Although I lost in two sets 4–6, 4–6, I was ultimately satisfied with my performance.

I had a sort of affinity for the US, perhaps because of the ten months there during my teens. Listening to the casual English the people speak is very soothing to my ears. Although the US doesn't have the sort of stately beauty of Europe's more seasoned, older cities, it's lively. It's a young, vibrant country.

The US Open's Arthur Ashe Stadium is the largest centre court of the four Grand Slam venues. It wasn't like Rod Laver at the Australian Open, awesome in my mind, but the venue itself was unusually large. Once I was with five teams of reporters from CCTV, and we stood on a terrace high above centre court chatting. This was the first time I'd been up there, and looking down really was horrifying. The CCTV reporter told me that, for security purposes, there were snipers over centre court. Thinking of dozens of snipers lurking around was enough to make my hair stand on end.

The US Open is held near an airport, and it's noisy. During the tournament, the airport ensures that aircraft are slightly rerouted so as not to affect the players' games. I hate noisy environments when I'm playing, but I don't mind the sound of aircraft. When I was in Texas at the tennis academy, there were often planes flying over the courts, so it's a familiar sound for me, and not at all upsetting. As I stood on the court at the US Open, the sound was a comforting reminder of my youth.

Chapter 14

Media Fiasco

After the US Open, I went home to prepare for the National Games in October that year. It was then that something unexpected happened, and it brought me more trouble and sorrow than I could ever have imagined. I was misunderstood, misread and misrepresented. It made me angry and regretful, and cost me many sleepless nights. I felt like a fish on a chopping board waiting to be slaughtered, feebly opening my mouth, but unable to utter a sound.

The story went like this: 'Li Na, playing in the National Games as the defending champion, was crushed by her teammate Peng Shuai in the women's semifinals. After the match, Li Na blasted the national team's system, leading to widespread rumblings and a very public rift. The National Tennis Centre director Sun Jinfang publicly criticised Li Na, saying Li would definitely not be allowed to represent China at the Beijing Olympics.'

I read various reports repeating this series of events, and every time, I had the same feeling. It froze the blood in my veins. How could this have happened?

I know I'm a very direct person, not guarded in my speech. I say whatever's on my mind, and my emotions come and go very quickly. If someone you like has this sort of personality, you call them 'outspoken'. If it's someone you don't like, you call them 'blunt'. I was just such a person. For me, hiding emotions is extremely difficult. It had been the cause of many of my failures on the court over the past few years, and was the main reason my results had been inconsistent in major competitions.

I'd been feeling very depressed over the loss to Peng Shuai when a reporter asked me how I felt about training with the national team. I told the truth: 'I think the measures the national team takes aren't quite perfect. There's no real systematic training geared toward individual players.' This really was, in my experience, the deficiency of the national training system, and I spoke honestly about it. But when these words appeared in the newspaper they seemed ambiguous, suggestive of something much more explosive. Soon, headlines reading 'Li Na Slams the National Team System' were all over the media, the story growing more exaggerated with every reprint. I never hurt anyone, and I didn't want to hurt anyone. I just wanted to go quietly about my business, live my life and be myself. But within twenty-four hours I became public enemy number one. There was talk of 'the gloves coming off' and 'earthquakes' within Chinese tennis. I was just a young girl playing tennis, neither a superhero nor a monster. As if I could wield such power over the national team!

After the first article was published, the same reporter who'd interviewed me went to Sun Jinfang and said, 'Li Na said the national team's training isn't good. What do you think of that?'

Is this not purposely stirring things up?

Sun spoke her mind, and the reporter immediately came to me for a response. I was hurt by Sun's words, but I didn't dare respond.

A single sentence, passed through three people's hands, was completely transformed.

Honestly, I was disgusted with the behaviour of the reporter who went back and forth telling tales. What I'd said had been transformed into something completely different. This experience also gave me a real fear of reporters. They were too smart, always laying traps for others to fall into. They would behave one way to your face, agreeing with what you said, but they would suddenly come up with a whole new theory in print. I felt betrayed and cheated.

This time was distressing for both Sun and me. Because I momentarily spoke freely, I made a rod for my own back and caused Sun to face extreme pressure. I'm a straightforward person, and I had never communicated well with the team leaders. I felt I gave Sun a lot of trouble, and I was even more embarrassed to approach her to chat.

I prefer to let my actions prove my words, but there are some things for which I can't produce any proof.

My Danish coach, Michael Mortensen, once told the media, 'After the 2011 French Open, Li Na became a superstar. But stardom always comes with a price.' In fact, even before I became a superstar, I'd started paying that price. Fame is a double-edged sword, and even if you only have a small amount of fame, you still have to consistently pay for it.

For a long time after that, I avoided talking to the media. On the occasions that I did, my words were carefully considered – the fruit of repeated discussions with Jiang Shan.

I felt that no matter what I said, it was wrong. Talking too much would cause me trouble. Talking less would cut down on the likelihood of mistakes. The truth is, even if I'd said nothing at all, the media could take that and write, 'Li Na is depressed and needs to lift her spirits', or something similar. It really got me down.

Before this, I'd always been very willing to talk to reporters after a match, sharing my feelings with them. Sometimes I would have a lot to say: 'Today my forehand wasn't very good', or 'I didn't have much stamina', or something like that. But comments that were actually related to tennis didn't get much attention. Instead, it was the irrelevant things that aroused interest. If I mentioned off-hand, 'I think there's a problem with the training regimen', the next day it would lead in papers nationwide with the headline 'Li Na Slams the National System'. I understand that everyone has their own ideas about the national system and that I'm just a tennis player. Ladies and gentlemen, let's stop forcing the issue, okay?

During this period, Jiang Shan also dealt with a lot on my behalf. He was usually with me, coaching me on how to express my ideas and how to deal with the media. But at the press conference after the National Games, when I made that fateful remark, only players were allowed in. If he'd been there to help me, I might have been able to avoid that pitfall.

When I feel depressed, I like to do something I've never done before to lift my mood. In 2001 at the National Games in Guangzhou, when Jiang Shan and I were forced to separate for mixed doubles play, I was really blue. When the games were over, I went and got a tattoo of a heart and rose. It wasn't for any deep reason – it was a nice design and the act of tattooing cheered me up, taking me out of the distress I'd felt on the court. Jiang Shan was annoyed by it, saying it made me look like a wild child.

I retorted, 'Can a tattoo determine if a person is good or bad?'

He said I didn't get it, and that other people would make the tattoo fodder for gossip.

Sure enough, many reporters noticed the tattoo, and pictures of it appeared everywhere. A lot of people thought it was a snake. Some thought it was yet another sign of my ego. Some said accusingly, 'Li Na got a tattoo! What right has she?'

Later, when I appeared on a TV program, the host asked me if it was a symbol of love. I gave a tight nod of agreement and, deciding to go with the flow, said that I'd got the tattoo to commemorate my feelings for Jiang Shan. Suddenly my tattoo was exalted as a romantic gesture. Overnight, everyone had swung to my side. 'The tattoo is to commemorate her love for Jiang Shan. How lovely!'

The human psyche is an amazing thing. A nineteen-year-old girl's capricious move could actually be interpreted as being loaded with so much intention and meaning. I was speechless. Truth and untruth are both produced from the same set of lips. After years of media experience, I finally grew numb to it. Let them say whatever suits them. Later, Jiang Shan showed me a quotation often attributed to Mother Teresa (I found out later that it was an adaption from the 'The Paradoxical Commandments' by Dr Kent M. Keith), and found it very helpful: 'If you are kind, people may accuse you of selfish, ulterior motives; be kind anyway.

'If you are successful, you win some false friends and some true enemies; succeed anyway.

'The good you do today, people will often forget tomorrow; do good anyway.

'You see, in the final analysis, it's between you and God; it was never between you and anyone else.'

My so-called 'slamming' of the national system was something I never spoke about again publicly, and it's remained a sore spot. I know that these types of situations can snowball out of control. Fortunately, the national team coaches and leaders all knew what I was like, and how this had been stoked by the media. Within the team, it didn't set off a firestorm. But in my own mind, it was difficult to get over, and I was very depressed about it.

When things settled down, I suddenly felt like going to get some professional photos done of us as a couple. Jiang Shan wasn't keen, but thinking of all I'd just been through and how down I was, he agreed to it. Although it was just a formality, some girls need this sort of formality.

The photos were beautiful, with both indoor and outdoor shots of us. Posing for professional photos is quite tiring. We'd only had a couple done before, right after I'd retired.

It was also then that I suddenly decided that I wanted to get married.

Chapter 15

Marriage

The culmination of my relationship with Jiang Shan in marriage was a natural thing. We didn't discuss it much before it happened.

At the end of January 2006, I encountered Serena Williams in the first round at the Australian Open. I lost in three sets. I was tired and didn't say anything, but just got a ticket straight back to Wuhan. Every time I finished playing, I wanted to hurry home. Playing exhausted me, and being home recharged me. I was very tired and wanted a good rest.

Jiang Shan made a special point of coming to the airport to meet me. We got home and put down my luggage, and some friends wanted us to go for dinner and karaoke. I nestled onto the sofa and said, 'I'm too tired. I want to sleep. I don't feel like going.'

Jiang Shan said gently, 'Let's just go for a while. Everyone wants to see you.'

After dinner, we went to karaoke, and when we entered the room there was a huge cake and an enormous bunch of roses. It was a very large bouquet, ninety-nine flowers in all. This was the moment Jiang Shan had chosen to propose to me. A friend helped me carry the roses home, and some girls who passed by looked at them and cried, 'Ooh!' They really were very eye-catching.

I was touched, but in the back of my mind I also felt it was a bit extravagant. Such a big bunch of flowers – something that couldn't be eaten or drunk – wasn't it a waste of money? The bouquet really was very beautiful, but we were past the age when we needed romance in our daily lives. That huge bunch of roses made me feel that the proposal wasn't quite real. The next day they withered, so I just threw them away. Jiang Shan didn't object. Flowers are good, and sweet-talk is fine, but his talents lie elsewhere. I think his main reason for getting me the ninety-nine roses was to make me happy. I was very happy – not because of the flowers, but because he put so much thought into it. Neither of us is much good at creating a romantic atmosphere. We're happier living in the real world.

The next day we went to the Civil Affairs Bureau and got our marriage certificate. We didn't even choose an auspicious date. We happened to have some time that day, so we went and did it. When we'd finished, we went home, ate a good dinner and felt more settled.

By this stage we were living together in a house we'd bought when we started university. It had four rooms: two living areas and two bathrooms. It was in a quiet, pleasant residential estate on the outskirts of Wuhan.

My ideal home would have a sea view. I love the sea and have always dreamed of having a house by the coast. Under the blue skies and white clouds, we could open the curtains and look at the ocean. Gazing at the vast sea, one can feel one's own smallness. In Wuhan, many houses have a view of the river, but I didn't like the idea of living by the Yangtze River, which is polluted and muddy. I like the cool, clear blue that's unique to seawater. It looks so clean.

But we had a house, and I was satisfied. We'd completely renovated it according to our own tastes. The designer had helped us turn one of the rooms into a small bar. After I won the French Open, we put the trophy in the bar. Along with the Suzanne Lenglen Cup, there's another silver cup. I forget which country's queen gave it to me, but it's inscribed with the words, 'To China's Li Na'. The queen sent it through the Ministry of Foreign Affairs, which sent it to the Chinese Tennis Association, which passed it along to me. Other than these two cups, my house doesn't have anything else related to tennis in it. The trophies I won earlier are all kept in a box at my mother's house. I don't like to hang pictures of myself playing tennis either. I don't want life at home to be constantly focused on tennis.

The biggest flaw in our decor is that we don't have a walk-in wardrobe, and I kind of regret not installing one. Nike has given me a lot of sportswear, and most of it has only been worn once during competition, then stored, since I try to showcase many different styles of clothing for my sponsor. Plus, bags and shoes are my weakness, and all of the cupboards at home, big and small, have been filled by me.

Our house has a lot of wine, and I like how imported wine comes in small bottles. Jiang Shan can put it away, and I'm not too bad either. Friends come to visit from time to time, and we all deliberately avoid topics related to tennis. But we're always aware in our minds that we can never really stray far from them.

Jiang Shan and I never had a wedding ceremony, and my mother wasn't very pleased. But I feel that marriage is between two people, and for me, such rituals are no more than an afterthought. Nowadays, many people's weddings are alienating, not a testimony of two people's affection. They're a waste of time, a waste of manpower and a waste of material resources, all for the sake of a boring ceremony. Jiang Shan and I both think that whether one finds happiness in life is completely independent of this ceremony. I can't see us deciding that we need to go through the ritual.

Despite my mother's unhappiness with our lack of ceremony, she was happy with my marriage. Like all Chinese parents, she can't wait to have a grandchild, but she also knows our current circumstances and that it's not possible to have a child in this situation. But she keeps on hoping, and she really wants to be the one to care for the child when the time comes.

This is absolutely not going to happen.

I don't particularly like my own character. Aside from a little talent at tennis, I don't think I have any extraordinary qualities. When I was young, I was shy and introverted, very much lacking in confidence. This has everything to do with my mother's way of teaching. When I have a child, there's no way I'll use the same methods I endured in my childhood. I want to teach my child respect and freedom. I want them to have the right to say 'no', and I want them to have their own spirit and dreams.

When I was younger, I had long naturally curly hair. If I left it down, it fell to my waist. Like all little girls I was very vain, always preening in front of the mirror. One day my mother pulled me up sharply, saying that I only cared about looks and didn't care about my studies like other children. After that, I rarely looked at the mirror. When I started playing tennis, I wore my hair in a ponytail or in braids for convenience. I never even used a comb on my hair, but just pulled my fingers through it and immediately tied it up. Those words followed me for many years. Whenever I saw a mirror, a sort of frustration born of that memory would seep out and surround my whole being.

Now that my financial situation is improved, I try to help my relatives as they once helped me. But this has become a weapon in my mother's hand. I'm very close to everyone on my mother's side of the family, and my two maternal uncles have never treated me like an outsider. My older uncle's daughter is only five years younger than me, and we grew up together, with a bond more like that of siblings than cousins. My younger uncle is only twelve years older than me, and when I was a child, he always played with me. My grandmother, an optimistic, open-minded old woman, resolutely refuses to take any money from me, saying, 'This is your hard-earned money. It wasn't easily acquired. It would hurt me to spend it.' My mother seems to take money as irrefutable proof of our mother-daughter bond. She readily accepts any 'respect' I pay in cash or other material terms, but any help I give to my uncles leaves her puzzled.

Of course, this causes embarrassment for everyone. I brought the issue up with my mother, saying, 'Don't be that way. Don't always think that others owe you. We have to remember that in our time of distress, it was our family who helped us. Other families don't necessarily enjoy the same unity and harmony that we do.'

My mother is also a person especially concerned with face. When my athletic achievements were good, she would ask me to call her to talk about it when she was with friends or colleagues so they would overhear. She seemed to think this was some sort of glory for herself, which made me feel awkward.

But it's hard to talk to her about these things. If I say too much, she thinks I'm opposing her. I don't know whether it's because of menopause or what, but she's often angry and aggrieved. So no matter what she says, I listen and try to endure without talking back.

My mother is my closest living relative. I often think back to my childhood at the sports school, how she came to see me every day, bringing me cold green bean soup to cool me during the hottest days. She's my mother, and I love her very much. I'm her only daughter, and I know she loves me. It's just that I don't know how to communicate with her any more.

Of course, my mother is more aware of this than anyone. After my father's passing, she was very lonely and really wanted to spend more time with me. But we grew apart, developing divergent views of life. Now if we spend too much time together, we argue, and this makes both me and my mother unhappy. She often complains that I don't visit her or keep her company enough. She's a very direct person. If she's grumpy, she says so.

Honestly, I would rather be with Jiang Shan's mother. Her ideas are very different from my mother's. Jiang Shan's mother has a 'whatever makes you happy' approach to parenting, respecting her child more. She doesn't interfere in our lives. My mother seems to feel that I'm still a child in need of monitoring and guidance, even though I'm over thirty years old. My mother thinks she's been through a lot and has a wealth of experience. When I talk to her, she has a habit of saying things like, 'Now you listen to me', and 'I've eaten more salt than you have rice'. I just say to myself, *That's not necessarily so*. She's very keen to use her own experience to guide my life, but she doesn't realise that the world has changed.

Chapter 16

Defeating the Top Ten

I only had a brief taste of marriage before I had to rush back to all the demands of my career. I wasn't in a good headspace. Following my defeat at the hands of Serena Williams, I encountered one of the world's top ten players at a tournament in Doha in February. Much like at the Australian Open, I was knocked out of competition after just one round. I was restrained tightly by my opponent and had no chance of reversal.

When I got back to the locker room, I was the only person there. As I took a shower, I couldn't control the tears.

From the age of eleven, I'd been hearing a coach behind me yelling, 'Stupid!' or 'Are you a pig?' Every little mistake I made would provoke more hollering. I hadn't needed other people yelling at me, because I always had the coach's furious shouts imprinted on my mind. But as it turned out, I didn't need the coach to humiliate me. I could sink myself easily in a morbid, uncontrollable state.

When I was restrained by my opponent, it was easy for me to fall into a state of irritation, anger, anxiety and agitation. After a loss, I felt like bashing my head against the locker room door. I felt like a trapped lion. The more frenzied my leaps for the sky grew, the deeper I fell into the pit. I hated everything that happened in my life, and the defeats made my mood worse. I constantly cursed myself, often bursting into tears.

Why was all of this happening to me?

I still hadn't defeated a top ten player. The cloud over my so-called criticism of the national system hadn't yet passed, and there was a new phrase being floated by the world at large: a 'top ten loser'. There were other similarly harsh, discouraging comments going around.

When I maintained good form, I could rouse my inner spirit to fight, but this particular defeat in Doha left me deeply disappointed. All the negative emotions I'd accumulated up to that point broke out. After the tournament ended, I suddenly lost all sense of struggle. I'd been travelling in the wrong direction, saddled with pain and ridicule. I was a joke – I didn't deserve to play tennis at all! I was a born loser!

Throughout my shower in the locker room, I cried so hard my body was trembling. My mind kept hovering over those negative thoughts: *See? What everyone says is right. As soon as you meet one of the top ten players, you lose. What's the point of training so hard?*

Jiang Shan was still studying at Huazhong. I was going to tournaments alone, at most accompanied by a coach and team leader. After my shower I could only send a message to Jiang Shan to vent. 'It seems that what they say about me is true. I really can't beat the top ten. I'll always be a second-rate player. Dog meat can never make it to the banquet table.'

He replied, 'Actually, you've already done very well. Don't stress yourself out. You're too hard on yourself.' He followed up with several more encouraging messages, helping me to quickly pull myself together and settle down.

But it was very hard. I felt my dignity had been shattered and left in tiny pieces. The newspapers were sharply satirical in their treatment of my failures. And they never forgot to mention the 'slamming' incident. Jiang Shan was thousands of miles away, and nobody around me cared about me, as though they were thinking, *Who asked you to attack the national system?* I'd become a universal sinner. Whenever I saw a newspaper, my hands turned cold, and I would stay well away. I refused to go online and read what anyone wrote about me.

Jiang Shan was especially busy trying to cope with school even while he tried to build me up emotionally. When I was down, he talked a lot of sense to me. I didn't believe everything he said, but I patiently listened to it all. Other than my father, no one had ever been so good to me. Jiang Shan is the only person who has ever been genuinely good to me without considering what was in it for him.

I'd always been a person who was very much bothered by what others said about me. When others made negative comments about me, it would take me a long time to get it out of my system. I didn't understand why they'd say hurtful things. I'd never done anything bad in my life, so why was this happening?

Jiang Shan gradually changed my mindset. He taught me to protect myself, and to be cautious about my speech and actions. He told me, 'We can't change other people's thinking. The only people we can change are ourselves.'

Gradually, I learned. I began to understand how to protect myself and control my emotions. Although there would be times when I couldn't, I knew Jiang Shan would always be there for me.

On the national team in Beijing, I didn't have a personal coach. We were all one big melting pot of players. In China, it's traditional to think of ourselves as part of a melting pot, and everyone's careful to blend in with the crowd. If you cross the line and depart from convention, it can immediately provoke a heated response from others. Many people live their lives by the values taught them by their coaches or their parents; few dare to apply their own style. I was just another piece cut from the same mould, struggling to make my own way. But some people thought I felt otherwise, and I suspect they wondered, *How come you're so special? What's so special about you?*

I'm not special. I just want to follow the voice deep inside me.

I've basically never lived even a single day for myself. When I was young, I followed my father's wishes and became a professional tennis player. After he passed away, it was unthinkable to go against his wishes. I struggled to earn enough money to allow my mother to live a better life. In 1997, I played my way to the National Tennis League finals and from then on, I was pressed even more into conformity: I had to live up to everyone's expectations as a champion. I was living in material comfort, but I was miserable. My inner Li Na was extremely unhappy.

The two years at university were the first in my life when I was able to do as I pleased, but I soon went back to the path chosen for me. I really wanted to be a good, obedient child and, most of the time, I was. But, that inner Li Na was always waiting in the wings, giving me trouble.

While I was on the national team, I felt marginalised and directionless. There was only one coach for the whole team, and with so many players, he couldn't put too much energy into individual training. There was no one to help me go through a more targeted programme. I needed people I could rely on. Most of the foreign players had their own private teams to help correct their individual flaws and manage their training. They could even hire a psychologist to build up the mental side of their game. In contrast, if us Chinese players wanted to improve our game, it was basically up to us. Coupled with this, there was a huge gap between the overall playing level of Chinese players and most foreign players. We had too few chances to face top players, we lacked experience in competition and we lacked confidence. The national team had hired the Swede Thomas Hogstedt as a coach, but he was responsible for all the high-level players and had no time to offer me specialised coaching. I felt like I was using a local-made rifle to face off with the first-class foreign cannons. And all the while I was constantly hearing sarcastic comments about how I 'couldn't defeat top ten players'. The stress was almost too much.

Fortunately, I had Jiang Shan.

Where would I be without Jiang Shan? We're two halves of a whole. If I hadn't met him, I wouldn't have become who I am. Many people around me ask, 'How come you always listen to Jiang Shan?' When I'm shopping, the only person whose opinion counts is Jiang Shan. When I hear him say, 'That looks good,' I think, *Okay, this really is a nice dress.*

He's my emotional rock, and in my mind he always represents a rational, strong will. As long as he's by my side, I'll never quite hit rock bottom, because there'll always be solid ground to stand on.

But Jiang Shan was in Wuhan while I was in Beijing, thousands of kilometres away. For me to play well, Jiang Shan had to find ways to spend time with me. He was like a special coach to the national team. He would patiently spend hours on the phone or online, counselling me. Whenever he could, he watched my games and made very sensible suggestions.

With his help, my game improved slightly. On 7 May 2006, I played my way to my second consecutive championship match at the Estoril Open in Portugal, meeting my teammate Zheng Jie. This was the first time two Chinese opponents had appeared in the finals of a WTA tournament.

I was very happy to face a teammate in the finals, as it indicated a rise in the level of play in China as a whole. Unfortunately, my old shoulder injury flared up before the match, and I ended up withdrawing from the final set. For two consecutive years, I was the runner-up.

Tennis is considered a relatively 'safe' sport, but professional tennis players will inevitably suffer injury. The bodies of professional athletes are usually covered in scars, and even the best athletes are rendered helpless in the face of injury. My shoulder injury was nothingtoo serious, but the knee injury I would later experience was terrible.

But when we compare physical pain to mental burdens, the former becomes trivial. Throughout my career, I've repeatedly seen great players brought down by their own mental pain. The adversary across the court is easy to defeat, but the enemy within ourselves is the truly terrible opponent. When we want to move to a higher level, we must first defeat the enemy within: our own inner demons.

Under Jiang Shan's guidance, I became more familiar with my own demons and, most of the time, was able to wrestle them for a few rounds and come out unhurt. When I was in the right frame of mind, good luck seemed to follow me. And in May, soon after the Estoril Open, for the first time in my career I defeated a top ten player: the 'Swiss Elf', Patty Schnyder. She was three years and three months older than me, petite, with a baby face. Chinese people called her 'the dragon maiden' because she had the Chinese character for 'dragon' tattooed on her right shoulder. Roger Federer as a teenager had been her ball boy. She was from Switzerland, along with Martina Hingis, and even when she was young she stood out from the pack with her superb technique.

We met at the German Open, which was a clay-court tournament with prize money of over a million US dollars. I met Schnyder in the quarterfinals. She was a very thoughtful player, and played left-handed. Her forehand pulls and her backhand slices were a style of play well suited to clay courts, and all of her best results had come in clay-court competition. She'd defeated many of the world's top players, including Martina Hingis, Jennifer Capriati, Lindsay Davenport, the Williams sisters and Justine Henin.

The 'top ten loser' moniker was still attached to my name, and I felt ridiculed and judged. I almost bought into this line of thinking myself, and as I stepped onto the court against Schnyder, I wasn't very confident.

Schnyder was ranked world number nine. Her shot placement was very unpredictable. She kept me moving from one end of the court to the other. I lost the first set. Naturally, my heart sank. The second set was going equally poorly, and I was down 4–1 when my mind suddenly went blank – whether from relief or anger, I didn't know. I let go and just focused all of my energy on my game. I clawed my way back in the second set to take it 7–6, and finally won the match 2–6, 7–6, 7–6. I went to shake hands with Schnyder and the umpire, then turned and waved to the crowd. It was a magnificent feeling. I'd done it! I could beat a top ten player!

Although I didn't get past the semifinals in that tournament, I'd finally crossed the hurdle that had been standing in front of me for so long. The pressure that had long lain on my chest was wiped out, and the curse was finally lifted.

Chapter 17

Wimbledon

It seemed that 2006 was the year my luck turned around. Just after the German Open I entered the main draw of the French Open for the first time. Defeating the twenty-seventh-seeded Anna Chakvetadze, my world ranking shot to thirty-two.

A couple of weeks later, in the Birmingham DFS Classic, I played my way into the third round. During the whole clay-court season my form had been pretty good. As a result, I became the first Chinese player to enter the top thirty. A lot of old friends called to congratulate me, and I was very happy. All that anxiety, pain and sense of crisis became a thing of the past. The old Li Na, full of positive energy, was back.

When I finished the Birmingham Classic, I was to go to the Netherlands for two tournaments, shuttling there by bus and plane. The trip left me fatigued, and the schedule for the tournament was tight. I arrived in Holland in the morning and started training in the afternoon because I had a match the next day. At least I wasn't lonely since there were other members of the Chinese national team competing too. On the day of the tournament, I played a set and, as I focused on considering how to break my opponent's serve, I suddenly twisted my neck. It hurt so much that I couldn't even turn my head. I immediately froze, and the umpire rushed to get the doctor. While I was waiting for the doctor, I sat in the lounge and went online. My teammate called me, but I couldn't turn my head to respond. I could only turn my whole body to face her, making me look quite awkward.

The tournament's doctor took me to the WTA Clinic and gave me a massage, applied some medicated plasters and told me to rest for two days. I didn't move my neck for two days, but it didn't do much good. Wimbledon was due to start soon. How could this have happened?

With a 'certain death' mentality, I travelled with several other teammates to Wimbledon. While I was training I played with a strange, stiff-necked posture. My friends were all very anxious on my behalf. Then we met a Chinese student who was working at the stadium. He said he knew a traditional Chinese medicine physician and that he could ask the physician to try some acupuncture for me. That was Saturday. Wimbledon would start on Monday.

I thought, *Well, things have got to this point. Might as well give the Chinese physician a try.* By this time, I'd already prepared myself to return to China.

Before I saw the Chinese doctor, however, an Indian doctor from the WTA infirmary at Wimbledon saw me with my stiff neck. I told him how I'd injured it. Without saying much, the doctor put his hand on my neck and with a crack and a pop, my neck was better. It was like magic!

Surprised, I thanked him profusely. I told everyone how amazing the WTA's Indian doctor was, how he barely touched my neck and it was healed. The doctor had obviously popped a lot of players' stiff necks as a lot of athletes apparently knew just who I meant as soon as I mentioned him. 'Oh, him! Yeah.' And then they would tell me how once, when nothing was wrong, they'd gone to this doctor for a massage, but he'd left them with a stiff neck instead. Everyone congratulated me and said I was one of the lucky ones. Heaven really helps good people!

And so I would play at Wimbledon for the first time. My luck was good: on Monday, the weather suddenly turned bad. It started raining, postponing the tournament for a day and giving me an extra day of rest. In Tuesday's match, my first-round opponent was from France. I defeated her easily. In the second round I beat Meilen Tu from America in straight sets.

This surprised me a little. Wimbledon was a grass court, and I'd never played on grass before. I wasn't very confident, and before arriving, I'd even told my teammates, 'I don't know how to play on grass. I'll just take the first-round prize money, then come home.'

We didn't have any grass or clay courts in China. I knew very little about play on either surface. A lot of players, Chinese and foreign alike, share this weakness. Of the four Grand Slams, two are on hard courts, so we battle on hard courts for about eight months of each year.

When I was a child, I played on the grey dirt in Wuhan, so I had an idea of how to play on dirt. Armed with this impression, I could improvise on clay courts; I could slide. That sort of footwork was like skating on any bit of dry ground. But playing on grass was an entirely different matter.

On grass, the ball has less friction when it lands, and the speed at which it rebounds is fast and irregular. So the demands on a player's response time, running method and technique are very high. Playing on grass, you must immediately drop your weight really low and not slide, which for many athletes is a great challenge.

Making the transition from hard courts to clay, I'd had some childhood experience to draw on. Also, I'd had two or three weeks during which I could practise and adapt to the court. But going from clay to grass was such a dramatic change that it was a little overwhelming. Every time I played on grass I felt a bit helpless. I hardly even knew how to move around. And the time Wimbledon allowed for practice was very short, so I could only adapt as I played.

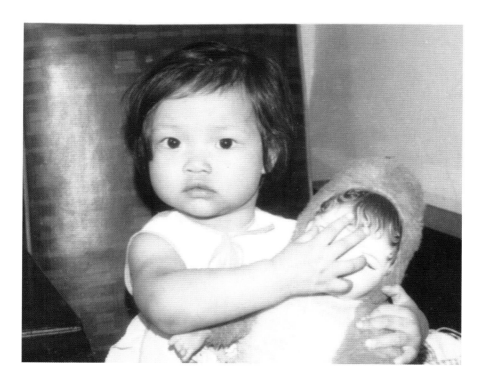

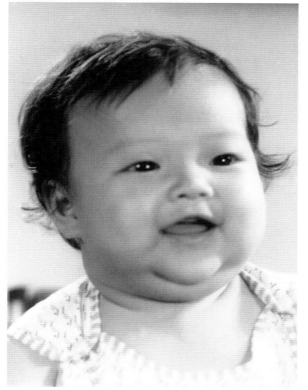

ABOVE A wide-eyed and precocious two-year-old Li Na

LEFT Happy and healthy at one year old

ABOVE Father and daughter smile for the camera

RIGHT Playtime at home in Wuhan, China

ABOVE Li Na (*top row, first from the right*) and some young teammates

LEFT A carefree Li Na poses for the camera on a family outing

BOTTOM LEFT Li Na in her early teens, outside the Liaoning Tennis Stadium in Shenyang, northeast China

TOP A national icon: Li Na shoulders the Chinese flag and the hopes of a billion people
LEFT Training with husband and coach, Jiang Shan, in 2006

RIGHT With trophy in hand at a photocall by the River Seine after her French Open win in 2011
OPPOSITE PAGE Preparing to backhand at Roland Garros Stadium, 2011

Serving on hard court

Triumphant en route to her career-
defining 2011 French Open victory

Because I was a low-seeded player, I met with tenth-seeded Svetlana Kuznetsova in the third round. This was more difficult. In the third set, I had a 4–1 lead but missed the opportunity to make it 5–1. Kuznetsova immediately followed up, winning two games in a row to make it 4–3. I started thinking anxiously, *Oh no, back to square one.* I didn't expect the next few points to go so smoothly. I finally won the set 6–3 and the match.

Defeating one of the top ten players in a Grand Slam is different from beating a top ten player in another tournament. There's something more official about it. I felt I was moving up, step by step, to a higher level.

After defeating Kuznetsova, I went into the fourth round, and my next opponent was the Czech Nicole Vaidisova. Coincidentally, we played on the same court where I'd met Kuznetsova. I was in a good state of mind that day and I won the first two games. Before the start of the third game, Vaidisova went to the bathroom, and I thought to myself that whichever of us broke serve first would win the match. When we got back on the court, I broke her serve. In my mind, I gave myself a loud cheer. And sure enough, I got on a roll and won the match.

After playing Vaidisova, I went on to the quarterfinals. All of my opponents were top ten players. It was the first time I'd progressed this far in a Grand Slam. I was making Grand Slam history, being the first seeded Chinese player to ever play at Wimbledon. In the quarterfinals, I met the very strong Belgian veteran, Kim Clijsters. She'd only needed two sets in the previous round to beat her Polish opponent in a total of just fifty-five minutes. I exerted all of my energy against Clijsters, but she still forced me to commit numerous errors. She won the match, and my Wimbledon experience came to an end.

But as I left Wimbledon there was a new tag attached to my name: 'the first Chinese player to reach the quarterfinals in Grand Slam competition'. Before this, the best record of any Chinese player was Zheng

Jie's entry into the fourth round at the French Open. I'd finally fought my way into the notice of the Western world.

With its long history, Wimbledon stands apart from the rest of the Grand Slams. Now, Chinese players were making waves there. Six days after I made it to the quarterfinals, Zheng Jie and Yan Zi defeated the former world number one international doubles team of Paola Suarez and Virginia Ruano Pascual to win the women's doubles championship at Wimbledon. Whether from a sports or business perspective, it was invigorating news for both the Chinese and the foreign media.

With my friends from the national team at Wimbledon, the lonely, restless feeling had left me. Even though I was standing on a grass court at Wimbledon, I could hear cheering from the East, from our motherland. At that moment, I knew I wasn't a lonely island. We were all interconnected.

On 16 July, at the Fed Cup World Group playoffs, I won two singles victories. In this tournament, the Chinese team defeated the German team 4–1. It was the first time in history that we entered the quarterfinals. The Chinese team's world rank rose from thirteen to seven.

That August, my own ranking rose into the top twenty. In September, I played in the US Open. Nothing unusual happened in the first two rounds, but in the third round, I lost one game, then won twelve, beating the French star Mary Pierce. It was my first time to break into the fourth round of the US Open. I'd made definite progress at the four Grand Slam events, ending the year with a ranking of twenty-one.

However, I began to feel a faint warning signal in my body. The tension that had gradually built up over the years was increasing, and I was worried. The beast that had swallowed up many great players was now beginning to sneak up on me. I didn't know if I would be able to confront it and come out victorious.

Chapter 18

The Australian Open

The year 2007 got off to quite a good start for me. I began by defeating the Russian star Elena Dementieva at the Sydney Open in January, successfully making it to the semifinals. This was the third time I'd defeated a top ten player after Schnyder and Kuznetsova, and my world ranking rose to sixteen, making me the highest ranked Chinese player ever.

I was seeded nineteenth at the Australian Open. In the first three rounds, everything went smoothly, including a defeat in straight sets of the ninth seed, the Russian Dinara Safina. In the deciding match for the quarterfinals, my opponent was the sixth-seeded 'Swiss Princess' Martina Hingis. As had happened before, the momentum swung after I won the first set, and my campaign ended in the fourth round, but this was my personal best at the Australian Open. Hingis was one of the best in the world, and in my match with her, I'd found ways to ward off her attack rather than passively take a beating. Even though I lost in the end, it made me realise that the gap between me and the world's top players wasn't so large. It was definitely a big boost to my confidence.

In March at the Indian Wells Masters in the US, I eliminated Vera Zvonareva and Jelena Jankovic in the fourth round and the quarterfinals.

It was the first time a Chinese player had made it to the semifinals in singles competition. In late March, I attended the Miami Masters, and it's worth mentioning that in the fourth round I reversed the tide in the third set to defeat Kim Clijsters. In 2005 she'd been ranked second in the world, and was fifth in 2006. She'd won several Grand Slam titles and she and Henin had the reputation of being 'the Belgian sisters'. After Wimbledon, I found the chance to turn the tables, and my confidence soared.

At the beginning of the clay-court season in April 2007, I planned to play for nearly two months in Europe. This time, Jiang Shan was able to join me. When I withdrew from Huazhong University, Jiang Shan had continued his studies and had successfully completed his four-year undergraduate program. He'd joined the Hubei team as a tennis coach soon after, and my repeated requests to the national team finally resulted in Jiang Shan being transferred to serve as my full-time coach.

Tennis is a lonely sport. For someone who was sent overseas alone as I was, it was especially so. The European season continues for at least three months, and if not for the other players and coaches from the national team accompanying me, it would have felt like three months of hard labour. Even with the coaches, sometimes you really wish you had a loved one keeping you company. As foreign players compete, most of them are accompanied by their parents, siblings or partners, as well as their coach, technical trainer and trainer.

As a player you can't afford to divide your attention. I'd often been afraid that I would lose focus when I was playing, thinking about distractions like, *Was I registered for the tournament?* or *Some other members of the national team had their own personal coaches.* I thought, *I also need my own personal coach. No one's more suitable for this role than Jiang Shan, so I'll apply to the national team to have him transferred over.*

After thinking it over, the team agreed to my request. I've always been an outspoken person, but Jiang Shan is more rational, more strategic in his thinking, and more thorough. Having him as a buffer between me and the national team would effectively reduce the friction between us. I would also be less lonely when I went overseas. Jiang Shan was an efficient coach and assistant. He would help me deal properly with all of the issues I'd not considered.

In late April 2007, Jiang Shan and I arrived in Europe. It was the height of spring, and as I was admiring the flowers in bloom, I found myself constantly sneezing at least thirty or forty times a day beginning upon our arrival and lasting for two months. It was really a strange, unprecedented occurrence. Suddenly one day, I felt a pain in my ribcage. I didn't take too much notice, but it kept growing. When Wimbledon was just a week away, I found that if I even took a deep breath, there would immediately be a sharp pain in my ribs.

I'd originally planned to play in a tournament the week before Wimbledon, but after discussing it with the national team, I cancelled, planning to allow myself sufficient rest that way. *Perhaps I've been training too hard recently,* I thought. *I should rest. The key is to be ready for Wimbledon.* Jiang Shan and I flew to London to prepare. The national team had rented a house in London for all of the players to stay in, and Jiang Shan and I were based there.

After arriving in London, I found that the situation was more serious than I'd thought. When I got up in the morning, I couldn't sit straight up but had to first turn onto my side, lean on my elbow and push myself up. For tennis players, the main problem areas are joints: wrists, elbows, knees and ankles. Few suffer injury in the area that was now bothering me. Feeling desperate, I told the coach that maybe I was injured, and then went to the tournament doctor. The doctor suggested we take X-rays and look at the area. On the way to hospital, Jiang Shan suddenly grew anxious and asked, 'It's not just that you don't want to play, is it? If you don't want to play, don't play. We can go home.'

I was speechless, in no mood to argue with him. My ribs hurt so badly that I couldn't think of anything else. I just felt miserable.

The X-rays confirmed the doctor's suspicion: it was a rib fracture. This sort of injury was more an occupational hazard for golfers and was hardly ever suffered by tennis players. I was very surprised. I'd never suffered a severe collision to this area. How could it get fractured?

After asking in more detail about the specifics of my recent activities, the doctor told me that he believed the fracture had been caused by my constant sneezing due to my pollen allergy a few months back.

Sneezing could actually break a bone! Incredible! With a cracked rib, I certainly couldn't compete. It was a big letdown.

When we got back to the house in London, Jiang Shan got me settled and went right back out. About an hour later, he came back with a lot of rib bones and condiments. It turned out that he had gone out to buy ingredients for pork rib soup for me.

The place where we were staying was about twenty minutes from the nearest supermarket. Jiang Shan had gone out on his own, with no language ability, and came back loaded with bags of food to cook. Despite my being in continuous pain, I felt very close to him. The next day, we went back to Beijing with the other members of the national team.

Two months later, I felt that my ribs were more or less all right, and I wanted to start competing again. To be sure, I went for another X-ray. I saw a young female doctor to find out the results, and when she looked at the X-ray she said, 'You're an athlete?'

I said I was.

The doctor said, 'Athletes don't need X-rays. Go back into training.'

I was at a bit of a loss, thinking that if the doctor was telling me to go back and train, it must mean the bone had healed. I went back to the training courts and practised for two weeks, preparing to compete in the US.

When I got to the US in August, I practised for one day and then, when I woke up the next morning, I could feel the familiar pain again. I found a local hospital to do another round of X-rays and asked about the results. The doctor who attended to me looked at the X-ray and immediately asked why I'd begun training again before the bone had healed. I asked, 'How long will it take to heal?'

'At least six weeks.'

It was August at the time, so that meant it would take until October. The season would be over by then. I was shocked. But I couldn't just keep playing injured. Finally, I decided to cancel the rest of my tournaments for that year and travel to Munich for treatment. It was at this time that I met my doctor, Eric Rembeck. He had previously served as the 1860 Munich football club doctor, and also as the Davis Cup German team doctor. The Chinese team's foreign coach, Thomas Hogstedt, had recommended him to me.

While I was sidelined, I lost a lot of weight, partly because my muscles atrophied. Jiang Shan comforted me, saying, 'Take it as a break, a time to adjust your mindset.'

I couldn't relax. I was in a bad place.

When I first started tennis, I didn't like the sport, but after so many years of training, tennis and I were inseparably joined. It's been my whole life. I've worked hard for it, and it has repaid me in its own way. I've experienced much grief and also much joy for it. It's made me grow up, forcing me to think. After so many years of life as a player, my feelings for tennis are very complex. As things are now, I can't use simple terms such as 'like' or 'dislike' to summarise how I feel about tennis.

I don't want to openly admit that I need tennis. I hated it for many years. But I can't leave it, and this puts me in a paradoxical situation.

When I was forced to take a break, my self-confidence and sense of fulfilment went out the door. The tennis court was my stage, the place where I'd gone through my proudest, most glorious moments. And now I was confined to bed, worse even than a toddler. It depressed me to no end. How could I get back on track and return to competing as soon as possible?

My performance in the first quarter of 2007 was good. If not for the rib fracture, who knows what might have occurred. But the unexpected happened. When people describe an unlucky person, they say, 'They get things stuck between their teeth when they drink cold water.' Breaking a rib when sneezing is a comparable situation. It was strange enough that I suddenly began suffering from allergies, and even stranger that I broke a rib. To top it off I encountered an irresponsible doctor. Beginning in April, I spent roughly half a season in a state of injury, and it was an injury of the most bizarre sort. But maybe some things just can't be explained. A sneeze can lead to disaster, like lightning in a clear sky. Just when I was soaring, I crashed to the ground and was banged up, both physically and mentally. But now, looking back, it's just a funny episode.

In life, everyone inevitably encounters obstacles. When it happens to you, it's unbearable. If you were able to somehow leave your body or move forward to a time a few years later and speak to that self currently going through the bad patch, these might be the words you want to say: 'Steady now. You'll get through it.'

Chapter 19

Injury

From 2007 through to 2008, I was tormented by injury. Just as the rib injury was almost fully healed, I developed a knee problem. During my recuperation period, Jiang Shan worked tirelessly on my behalf.

To be more accurate, Jiang Shan always works tirelessly on my behalf. I'm a moody person, and when a situation gets out of control, I often lose my temper. Actually, I'm quite a coward; not daring to yell at outsiders, I vent all my frustration on my husband. If it were someone else, maybe they would have called it quits long ago. It's only Jiang Shan who can forgive and forget, continuing to put up with me.

When we were both professional players, we both carried out our duties in the relationship and had our own space. After I made my comeback, I wanted to play at the top of my game, and Jiang Shan took on the responsibility of being my 'nanny', helping me take care of a lot of things. I wasn't eloquent, I was ignorant of the ways of the world, and when I became emotional, I acted like a child. Jiang Shan helped me grow up while also teaching me to adapt to my environment. Sometimes when I was too arrogant, he wouldn't say anything. Soon, I would realise I was in the wrong and take the initiative to make up.

If we're frightened or hurt by something as children, our first response is to go to our parents for help. When we grow up, we have to be more independent. When we find ourselves standing on the brink of disaster, we must be prepared to 'swallow the blood if your front teeth get knocked out and thank those who have helped you'. I can only thank God for sending me Jiang Shan. He's my security blanket, my confidant and the one person I can rely on. He's my biggest blessing.

When two people have been together for some time, many characteristics and little habits or quirks will start to grow on each other. I'm always biting my nails, and Jiang Shan never did. But when he nursed me back to health after my first knee operation, I noticed that his nails were very short. He'd been biting them. Jiang Shan is a deep, strong man. He never lets his stress be a burden to others, choosing to carry the load himself.

Jiang Shan has said that what he most appreciates about me is that I can face reality and break through boundaries. We Chinese have a habit of saving face, and are used to making all sorts of excuses to justify ourselves. In the sports arena, when we fail everyone says, *It's because we Asians don't have as good a build. We can't compete with Westerners.* I don't think this is the right attitude. Often, people don't understand the limits they can be pushed to achieve, regardless of physique.

Fluid build-up in the knee is a common sports injury, and many well-known athletes suffer immensely from it. For ordinary people, one need only undergo acupuncture, massage, traditional Chinese medicine, physical therapy or other similar treatments while avoiding over-exertion, and the injury's likely to improve. But for an athlete who's going through intense competition practically every week, sports fatigue increases the damage, making recovery difficult. If you want a full recovery, it's not only a matter of withdrawing from competition, but also involves the studious application of scientific, rational rehab coupled with a precise treatment. This is clearly very difficult.

I knew my knee had problems. In January 2008, when I was competing in Australia, I felt something was wrong with the joint. After an examination, the tournament doctor said the cartilage was worn and there was a build-up of fluid on the knee, and he helped me drain some of it. I asked him, 'Where is best to have surgery to drain the knee?' The doctor said that Australia was quite good, but that Germany's rehab was the best in the world.

At the time, I had a full schedule. There was always another tournament to play, and I felt okay playing, so my knee problem was shoved to the back of my mind. I took medicine for the swelling each day, then kept training and competing, thereby delaying dealing with the knee. In March, I flew to the US for the Indian Wells Masters and the Miami Masters. Indian Wells arranged for every player to have a physical. When the doctor checked my knee function, I found that there were already many movements I couldn't perform.

The doctor told me harshly, 'You can't play tennis any more.' In order to make me understand how serious the situation was, he used this example: on a scale of one to ten, the damage to my knee was a seven. He said he couldn't understand why athletes still wanted to play under such conditions. As the tournament doctor, he was obligated to explain the situation to the organising committee, sending a report advising that I should immediately stop training and competing. The Chinese team's head coach, Jiang Hongwei, was with us then, so it wasn't up to me to call the shots about whether I would withdraw from the tournament. Coach Jiang met with the doctor, then decided that I should go back to China to rest.

I felt quite grateful to this American doctor and asked his advice about the best places to have treatment. His answer was similar to that of the Australian doctor. Surgery would be the same almost anywhere, including the US, but Germany had the best rehab.

Since everyone seemed to agree that Germany's rehab was the best,

I decided to go to Germany for the operation. Jiang Shan immediately arranged for plane tickets and took me straight from the US to Germany. Everything went very smoothly as we booked accommodation and a hospital, arranging for the surgery with my doctor, Eric Rembeck. He told me that he could arrange the surgery for the next day. Only then could I relax. But right at this time, word came from the national team: *The surgery must be suspended!*

The reason for the delay: the Olympics were just five months away, and the team leaders were afraid that my post-surgery recovery time would be too long, affecting the competition. They asked Eric to write a report clearly indicating the time required for the operation, how long after surgery it would be before I could walk and how long before I could play.

The doctor wrote a long letter addressing these issues very plainly and sent it to the national team leaders. But the Chinese side expressed doubts about what he'd written. They thought the doctor gave too little leeway in the recovery time, and that it would be difficult for me to make a full recovery in such a short time. So they wanted me to delay the surgery and return home immediately.

Things being what they were, I had to apologise to Eric and follow orders. He said it was no problem. He could understand my situation, and if I needed him, he would do his best to help.

This was 21 March 2008, and Jiang Shan and I bought our tickets home that very night. After we got back to China, I had to undergo more medical consultation. The results were presented two days later, with all of the leaders present, and included a recommendation for conservative treatment, followed by surgery post-Olympics. But the decision was in my hands.

Since it was to be my decision, I needed to understand the situation clearly. I asked the doctors, 'What's involved in this "conservative treatment"? Will I be able to go all out in training?' If an athlete can't go full bore in training, there's no point. The answer to my question was very vague, and no one could give me a straight answer. That seemed to indicate that during my 'conservative treatment', I'd get up every morning not knowing what my situation was and not knowing how much training I'd be able to do. Even worse, I wouldn't know whether my body would be able to endure the stress when the Olympics finally came around. Everything was uncertain.

I've always been a person who likes a straight answer. Yes is yes, and no is no. Leaving me hanging like this, in limbo, was even harder for me to bear than the pain of the injury. In contrast, the German doctor had a definite timetable and a plan for the surgery that we could adhere to, instead of leaving me haunted by fear for five months, waiting for uncertain results. I would make a clean decision myself once and for all. I told the leaders I'd decided to go ahead with the surgery.

I booked tickets and got my visa, and sent word to Eric. At the end of March, I once again flew to the hospital in Munich. At eight o'clock on the morning of 31 March, my surgery began. The procedure, delayed by ten days, was finally underway.

No one tried to stop me. Perhaps no one wanted to bear the responsibility. Going overseas for treatment was my own choice. If the German surgery failed, or if there were problems with my recovery, the blame would be squarely on me. 'We suggested a conservative approach, but Li Na would not agree to it,' the team would say.

Even more exasperating was that if my results at the Olympics were good, the team might even claim that it was they who encouraged me to have the surgery. Well, what could I do? If my results were bad, wouldn't they just say, 'Li Na wanted her way and was hell-bent on surgery'?

The year before, Eric had introduced me to an excellent fitness coach, Johannes Wieber, who would help me with my rehab post-surgery. Both Eric and Johannes had both been athletes before. Eric ran marathons when he was younger, and Johannes was a handball player. Handball is not very popular in China, but in Germany it's second only to football.

I was very impressed with Johannes. He was twenty-nine when we met, and a typical German man – tall and with a loud voice and imposing appearance. He worked in a community sports centre open to the public, and many elderly people would come to do their exercises there. After I won the French Open, Johannes even displayed my photo on his wall for everyone to see. On it was a note I'd written to him: 'Thank you for helping me become a champion!'

Despite having Jiang Shan by my side, my trip to Munich was the most difficult, lonely time of my life. From making arrangements for the surgery through rehab and training, it was only the two of us. The hospital where I stayed was very good. It was simple and beautiful, not really like a hospital but closer to a sanatorium. The doctors and nurses had very good attitudes toward the patients. The pre-op nurse chatted to me as she pushed me to the operating room.

I remember that the operating theatre was a transparent glass room with good lighting. On the operating table there was a row of shining silver needles, scissors and other instruments. It all looked very clean. I gradually relaxed. The nurse covered me with a blanket, then Eric came over wearing a white cap and lab coat. He looked cool and bright, and very kind. He'd admitted to me earlier that previously he'd had a bit of a bias against Chinese people, but he said that, in getting to know me, I'd changed his impression a little. He once told me that his daughter and I were about the same age. In fact, the way he talked to me was like a father talking to a daughter. When the surgery was about to begin, he told me, 'Now I'm going to give you the anaesthetic. You'll be asleep after a few moments.'

I nodded. I found the doctors here a little funny. They explained every tiny thing before they did it. This was my first time in surgery, and I was very curious. After I'd been given the anaesthetic, I still wanted to open my eyes and see what was going on. Eric patted my face and asked, 'Nervous?'

I whispered, 'No.'

As soon as I spoke, my eyelids grew heavy. I was soon fast asleep.

It took a little over an hour for the operation to be completed. By the time I woke up, it was midday. The nurse had wheeled me back to the ward while I was asleep. I saw my leg in a sling over the bed, with a tube sticking out of my thigh attached to a bag that was used to drain the blood. There was no cast on my leg, just an elastic bandage. The anaesthetic hadn't worn off completely. I lay there, feeling a little dizzy.

Eric was in theatre all day, but before he left he came specially to my room to see how I was doing. When the anaesthetic wore off, the wound was painful but bearable. The most depressing thing that evening was going to the bathroom. When I got up, I felt dizzy. I still had tubes poked into my arms and legs. The short trip was very strenuous. It was only with great difficulty that I walked back from the toilet. I felt like I wanted to collapse, and I was covered with a cold sweat.

Two days later, Eric came and taught me how to walk on crutches. It was also on this day that he removed the tube from my leg. He warned me that it would be a little painful, but when he really started pulling, the pain caused me to grit my teeth. It felt like a bone was being sucked out of my body. I had to rest for a couple of hours before I finally felt better.

After the surgery, I didn't quite dare to bend my leg. Even a slight bend was rather scary. Eric took off the elastic bandage, then covered the wound with a white cloth bandage, using an ice pack to reduce the inflammation. My surgery had been only minimally invasive. Later, there would not be any permanent scars.

I was in the hospital for five days before being discharged. After this, I still had to be on crutches. Because it'd been so long since I last trained, my muscles had atrophied badly. While I was in hospital, the doctors had administered a massage twice a day. They were very skilled, and it didn't hurt at all.

I immediately began working with my fitness coach, Johannes, doing rehab exercises. Since my legs were temporarily unable to move, we began with arm exercises. A week after surgery, I went to the hospital to have the stitches removed from my knee. I had to use crutches for another ten days after that, then the doctor said I could walk on my own.

When I'd finally got rid of the crutches, I still couldn't put my full weight on my right leg. Every time I tried to, I would immediately feel discomfort. Johannes kept me busy with a full schedule of exercise. Every hour was occupied, both morning and afternoon. Would my leg ever fully recover? I had no clue. This question weighed like a stone on my heart.

Based on my physical condition, Johannes developed a full programme for me. We faced the mirror, doing rehab exercises. When we first started this training, I found that my legs were uneven. With the regimen Johannes prepared for me, my left leg could accomplish all the tasks, but my right leg couldn't do them at all. Before surgery, my right leg had always been stronger, but after surgery, it was weaker than my left leg.

While training, Johannes sometimes asked me to 'squat down lower', then would urge, 'a little lower.' But the right side of my body wouldn't go down any more. It almost felt like this weren't my leg but someone else's. You try like crazy to make this sort of programme work, and when you can't, it's infuriating. I was desperate, extremely anxious, really wanting to do it, but my right leg hurt as soon as I exerted any strength. And on top of that, it was only four months before the Olympics were due to start at the beginning of August.

I could almost hear the second hand on the watch ticking. Johannes said it didn't matter whether I made the Olympics, I should just believe in myself. He asked me to set goals, including playing at Wimbledon.

But I had many doubts. Could I really recover? Could I still play tennis?

During that time, I was often caught up in an extreme state of panic, despair and anxiety. I watched others in competition, but I couldn't even take up my racket. I would often lose patience, saying to Jiang Shan, 'Why is everything always okay for other people, but I have an injury every year? Why can't I for once just play through the whole year? What's the use of training so hard? I still can't play!'

Jiang Shan didn't rise to the bait. As he was taking care of me, he was also actively exploring my condition with Johannes and Eric. One good thing about staying in Germany was that I had my doctor and trainer readily available. For instance, if one day my leg was sore, we could immediately inform Eric. He would tell us what the problem was and immediately call Johannes to make appropriate adjustments to my exercise plans. This was crucial to my rehab.

At that time, I had no idea I would be able to achieve what I have today. I couldn't move my leg. It was like I'd fallen into a chasm and all I could see in front of me was darkness. I was a lame, retired tennis athlete – what else could I do? Undergoing the surgery was my own choice, but every doctor, no matter how good, had a certain percentage of cases that failed. Did I make the right choice? Or should I have opted for the conservative treatment? This was the first time in my life I'd taken such a gamble, and I was completely unsettled as I awaited the results.

Fortunately, over time, my leg started to improve. The programme began to show some results. Since I only had a three-month visa in Germany, I had to leave the country before 30 June. I wasn't quite ready to leave, still feeling that I wasn't one hundred per cent recovered. But Eric said I could start training. He asked me to believe in myself and try playing a little.

And so I took part in Wimbledon in 2008, less than three months after my knee surgery, and even defeated my first-round opponent. Although I lost to a young player in the second round, that one precious victory was the irrefutable evidence that my competitive state was picking up. I was so excited I almost cried. After the loss, Jiang Shan and I packed up and happily returned to China to prepare for the Olympics.

Chapter 20

The Olympic Games of 2008

By the time I'd undergone three months of rehab, the Olympics were already very near. The 'Bird's Nest' arena and the 'Water Cube' pool were both ready to be packed with people, and the countdown appeared every day on television. My teammates and I arrived together at the training base in Jixian and began training there. The base was in the hills between Beijing and Tianjin. We could see the Great Wall in the distance, and the air in the valley was fresh and clean. There weren't many people around, and it was a very pleasant environment.

Upon returning home after Wimbledon, my right knee once again started swelling a little. I quickly contacted Eric, and he told me the name of the medicine I should use. He suggested I consult a doctor locally, getting an injection once every five days. So while I was training in Jixian, I went to Beijing once every five days, with Jiang Shan accompanying me on the bus, to see Dr Hu from the Beijing Number Three Hospital for the injections. This required three or four hours of travel time on each occasion, but because of my training, it was really the only option.

The increased intensity of my training was quite hard on my knee, which was damaged more seriously than I'd imagined. Once, it swelled quite badly, and the doctor had to drain fluid from it before he could give me the injection. I got the injections regularly, only missing a couple. Even now, I get an injection once a week. The medication injected in the knee is the medical equivalent of lubricant in a machine. It works to protect the cartilage.

Would the injury affect my play at the Olympics? Even I couldn't be sure about this. I could only go into the Olympics with a mindset of 'participation', and not put too much pressure on myself. Fortunately, everyone was more focused on the women's doubles team, not pinning much hope on the singles competition. We trained for quite a long time in Jixian before the Olympics, and the head coach focused most of his attention on the doubles players Zheng Jie and Yan Zi, often watching them train. He only came to my court a couple of times.

The eighth of August was the day of the Olympic Games opening ceremony. Despite all of the pain and frustration, now that the Olympics were really here, I was really excited. This was the first time my home country had hosted the Olympics, and it was an especially significant event. In 2000, I'd taken part in the Sydney Olympics, the first time I'd played in the games, but this was on my home soil, and the feeling was totally different.

It's hard to describe that sense of elation. Whether you were an athlete or an ordinary spectator, watching the ceremony live in Beijing or at home on TV, every Chinese person must have swelled with pride.

National Tennis Centre director Sun Jinfang was afraid the opening ceremony would exhaust me. She said, 'Don't go. It will be very tiring.'

I told her not to worry. I wanted to witness this grand event with my own eyes. I paid careful attention to my appearance, trying to look my most photogenic for the occasion.

As the host of the Olympics, the Chinese team was the last to enter the main venue. Along the way, volunteers around the Chinese delegation kept shouting, 'Go China!' In the stands, people held small flags, and everyone shouted enthusiastically. For a moment, I really wanted to cry. Words are insufficient to describe the feeling, and I could only let the tears roll down my cheeks.

After entering the stadium, the performance began. Jiang Shan and I both kept taking photos with others. Actually, at the time, I really wanted to find Roger Federer to take a picture with him. That day, he served as the flag-bearer for the Swiss team, and from the moment he stepped on the field, he'd stirred up quite a response from the spectators. Usually, we only see Federer in sportswear, but at the opening ceremony he was wearing the Swiss national colours. I searched the crowd a long time for him, but I couldn't find him. Perhaps he slipped away early. That day was his twenty-seventh birthday, so I think it was a very meaningful day for him.

I found Daniela Hantuchova and many other players I really liked in the crowd and took photos with them. The Chinese contingent also took many photos of one another, and everyone was very excited. When we arrived at the ceremony, it was all very orderly with us sticking strictly to the buses we were supposed to ride on, but afterward, it was a mess. Whatever bus we saw, we just climbed aboard. The shoes the Chinese leaders made us wear were very uncomfortable, so by the time we got to the Olympic Village, I'd taken them off and walked home barefoot.

In contrast with the joy the Olympics brought, the tennis team was a little gloomy. The start of the games didn't go well for the Chinese team. I remember that as soon as the draw was completed, Coach Jiang's expression changed. Almost all of the Chinese team members would be facing seeded players in the first round. My fate in the first draw was the worst of all. I would be facing one of the most outstanding players: Svetlana Kuznetsova.

Kuznetsova was at her peak at this time. Before the Olympics, she was ranked third in the world. It looked like a one-sided battle. Almost everyone agreed that she would get this win. Even I couldn't help but think so. The media headlines read, 'Fortune is against China; Kuznetsova in first round for Li Na.'

I hadn't had much luck at the Olympics. In the first round in 2000, I encountered a top ten player, Arantxa Sanchez Vicario, and was eliminated without ceremony. Now, when I saw the result of this draw, I smiled wryly at Jiang Shan and said, 'That's it. This will be another quick tour!'

Still, I did my best and trained hard, preparing for the match. I watched a video of Kuznetsova's matches, viewing them repeatedly. There was a competitive little flame secretly burning in me. I considered Kuznetsova an old acquaintance, and I'd even defeated her once at Wimbledon before. After that, whenever we'd met in competition, the score had always been relatively close. Although I said aloud that she would beat me, inside I knew that she wasn't invincible, and that I might just have a chance.

This proved to be true. That match didn't get off to a smooth start for me, and I was still a little worried about my leg. Kuznetsova displayed her strength by breaking my first three serves, establishing an early lead. She had a powerful serve, and her forehand was also very strong. But during the match, I found confidence. I didn't think about winning or losing, but just concentrated on attacking her forehand. I succeeded in breaking two of her serves.

Kuznetsova was serving to win the next game, and I broke her serve, and caught up to even the score at 5–5. In the tie-break, I finally won the first set 7–5.

The spectators cheered loudly. I grew calmer. *No matter what, Kuznetsova, this is my home court!*

The second set began exactly as the first set had, with Kuznetsova breaking my serve. But she didn't take the advantage. I broke her next two serves, powering through the following five games to a score of 5–2.

I watched Kuznetsova's face. She looked restless, like she'd lost confidence. I'd often seen that same expression on my face in the locker room mirror. It was the sign of failure.

By this time, the match had completely lost its suspense. In the crucial tenth game, I served the victory break point and crushed all hope of reversal for Kuznetsova. The final score in the second set was 6–4. We played the match in one hour, forty-five minutes, and I served three aces.

The second round was uneventful, and I proceeded smoothly on to the quarterfinals. And suddenly the head coach was there at my court to watch. One particular day, I was training with many reporters there to observe me. The head coach arrived unexpectedly and inspected my play and even helped me pick up one tennis ball from the ground. It was stressful, though, because this sort of deliberate behaviour meant that everyone believed I could win an Olympic medal.

My next opponent was a majestic one, and even to the relatively ignorant Chinese tennis audience, her name was well known: Venus Williams!

Once again, this was considered a very one-sided match. Everyone felt that Venus Williams advancing to the semifinals was a foregone conclusion. Even people who didn't follow tennis knew the names of the Williams sisters. Venus held seven Grand Slam titles, and just a month earlier, she'd taken both the singles and doubles championships at Wimbledon. She won her first three matches at the Olympics easily, and it was clear she was in quite a good competitive state. I'd never faced Venus Williams before, and to be playing such a strong opponent in the quarterfinals was enough to make everyone break out in a sweat on my behalf.

If you followed tennis news, you could see a subtle change in the headlines at this time. It went from 'Li Na bravely conquered Kuznetsova' to 'China's golden flower faces major test' and 'Formidable adversary blocking the road to the semifinals'. The Chinese media had a unique way of expressing its concerns about the match. Obviously, they had a cautious 'wait and see' approach (or, you might say, not many held any real hope), but you could feel that the Chinese people were behind me.

On the day of the match, it rained, and the match was delayed several times. It didn't stop raining until six o'clock that evening. I hadn't even begun to prepare when I received word that we would start the match in forty-five minutes. I hurried to the court in time to catch the end of the previous match, James Blake versus Roger Federer.

It seemed that Federer had lost. Venus Williams and I walked onto the court as the male players were leaving. I saw Blake looking very pleased, surrounded by reporters. When Williams passed by, the pair of them high-fived. Their meaning was clearly, 'Let's go!' I didn't think too much about it, but just went to the court and started warming up.

The sidelines were packed for this match. Despite the fact that the umpire asked the crowd to be quiet, I still heard the audience calling my name when I entered. During that match, I really came to know the meaning of the phrase, 'It's hard to get off when you're riding a tiger'.

Home-court advantage is a very subtle thing. Seeing the stands full of cheering crowds can be empowering, but it can also be stressful. After many years of playing tennis, I was more used to playing away from home. I'd weathered vicious storms while clashing with Russian players in Moscow, and I had played at the US Open, where the crowds really loved their hometown players. That had never been a problem. Most of the time, I can block out English, Russian, French or Spanish, no matter what the disturbance. They're not my mother tongue, and when I concentrate on tennis, they float in one ear and out the other.

The one thing I hadn't experienced before was playing in China, in front of so many cameras, with so many of my compatriots' gazes upon me. Many people didn't know much about the etiquette of the game, so often there would be a lot of cheering before crucial points, and I felt very touched. To a certain degree, the noise affected me, and I couldn't focus on my opponent or think strategically. But I said to myself, *Don't worry. You're playing on your own doorstep. This is your home court. Stop worrying and just play.*

Williams is worthy of her reputation as one of the best women's tennis players in the world. She began with authority, putting so much power into her serve that I couldn't return it. She soon established a 3–0 lead.

Starting poorly seemed to be my trend in that year's Olympic matches. I tried hard to calm myself, looking toward the box. Jiang Shan was in the same state I was, trying to remain calm. He made a 'take it easy' expression.

I steadied my mind, then turned to receive Williams' serve, trying to return the ball to my opponent and turn the momentum of the game in my favour. This seemed to work, and I successfully saved consecutive points. I slowly pulled the score a little closer. Finally, I won the set 7–5.

The Chinese fans were even more excited than I was. I heard them cry loudly, and some people even started singing 'The Dragon'. The match wasn't even half over at this point, and everyone was already happy, as if I'd defeated Williams.

The desire and motivation to win hit me hard. I knew I had to win this match. I *had* to win. Victory was the only option. I didn't have the right to fail. This wasn't just my own personal battle.

After the second set started, I pulled ahead 6–5, but the score had stayed close throughout, with the lead going back and forth. When I got to match point, I was very nervous. Williams was experienced and immediately noticed this. She returned my serve very forcefully, and when I went to return it, I made an error.

I comforted myself, thinking, *Never mind. I'm still in the lead. Put this one away and it will be no problem.*

But Williams also understood the significance of this moment. We fought for a long time for the point, until Williams was losing patience. I seized the opportunity and went for the ball. I finally won that valuable point.

This put Williams under a lot of pressure. When I served for the second match point, she hit a shot straight into the net. I couldn't help but jump up. 7–5! I won! I beat Venus Williams!

It was only after the event that I learnt that among the spectators that day, not only was Sun Jinfang cheering for me, but Bill Gates was there to watch Williams. What was most touching, however, was that after I defeated Williams, when I'd shaken hands with my opponent and the umpire, the audience was shouting in unison 'Li Na! Li Na!' At that moment my ears were buzzing with the continuous uproar. Even when I left the court and went to the locker room, I could still hear those seated on the sidelines shouting my name.

Later, reporters told me that this was the best result any Chinese player had achieved in Olympic play. Many sites immediately updated the latest news. Most of the headlines included words like 'upset' and 'dark horse'. More provocative terms like 'defeat' or 'pummel' also appeared frequently. One even read, 'Williams has become a spectator under the Li Na racket' (what an exaggeration!).

One website was particularly interesting. It even made a comparison chart: seven-time Grand Slam champion versus two-time WTA low-level-event champion; number seven seed versus number forty-two seed; five-time Wimbledon champion versus Wimbledon quarter-finalist. Below, it said, 'Our "Chinese sister" Li Na eliminates Venus Williams'.

Victories and losses are common for professional athletes. Venus Williams was a talented player without equal. After that match, we played several more times in succession, and each of us won a few. Our first match in the Olympic arena didn't really mean anything. What most shocked me was the invisible force of the audience, the weight of a nation needing this win to prove itself. Before that, I'd thought that tennis was just a sport, but during that game, the frenzied audience made me realise that it assumed a significance well beyond sports.

In the next match I played the Russian Dinara Safina. This game was harder than I'd expected. I'd played Safina twice, and won both times. I thought my chances of winning were good. But as it turned out, Safina not only had extensive experience, but she also possessed the same stamina and explosive power as her brother, 'the Czar of tennis', Marat Safin. And my own lack of play the previous few months had made me regress. I really exerted myself during the first set, trying to play close to the net offensively. However, under Safina's powerful serve, my own attack seemed a little sloppy. My damn knee was flaring up, and I felt quite weak. In the end, I lost the crucial tie-break.

In the second set, the situation was a little better. In order to try to quieten the energetic Safina, I constantly shifted my placement of the ball. This helped some, and I gained a 4–2 advantage.

But Safina picked up on my strategy and went on the counterattack. This Russian woman, four years younger than me, was indefatigable. I couldn't let my guard down at all, my mind growing taut as a rubber band. If I made the slightest mistake, I'd break. Just at that moment, I heard someone yell from the audience, 'Charge the net! Smash it! Move the ball!' It was very loud. Safina's return had not yet hit the ground, and I heard the spectator yell, 'Out!' Some of the other spectators shouted along with him, and it grew quite chaotic. The umpire said 'Quiet!' in Chinese several times, but with little success.

After defeating Venus Williams, I knew my mental state had changed. Before that, I thought, *Just do your best and it'll be fine.* But now, my expectations of myself were much higher. I was eager to defeat Safina, and in my haste I double-faulted. At the moment, I felt like I was rowing against the current. I was fatigued and irritable, having expended much energy on the match. My mind had grown numb, and the clamour from the audience made it very difficult for me to focus on the match. It was 5–4 my way, and the match was within reach, but just as I was returning the ball, the voice sounded again: 'Charge the net! Smash!'

Oddly enough, I did move in to smash. The ball went out, and I lost the point.

Before I even knew what I was doing, my body got ahead of me. All the pent-up frustration broke out. I turned to face the crowd and yelled, 'Shut up!' in English.

The scene suddenly grew very quiet. The faces of the spectators wore expressions of disappointment and hurt. I was shocked by my own impulsiveness. What was I doing? I was speechless, guilt flooding over me. I lost interest in the game, and it was soon over, with Safina the victor.

After the match, I was furious, but also tormented by guilt. I owed a big 'I'm sorry' to the audience. To me, 'shut up' merely meant, 'That's not right; you're disturbing me'. My frustration had usually been vented on Jiang Shan, but this time, I lost control. Obviously, this wasn't the way a mature athlete should behave.

Training year-round overseas, I was used to speaking English on the tennis court because English is the medium of communication with the referees, umpires and coaches. After the match, the internet community began vigorous discussions about why Li Na had used English to 'insult' people. Just 'insulting' the audience was bad enough, but to do so in English was even worse, dragging me into a quagmire. The national sentiment was all stirred up by the phrase 'shut up'. If I'd known before how much trouble this moment of anger would bring me, I would have rather played with my mouth pasted shut.

Full of ups and downs, my Olympic tour had come to an end. From this moment on, I began to take on a real professional athlete's mindset. The Olympics is a high-stakes event. When my father was alive, he'd said he hoped I would win a national championship and an Olympic gold medal. It was with great difficulty that I made it to this Olympics, which was hosted by my own homeland. Failing to rise to expectations, after having reached the semifinals, is still a lasting regret.

Chapter 21

Going Solo

I'd now passed through one Olympic cycle, from 2004 to 2008. I'd been plagued by injury for a few years, and my results were not what I'd hoped they would be. The idea of retiring again sprouted in me, and I discussed it with the personnel of the national team. If I couldn't make my own decisions concerning tournament participation I would retire and go back to finish my degree. If I could play on my own, then I would continue to play.

In 2008, I was already twenty-six years old. For a professional tennis player, this is a ripe old age. I was tired of playing under the national team. I wanted to experience what it was really like to be a professional. I wanted to hire my own coach, like foreign players did, and be free to choose my own tournaments and to equip my team according to my own physical condition and skill level, propelling myself to more success and improvement. This was professional tennis. Having played more than a decade of tennis, I'd never really *experienced* professional tennis. I never thought about winning a Grand Slam. It was like looking through a paper-covered window, knowing there were stars and a moon out there, but feeling it was all hazy and distant.

In September 2008, after the Olympic Games had ended, the

Chinese Tennis Association announced that four players – Zheng Jie, Peng Shuai, Yan Zi and me – could all choose to go solo.

This news was something I'd long waited to hear, a groundbreaking 'restructuring' marking a new era in Chinese tennis. I don't know how Sun Jinfang convinced the General Tennis Administration to allow Chinese tennis to reform, but upon hearing the news, I was ecstatic and went immediately to sign my contract. The agreement stipulated that, beginning in 2009, individual athletes would be entitled to autonomy in managing their own coaches, bonuses, participation schedules and income, with a required revenue of eight per cent and a match bonus of twelve per cent to be paid to the state. The agreement included a stipulation that when the athlete's personal arrangements for tournaments and training conflicted with the Olympics, confederation cups or other similar events, she need abide by the Tennis Association's arrangements and shoulder the responsibility of playing for the relevant provincial team.

I accepted all of these terms. It was a fundamental change to my training and life, really sending me fully into the professional arena. Playing under the auspices of the national team could protect a young player's interests and open up more opportunities for experience, and was a good example of the 'big rice bowl' concept that's well known in China – everyone eating from one big bowl, sharing resources. But when it came to helping more mature players to compete at a higher level, this arrangement was useless. What the state system can't accomplish, the private model can do quite well.

I'm especially grateful to Sun Jinfang. I know she must have put a lot of effort into making this happen. When the reform of the programme was first proposed, the resistance from the Sports Authority was strong. Sun explained that tennis was a very special case. The administration's response was 'What's special about it? If it's because it's an individual sport, well, so are table tennis and badminton.'

In fact, there's no distinction in the sport itself. What sets tennis apart is that it's already a highly professional mainstream sport globally. It's the biggest of the small balls, which is why there was a good case for reform.

At that time, the national tennis team wasn't performing as well as it is now, and the consensus was that reform would be a mistake. If it hadn't been for Sun's unflagging insistence, this crop of athletes would most likely have been silenced and buried, just as our seniors had always been. Until I won the French Open in 2011, there was constant tension over 'reform'.

I'd always wanted to go solo in order to access a more professional style of training. As early as 2004, when I made my comeback, I'd harboured this desire. When I'd first asked permission to continue with my own training instead of going back to the national team in 2005, permission had been denied. According to the state system, it wasn't up to individuals to make their own decisions about things like this. In the end, I went back to the national team.

Honestly, I'm too direct. I don't know how to act sometimes, and I'm not good at dealing with delicate situations, and this made it appear that I wasn't a team player. In the national team, I wasn't a very well-liked player, or at least that was how it felt to me. My teammates must have thought, *How did this camel infiltrate our flock of lambs?*

Of course, no one would say this publicly, but there was always a subtle sense of distance. When there was no tournament, I felt that I didn't exist for the team. People looked at me like looking at a glass door, seeing right through me to things beyond. But when a major event was approaching, I suddenly became a hot item once more. Everyone lined up to express their care and concern. There was no place to hide, nowhere to escape notice. Even hiding on the court wasn't possible, because everyone knew where to find me.

This sort of thing happened often, and I gradually came to understand why it was the case. After a long time, I got used to it, but I also grew unhappy, and the leaders were also unhappy.

Go solo, then. Going solo was win-win. Everyone would be happy.

To be fair, there wasn't a lot of tension in my relationship with the national team. On some level, we were still a community. A loss for one was a loss for all, just as we shared all of our victories. But sometimes there was a lack of timely communication, and messages got passed through a number of people, causing the original meaning to be lost. Once the team's instructions had made it through all the layers of communication and finally found their way to me, the message was distorted beyond recognition. Sometimes I got so fed up I went directly to the leaders to complain. They were often surprised by what I'd heard, saying, 'Where did you get that idea?'

Jiang Shan told me, 'Sometimes you just have to put up with it.' But there were some things I couldn't put up with. If you ask me to endure hardship, that's fine, but you can't just humour me or lie to me. I was also not very willing to explain myself. If you believe this is a cup then it doesn't matter how many times I tell you it's a bowl, you won't believe me, because you already have your own ideas. If you want to call it a cup, fine.

Being my own boss now, bearing my own risks and forging my own achievements, even though it would be more tiring, meant I also had less mental stress. Life was good, and at least I wouldn't be so distracted by things that actually had nothing to do with sport.

When I signed the agreement that allowed me to go solo, I felt I was ushering in a new beginning. Now I could fully enter the ranks of professional tennis players.

Going solo meant more autonomy, but it also meant increased pressure. If you played poorly, there would be less money, and you couldn't hire the best coaches or access a high level of training, which might ultimately result in elimination. It meant new opportunities, but also new challenges. I joked with Jiang Shan, telling him to prepare for the worst; if I failed I might end up spending everything the two of us had saved. He just said, 'If that happens, we'll start over.'

Of course, I was only kidding around. Talk of 'starting over' was a joke. I was firmly committed to embarking on this professional path. Before, when I played in tournaments, I invested my physical strength. Now I would also have to invest my money. Both the financial and physical investments resulted in my returns.

When I was with the national team, all the expenses were borne by the state. All I needed to do was put my physical strength on the line, so the burden was much smaller. In all honesty, if I'd been free to set my own competition schedule and have my own small team to accompany me, I would have been very willing to stay with the national team. The burdens that I had to bear would not have been nearly as great, and the risks would be much smaller.

When the national team nurtures you, they have administrative rights over you. That's a given. Our national tennis team is actually fairer than many other sports teams. For tennis, as long as a player qualifies, the team will send her abroad for a tournament, provided it doesn't affect the team's plan or training regimen. In the national team, players eat, live, train and compete under the management of the team. So we had no expenses, but our income was also much lower, accounting for about a quarter of any prize money we won.

From a purely economic perspective, going solo was a bad idea. At that time, my income was only about seventy or eighty thousand US dollars a year, but the expenses of a team were considerably more. Obviously, I would not be able to make ends meet. But after playing tennis for so many years, I desperately wanted to experience the life of a real professional.

After going solo, my expenses for training, airfares and my team were my own responsibility. In addition, I still needed to pay a fixed revenue to the government. I was very willing to do this, and I hope to see the nation's tennis programme consistently improve. I hope there are many more young players and promising newcomers breaking onto the international scene, showing everyone that Asians can also possess a first-class physique and compete at the highest levels. I feel that when it comes to giving back to the nation, actions would be much more effective than shouting slogans.

The biggest problem I encountered after going solo was the visas. A tennis player needs to fly all over the world throughout the year, and every country requires a separate visa. If I went through the regular channels of visa applications, I wouldn't be able to get anything in time. Fortunately, the National Tennis Centre has been very active in helping me settle visa issues.

Another test after going solo was the language barrier. Most of the staff, coaches and trainers around me were foreigners, just as most of the reporters I faced when overseas were foreigners. They all spoke English, so if I didn't speak English, I couldn't communicate with them. It was at this time that my English began to make rapid progress. Many online fans were interested to know how I learned English, but the truth is, I was in an environment in which I was forced to learn. If you ask me what's the most important part of learning English, I'd say you have to have thick skin. You can't be too shy to speak up. You have to dare to try. Don't worry about whether your grammar, tenses or pronunciation are all correct. My English isn't very good, but it's good enough to communicate. And for me, that's enough.

Chapter 22

A New Team

After going solo, the most pressing thing was to form my own team. I asked a friend of mine in Hong Kong, an avid tennis lover, to help me retain the services of the former national team coach, Thomas Hogstedt (at the time, I didn't have the financial foundation to employ a coach myself). Thomas became the first foreign coach I employed.

Jiang Shan was naturally an integral part of my team. The others were my doctor in Munich, Eric, a physiotherapist, a technical trainer and my fitness trainer, Johannes. Of these, Johannes didn't always travel with us. His work was mainly to help me do my rehab and occasionally to help if I needed a hand in my physical training. Aside from Jiang Shan, everyone's fees were calculated weekly. So every year I would talk through a year-long plan with my therapists, telling them which tournaments I'd need them for.

My current physiotherapist, Alex Stober, who has been with me since March 2010, was first introduced to me by Thomas Hogstedt. Alex, a German man of fifty-something, has been working in the tennis circuit for more than thirty years, over ten of which were spent as an official therapist for the Association of Tennis Professionals, the international men's professional tennis association. He's worked with top players like Pete Sampras and Andre Agassi.

Alex has followed me all over the world, working about twenty-five to thirty weeks each year. His job is to give me relaxation therapy, including roughly two hours of massage therapy after training each day, which helps in recovery. Thanks to his superb technique and skill, I've no longer been plagued by injury. When I first met him, I couldn't even straighten my knee. Since then I've made a lot of progress, and it's largely due to Alex's work. I'm very grateful to him, and I really trust him. I can dedicate all of my attention to the court, not having to worry about my physical condition.

When Alex and I chat, he shares anecdotes and gossip from tennis circles. Although I know he's a veteran in the field, I'm still often surprised at his impressive knowledge, breadth of experience and huge circle of friends. How can he know so many stories from tennis circles? How can he have so many friends? When we travel to a tournament, as soon as we finish checking into the hotel he's nowhere to be found – he's already out looking for old friends to catch up with.

When we're travelling for tournaments, we usually choose to eat at Chinese restaurants. If there are no Chinese restaurants, we choose a Thai or other Asian eatery. I usually ask the staff for chopsticks and often, the waiter will ask if the other members of my team want chopsticks. At this point Alex often jokes in an exaggerated style, 'I'm Chinese. I want chopsticks.' He uses chopsticks, and does so very well.

For a period of time, every time Alex arrived for my therapy, the first thing he did when he walked through the door was ask Jiang Shan, 'Did you win?' Jiang Shan spends the hour while I'm undergoing therapy sitting there playing video games. Alex often says, 'I can't even sit still for a minute. Strange how Jiang Shan can play video games for hours.'

When I first went solo, my diet was a standard one, not one tailor-made for athletes. With my new training regimen, my body couldn't cope, and I employed a personal nutritionist to help. After a period of conditioning, I gradually recovered stamina.

When I embarked on my solo journey, many people wondered how I'd go. I didn't argue with them. I had no time to engage in senseless verbal sparring. Only by producing good results could I silence the critics.

Until that point, I'd felt that I was one of a large family, and all I had to do was listen to my 'parents'. Creating my own team and becoming a true professional athlete changed my life completely. Before, everything had been managed by others, all the arrangements made by someone else. Now, all of this was in my own hands. Put plainly, I was the team's boss, with the right to choose and to dismiss employees. This wasn't only a sort of freedom but also a responsibility. I wasn't only leading myself, but also helping the team to be its best. To me, this was no small challenge.

I had to learn how to book hotels, flights and do other travel-related tasks. Thomas played a very big role, taking the initiative to assume this job so that I could spend more time training. Imagine a coach who, on top of offering instruction on the court, has to sit at the computer keying in itineraries letter by letter. It wasn't ideal.

It's fair to say that it was Thomas who really put me into the professional circuit. He was always very positive during training and very dynamic on the court, as if he didn't know what it meant to be tired. From the time he first started training me, he was convinced that I could become a top ten player and that I could make it to a Grand Slam semifinal. He was the first coach who made me believe that I could make it.

Thomas had been in tennis for a relatively long time, and he offered a high level of training. When we were both with the national team, we got along very well, becoming good friends, but Thomas had to take care of all the players and my time with him was very limited.

After becoming my personal trainer, it was a different story. Thomas was a very optimistic person, and quite chatty. To be more accurate, he was talkative, and when chatting with him, you didn't need to say much. Thomas can singlehandedly offer a full analysis of international tennis, and sometimes his topics veer outside tennis, covering everything under the sun. Training with him was relaxing and pleasant. But if you didn't speak for a while, he would suddenly grow alert and ask, 'What are your thoughts?' or 'I've been talking so much. Maybe you have something to say?'

I would try to offer some thoughts of my own. When listening to players, Thomas was very patient. Regardless of whether he liked the ideas or not, he was always very respectful. Foreigners are different from Chinese people, preferring not to beat around the bush. If what I said was in line with his own thinking, Thomas would immediately and enthusiastically express his agreement. When my ideas were not in line with his, he would speak up and set me straight. This approach was a lot like Jiang Shan, in that Thomas often refuted me mercilessly. He had a sharp eye, and was very professional in analysing a problem. He gave me a lot of good suggestions. He is, without question, a very good coach.

What I most appreciated about Thomas was how positive he was. He was bold in speech and action. As long as he thought it was possible to achieve something, he would keep telling me, 'You can do it! You should try this!' When I entered the top twenty, many of my peers thought it was the peak of my career. But Thomas said decisively, 'You can get into the top ten. In fact, you have a chance at a Grand Slam title!' Maybe it's the way Westerners do things, giving you confidence and affirmation, constantly reminding you that you can do better, and praising players without restraint. Even when I'd just lost a match, Thomas would be on the court the next day, analysing my successes and failures. And he always added at the end, 'Never mind. We lost this time, but we'll do better next time.' During the two years that Thomas coached me, I experienced an unprecedented sort of confidence. I never thought myself invincible, but I did feel I should have the courage to push myself to a higher level.

For a professional tennis player, language skills are very important. South American athletes have a major advantage over Asian athletes because most of them speak Spanish and French, and they can communicate well with their European counterparts. Professional players will usually spend time with their opponents while competing. Those who are friends greet each other and train or hang out together before the match. After the match, they also sometimes encourage each other and discuss their own thoughts about the game. All of the bigger tournaments have a player party, but I usually only attended those events I was required to. I wasn't really adjusted to this new scene, and sometimes I asked some of my team members to accompany me to the events.

Thomas did very well in cross-cultural settings. He'd spent many years in the international tennis circle and was at ease interacting with other people. During the tournaments, he often took the initiative to help me find top ten players to train with so that I'd have more opportunities to connect with them. When playing a match, I would try to arrive early. For example, if the match was on Monday, we would arrive at the stadium on Friday so that Thomas could spend the weekend introducing me to the top players, or even arrange for me to train with them. Before this, as a player ranked in the top twenty or thirty, I was unlikely to take the initiative to seek out these top players and compare notes with them. But Thomas's enthusiasm and initiative made it all possible. These training sessions gave me a lot of confidence. As I played more, the mystique veiling the top ten was lifted from my imagination, and with Thomas's help, I learned to take the initiative in talking with them, asking them to train with me, and raising my own level of play. I was learning to really integrate myself into their circle.

In addition, Thomas took me to meet the umpires. It had never before crossed my mind to get to know the umpires. Most Chinese players have this same attitude, resulting in us being isolated and closed off. My newfound networking also helped break me out of a sphere of anonymity, and the Western world began to remember my name. This was a very big step.

For the first two years, things carried on in this manner. From late 2008 through 2009, Thomas was also coaching a male player at the same time as me. Throughout 2010, he focused solely on training me. For that first year in my team, he took on the extra work of booking hotels and airfares, but by the end of 2009, I employed a firm that managed all of these arrangements for me so that Thomas could focus more on training. Besides improving my ties with other players, Thomas also helped me hire Alex, and had already introduced me to Eric, my doctor. Thanks to him I made connections with many outstanding insiders, truly propelling me to the international arena at last.

Chapter 23

The Agency

On 22 December 2008, I was in Munich, Germany, preparing to undergo my second knee surgery. The whole operation had been arranged by me and Jiang Shan alone. Christmas was coming soon, and my doctor, Eric Rembeck, deliberately scheduled my surgery for Christmas Eve, so that I would be in the hospital on Christmas Day, eating regular meals at set times. He told me that all of the shops would be closed during Christmas and if he discharged me, he was afraid I wouldn't be able to eat.

When I got out of the hospital, it was 26 December. Jiang Shan and I quietly thanked the doctors and nurses and left. Jiang Shan took the prescription the doctor had given me and went to the pharmacy to get anti-inflammatory medication. On crutches, I waited in the subway station until he got back. Germans like to spend the holiday period at home, and all of the shops, big or small, were still closed, the city was empty and the streets were ominously quiet. Only the pharmacy was open, and even that was just a side door. The contrast with the usual bustle was stark. Fortunately, Christmas holds no significance for us Chinese, so it didn't evoke any sense of homesickness for us. Jiang Shan escorted me back to our lodgings – we were staying in a guest room at a local sports school at the time. We began the process of recovery, relying completely on ourselves.

The small apartment was equipped with everything we needed. There was a kitchen stove, so we could cook our own food. Jiang Shan had followed Eric's suggestion and stocked up on food before Christmas, and he used that now. While I was recuperating, Jiang Shan busied himself in the kitchen every day, washing and cooking rice, frying vegetables and so on. His cooking was passable; at least we didn't have to go hungry. Every day, I ate the meals that Jiang Shan had lovingly prepared, then watched television and went online to pass the time. The leg that had undergone surgery hung in a sling over my bed, and I didn't dare move it too much.

When I was tired of watching TV, I turned on the computer and chatted with friends in China, watched Korean soap operas we'd brought over, and spent my time happily. It was rare that I got to spend a few days without touching a racket. If you don't count the pain of surgery, then honestly, those days were quite pleasant.

The greatest distress was the injections. During the Christmas season, Eric couldn't give me the injections himself as he was with his family. He taught me the simple procedure so that I could do it myself. When he gave me the injections, he did it easily. It wasn't painful at all. But when I held that thin needle in my own hand, I suddenly found that it took a lot of courage to administer the injection.

Jiang Shan volunteered, but I declined. Men always have a heavy hand, and I didn't quite trust him. I felt better doing it myself.

But where should I administer it? In the backside? I couldn't reach it myself. The thigh and belly looked like good, meaty options. I squeezed my thigh, then pinched my belly, and felt that there was more flesh on the stomach. Okay, belly it was!

I was clearly not as skilled as Eric. I hesitatingly poked the head of the needle into the skin. It didn't hurt that much. I wiped the sweat from my palms, and slowly pushed the fluid through the needle, then withdrew it. I'd done it! Jiang Shan helped me clean the site with alcohol. This wasn't so difficult after all!

I gave myself an injection every day for five days. Then the Christmas holiday was over, and Eric helped me do the final few injections. Rehab had already begun, and just as had happened on the previous occasion, my leg was temporarily unable to move, so I had to follow my trainer's regimen for upper body exercises.

After surgery, you usually need to use crutches for a week or two. The first time I had surgery, I wasn't sure that I would be able to recover according to schedule, and with the upcoming Olympics weighing heavily on my mind, my spirits were very low. This time, I was much steadier. Eric told me it would normally take about four to six weeks to fully recover. He thought, seeing my physical condition, it might take me five weeks. Sure enough, five weeks later, I resumed training. It was really amazing.

After two operations, Eric and I had developed a good relationship, and we became good friends. In the months after my surgery I went for an injection once every five days, and sometimes my trainer, Johannes, would also seek the doctor's advice. When my training was very busy, Eric would bring his small medicine chest and make the twenty-minute drive to Johannes's office himself, then return to his office after administering the injection.

A few years later Eric decided to move his surgery to a place above Johannes's office so I didn't even have to travel twenty minutes for my injections.

Some people say that Germans are old-fashioned and arrogant. I disagree. In fact, I feel that 'arrogance' is what some of the leaders in China felt toward the Germans. In China, the leaders hold a lot of power and their subordinates work to please them. Germans don't behave like that. Instead, everyone has a cooperative relationship, treating one another as partners. At least, this has been my experience with the Germans I've been in contact with. They are very generous and respectful toward their foreign friends and their culture. Once when I went to see Johannes, Eric even joked as he was taking our photos, 'Today is our China day!' I've never trusted others easily, but with this group of German friends, I felt very safe. They're all good people.

Many people also say that Germans are rigorous and punctual, a point I agree with. My doctor has a very real concept of time and also a spirit of service. He would change his holiday plans for the sake of a patient. When there was a volcanic eruption in Iceland, he was on holiday in Spain. I was originally scheduled to have an injection on Monday, but planes weren't allowed to fly due to the eruption, so he rented a car and drove back from Spain to Munich to administer my injection. I was very touched. But he seemed to think this was normal, and that it was simply a matter of his doing his job.

The injections Eric gave me were indeed very effective. The problem with my knee amounted to cartilage wear and tear, and a lot of fluid built up when this became serious. Human cartilage tissue is usually flat, but because of the constant friction on my knee, there was excess cartilage that had built up. When it was at its worst, I couldn't even walk to the toilet, and when I slept, I needed to place a pillow under my knee, as I couldn't fully straighten my leg. The goal of the surgery was to flatten the cartilage, but the effects weren't permanent, and after the surgery, the cartilage would continue to grow. Eric told me that as long as I continued to train, the knee wouldn't fully recover.

Before my third operation in 2009, I asked Eric if there was any cure. He said there were only two options. Either the cartilage above the bone could be smoothed away and then given eight months to grow back, or we could opt for artificial cartilage. However, this artificial cartilage was only suitable for general use and couldn't withstand an athlete's regimen. If we opted for artificial cartilage, my sports career would be at an end. No player had ever returned to the court after this kind of operation.

I didn't dare to try either option. The artificial option was definitely out of the question, and I couldn't afford eight months of downtime. So in the end, I followed the same procedure as before and underwent a third operation. But that all came later.

Most tennis tournaments are held in Europe, so I spend about half the year in Munich, basing my team there. Being near my doctor and trainer, I can easily continue my training and recondition myself. It saves me the hassle of applying for visas, plus I can have my regular injections – basically once every five days. Over the years, I've gone from fearing needles to being able to chat idly while undergoing the jab. Sometimes I think, *Am I becoming one of those people who depend on shots to maintain my athletic life?* (Of course I'm clean. I've never touched an illegal substance, and I would never do anything to hurt myself.)

Although fitness training is usually very boring, especially the early stages of rehab immediately following a surgery, I've stuck with it. When you repeat the same programme every day, you sometimes wonder why you bother. It's a battle with the will, a sort of self-torment. But when you see the atrophied muscle become stronger and your form improving, you can only thank those ice-cold exercise machines and the rigid plan that you stuck to. You realise then how important your own early persistence was.

My team support me unconditionally. No matter where I am in the world, no matter what tournament I am at, I know they're rooting for me. No matter whether my results are good or bad, I know that when I return to Munich, they'll greet me with the warmest hugs and that will be enough.

Generally only Jiang Shan and my physiotherapist travelled to tournaments with me. My team didn't have a press spokesperson, and during competitions, there was a tournament doctor to take care of the players, so I didn't need to bring Eric with me. Though my team was small, every year my expenditures totalled between US$115000 and US$165000. This included a salary paid to the coach, and his airfare and hotel expenses when he accompanied me. If my results were good, he also got a portion of my earnings. All of these expenses relied on my bonus money and brand sponsorship. During the French Open, my team spent at least US$1500 a day.

Sometimes I chatted with the kids on the national team, and I couldn't help but think, *You've got it so easy.* Honestly, for younger players, being a part of the national team is good. Although you only get to keep twenty-five per cent of your bonus money, you don't need to invest any of it. Tennis is a project that requires a very large financial investment, and it's difficult for young players to afford it. In other countries, for younger players to succeed, either the family needs to be financially strong, or at a very young age, the player needs to earn corporate support (like the sponsorship I got from Nike). It's very difficult for a person of average financial means to succeed on his or her own. This is the cruelty of professional tennis. It's a world where achievements speak, and they don't come cheaply.

On the professional circuit, I felt isolated because of my nationality. Not many Chinese faces were to be seen on the international scene, so I had to work hard to keep pace with European and American players and adapt to their culture. And I felt lonely because of my age. Of the four of us who had gone solo mere months before, Yan Zi had already retired. Many European and American players my age were also retiring. I was approaching thirty years old, a true 'veteran'. Eric told me that since I'd earlier retired for two years and gone back to university, in terms of wear and tear on my body, I had a distinct advantage over players of the same age. Still, seeing players I knew leave one by one, only to be replaced by younger faces all full of childlike enthusiasm, made me miss the old times and feel nostalgic for the teammates I had fought shoulder to shoulder with.

One good thing happened during this time. When I was with the national team, there was no way I could sign an agent. After I left the national team, there were many trivial matters that I had to deal with personally. Even with Thomas's help, I found it tedious. Several agencies started contacting us, and I kept receiving solicitations.

I considered for a while, then finally decided to sign with IMG at the end of 2009, allowing the professionals to take over and do things the right way. Sports agents are very different from entertainment agents, and their influence is somewhat less. They are mainly there to serve the athlete while the athlete's focus remains firmly fixed on the court. Signing with IMG greatly reduced my burden and put the entire team's work on the right track. Now, when I went to tournaments, I just let the management firm know where I was going and how many rooms I needed. The firm would make bookings and arrange for ground transport. The events I took part in each year were up to me, though of course there were a few that I had to attend. If I needed a new coach or trainer or assistant, I just had to consult the management firm and it would give me a few reasonable suggestions.

Endorsement and brand sponsors were also arranged by the firm. When it received an offer for an endorsement contract, it would contact me and tell me the details and whether or not to pursue it. IMG has been very happy with my work with Nike. According to my sponsorship contract, I have to shoot two advertisements for Nike each year, and I've been portrayed in a 'healthy, sunny, athletic' way, an image I like and that fits me well. Nike has produced two ads, both of which I like: 'Strong is Beautiful', shot by the WTA, and 'Movement Changes Everything', shot by Nike.

As a result of IMG's management, I can basically control my own time. My tournament schedule is booked a year in advance. The specific times and places have been planned, and I can always adjust my conditioning according to my tournament schedule. When a tournament finishes, I can relax for a while, rejuvenating at home. Whenever I can, I return to Wuhan. It's the place I grew up, and many of my childhood friends and teammates are still there. We like to get together to watch movies, hang out at pubs, eat and talk. My friends' opinion of me doesn't change according to whether my career is going smoothly or not. In their minds, I'm the same old Li Na.

Except when I play at tournaments, I always choose my own clothes. I don't have a stylist. I'm an athlete, not a fashion icon, and would rather allow my play on the court to speak for me. I don't like to spend too much energy on my image. I'm not really crazy about luxury brands, and I often wear designer and high street brands all mixed together. I'm proud of my own sense of style. I don't like to put on make-up, and I find it very troublesome to remove it. I'm not a very careful person – what if I touch my face after applying make-up and smear it? I'd have to spend time touching it up then. It's just too much trouble.

Sometimes if I attend a party or go to some special event where everyone is going to be dressed up, I wear a pair of sports shoes on the way there. I ask Jiang Shan to drive me to the door while I change into high heels in the car, and then I confidently and elegantly walk into the party. I sign my name on the attendance register then walk back out, pretending to take a leisurely stroll in the parking lot, where I go to the car and change back into my sports shoes.

On one occasion, I wore high heels to a party. We drove there, but had to walk back. The walk would usually only take about ten minutes, but in heels it took me at least twice as long – and it was all uphill. All I could think of was throwing off those shoes. But I had to fight back the urge, because along the way we met many other athletes who were arriving late, and I thought if they saw me all dressed up but walking barefoot it would be quite humiliating. So I bore the pain and made a special effort to look poised. As soon as I walked in the door I rushed to take the shoes off. What a pain!

I now try to buy shoes with an especially low heel to wear to such events. Occasionally I will buy high-heeled shoes if I really admire the design, but I almost never wear them out.

Once I wore the same casual outfit to two different media events. My agent immediately cautioned me, saying, 'Online fans have noticed that you wore this outfit twice.'

Aiyah, surely you won't die from wearing the same clothes twice.

I told my agent, 'I'm not a movie star. They expect too much. It was just casualwear, and it wasn't what I wore at the tournaments, so it shouldn't be a problem.'

I find it a waste to only wear expensive clothes once. People like me not because of my clothes. But I gave in to my agency's suggestion, and a designer helped me settle the problem. If I sell the clothes I've worn, I can donate the money to charity. This helps many people and also makes tennis fans happy.

Usually after a match there's a press conference, during which one WTA official will accompany the players. After the conference, I don't give more interviews, as everything's already been said. Reporters on the tennis circuit know my character and don't expect me to give an interview without prior arrangement. Sometimes they send text messages, which I usually forward to my agency, so that it can follow it up. This might not be the most convenient arrangement for the media, but circumstances force me to do this. I can't possibly take the time to be thinking about other things. I just want to concentrate on training and competing.

As a professional tennis player, you have to update your whereabouts every day on the internet, because at any time you might be required to submit to a drug test. In 2010 alone, I gave twenty-five to thirty urine samples. Some people feel that such frequent checks are a pain, but it ensures that the sport won't be tainted. Let's say I'm in Munich today and need to go back to China for some reason; if I fail to update my location the following day and the Munich authorities don't find me at my reported address, it will be seen as a deliberate escape. In accordance with International Tennis Association requirements, if this happens three times, the player will be banned from competition for one year.

Some players have complained that we have no freedom and no privacy, because the ITA always knows where you are. Even for a vacation, we need to fill out forms to facilitate testing at any time. So far, everyone's complied with this system. For the four Grand Slams, it's not only urine tests, but blood tests as well. In the 2011 Australian Open I found out that blood tests would be conducted on everyone who made it into the quarterfinals. The programme is designed to be very strict.

Chapter 24

A Third Operation

Following my second operation late in 2008, I didn't play in the 2009 Australian Open but went directly to Dubai in February for the Dubai Tennis Championships. I didn't do well. After the match, Jiang Shan couldn't find me; I'd sought out a corner where I could have a good cry. Thomas had a lot of encouraging words, reminding me that this was my first tournament since the operation, and that I just needed to believe in myself.

After playing in Dubai, I went back to training in Germany for a while, then went to Indian Wells and Miami to compete in March. In May, I went to the French Open and made it to the fourth round at Roland Garros. This was my first real step forward since my surgery.

On 5 June, Jiang Shan and I successfully graduated from Huazhong. Jiang Shan met all the requirements without dropping any classes, while my final two years were done in a sort of self-study programme. At the end of each term, I would go to the university for exams or to hand in papers, which meant that what would normally have been two years of school dragged on for four years. To be honest, the teachers were very gracious, and I was relieved when I finally managed to graduate.

Jiang Shan should have graduated two years before me, but because of an oversight, he found he lacked one elective credit before graduation. Since he was always accompanying me to matches, it was a while before he could go back to make up that one credit. This marked the conclusion of one small episode in our otherwise tennis-centric life.

Good things just kept coming our way after graduation. On 14 June, I made it to the semifinals in grass-court play in Birmingham, where I defeated my old rival Sharapova to get into the finals. This was the first time a Chinese player had made it to the finals in grass-court competition. In September, I got into the quarterfinals of the US Open. I advanced five spots in the world rankings.

I was very pleased with my progress, but this year of globetrotting caused me to have a relapse. After playing in the US Open, my knee couldn't make it another day. I approached the national team's personnel to ask whether it was all right for me to miss the National Games. If I used the time to have surgery, and if my rehab went well, I thought I would be able to play in the 2010 Australian Open. I felt my enthusiasm rising. I was getting better, and if I played well in this Australian Open, I'd have the chance to enter the top ten!

The team leaders apparently weren't too keen on this idea. Unlike the Australian Open, the National Games was our nation's premier sporting event, and it was highly valued. The head of the Hubei Sports Bureau spoke to me and said something shocking. 'Li Na, trust me! I've been through it. The world's top ten is not nearly as important as a National Games championship.'

Hearing this, I was deflated. I told Jiang Shan, 'I can't talk to him. There's nothing to say.'

The China Open was held in late September, and after that was the National Games. By that time, I'd already prepared myself for a third knee operation. My plan was simple. I thought, *I'll have the surgery, then return to China. If they won't let me back out, I'll just play on one leg. If they really force me to play in the National Games, then I'll just play in that condition.*

Jiang Shan didn't agree. He said, 'We can't do that. Even though they're being unreasonable, we can't do anything that will allow others to point fingers.'

The most annoying thing about Jiang Shan is that he's always right.

In the end, I delayed the surgery. When I first spoke to Eric I'd told him that I would be ready for surgery the next day. Jiang Shan called and told me not to be impulsive, but to return to the national team and talk things through clearly before settling on anything. Apologising to Eric, I made my way home to determine my next move. Fortunately, Eric was very understanding.

I rushed home and went to Jinan, Shandong, where the national team was training. I explained my situation. I'd already rested for two weeks, but the fluid in my knee hadn't gone down.

The team leaders expressed concern for my leg. Then they said, 'No matter what, we hope you can make it to the quarterfinals.'

I said, 'It's not that I don't want to play. I really *can't* play. If I were able to, I wouldn't keep discussing this with you.'

Finally, they gave in. 'Okay, then, you can withdraw.'

But I couldn't openly withdraw from the National Games. There was simply too much pressure. I had to go through the formality of playing a match. I remember that I faced a girl from Guangdong. We played one set, and I didn't win a single game.

I was finally able to return to Germany for my third operation. I remember the date of that operation very clearly. It was 22 October 2009.

My three surgeries were all performed by Eric. The first was the most major, because we had to release the ligament. It cost about ten or twenty thousand yuan, paid for by the Hubei team; the national team didn't pay. The two later surgeries were at my own expense, since I'd gone solo.

Charges overseas work like this: if an operation costs five thousand, the doctor takes about two thousand or so, and the rest is to cover hospital and pharmaceutical costs. When I had the second surgery I'd just gone solo and was under great financial strain. Eric didn't charge me for his portion of the fee. I only needed to pay for the hospital, pharmaceutical and anaesthetist costs.

Though Eric and I had known each other for a little while, our relationship wasn't so close that we would regularly 'share our wealth' like this. But Eric is German, and has a great sense of integrity. He simply said, 'I hope you can return to the battlefield. You belong there.'

After my third operation, Johannes helped me with my rehab as usual. One day I even met a great predecessor: Boris Becker. He was doing rehab with Johannes too. When Becker was younger, he won six Grand Slam titles, and he and Steffi Graf were known as the 'dream couple' of German tennis. Even though he'd been retired for years, he still had the admiration and affection of the people. Whenever he started training, the room would suddenly fall silent, watching him.

Becker stopped by Johannes's office once when I was there too, and he wanted to say hello to me. I was training and didn't realise he was there. Becker didn't let Johannes send anyone in to tell me, saying he didn't want to affect my workout, and that he would just say hello next time.

When Johannes told me afterward I was a little surprised. I didn't expect a young athlete from overseas to get that much attention and concern from a legend of the game. Becker was a name that, before, I only knew from television and newspapers. To me, he was like a hero who'd stepped off the murky pages of a novel. I never imagined I would catch his attention.

In late 2011, I once again saw Becker at Johannes's sports centre when I was playing there. He called, 'Hey, Li Na!'

I looked over and immediately recognised the legend.

He asked me, 'How's your leg?'

We talked for about ten minutes. Though he looked so imposing, he was actually very warm and kind. When he heard that the next tournament I was planning to play in also included Pete Sampras and Carlos Moya, he said, 'So many people will be there. That's good. Say hello to them for me.'

That was an amazing moment. After Becker left, I was bathed in excitement for a long time. It felt just like when Martina Navratilova took the initiative to talk to me after the French Open a few months earlier.

At the 2011 China Open, Pete Sampras played an exhibition match, and I was there. When Sampras came out of the stadium, I was just on my way in and we met in the passageway. He shook my hand enthusiastically and said, 'Hello, I'm Pete Sampras. Congratulations on your French Open title!' I felt a thrill run through me. Sampras was the best player of his generation, and here he was now taking the initiative to greet me! I suppose one big reason these tennis legends bother to talk to me is because I'm Asian. They probably feel that it's unusual for a Chinese woman to have reached this level.

Even though I hold one Grand Slam title, I know I can't compare to the likes of past greats such as Navratilova, Becker and Sampras. They stand in the temple of the tennis gods as idols that tennis enthusiasts around the world worship. And yet in person they're so kind and friendly. This makes me respect and admire them even more.

Besides seeing personal idols at Johannes's centre, I also became friends with many fellow sufferers. There was one girl from the Bayern Munich football team who was still very young. We trained together, and sometimes I would play with her. We had quite a good rapport. I also met a Russian figure skater who was a European champion. He'd had surgery in Russia and hadn't been able to recover. Later, he found Eric. After seeing his X-rays, Eric told him, 'If I'd done this procedure here in Germany, they would put me in jail.' The champion had to spend a long time in rehab with Johannes.

The rehab and fitness training I did with Johannes did me much good. My health would no longer be an impediment. By the end of 2009, I entered the top fifteen for the first time, and that was where I ended the season.

Chapter 25

Haven

Munich was a haven for me. The scenery was beautiful, and the training facilities and equipment superb. When I needed to escape from my numerous daily chores and immerse myself in the world of tennis, I would travel to Munich. My trusted doctor and fitness coach were both there, and when my injuries were acting up and affecting my performance or I needed a place to relax and recalibrate, there was no better place. When you add to all this the fact that Europe is the cradle of tennis and that I play in Europe for more than two months out of each year, it made sense that Munich would gradually become my stronghold in Europe.

Whenever I had a longer period of time to rest, I would usually go home to China for a few days to adjust, then go to Munich for training. Sometimes it would take me two or three weeks to settle everything in Munich – seeing my doctor, doing physical therapy – and at the end of the tournament season I would also return to Munich for offseason training. Every year after the Australian Open in January, I head to Germany, then come back again after playing in Dubai in February. After the tournaments in Indian Wells and Miami in March, I go back to China for a few days, then return to Munich. After the

French Open, I go to Munich for reconditioning in June, then head to Wimbledon. After Wimbledon, I hurry back to Wuhan to see my family and friends, then go back to Munich before heading to the US in August for the US Open.

When I think about it, I spend more time in Munich than I do in China.

I really like Munich. The environment is good, the weather a little humid, and it's a very quiet, beautiful city. I first went there in winter 2007, and from March through June of 2008, I was there recuperating. While waiting for my injuries to heal, I got to see spring arrive after the melting of the winter snows, exposing the bright green grass beneath. The whole city is very tranquil, the residents gentle and polite. It's said that the literacy rate is one of the highest of any European city. I especially like the people here. Whether old or young, they all look well, and they walk very fast. Everyone seems to live a relatively simple lifestyle, which impresses me.

The city architecture in Munich is quite distinct. It's an ancient city, but the modern-day residents have carefully maintained the traditional style of Munich as the capital of the Kingdom of Bavaria. That's why Munich is a so-called 'village of a million people'. Its urban infrastructure and transportation are designed very carefully and precisely; all the bus and subway schedules are accurate, letting passengers know how many minutes there are before their transport will arrive. From any metro station, it's easy to transfer to another train or a bus.

For the first few years, Jiang Shan and I stayed in the outskirts of Munich. In early 2010, we finally moved into the English Garden training centre's hotel. This training centre is mostly for tennis and equestrian sports, and there are quite a few indoor and outdoor tennis courts. The garden itself is a huge park, even bigger than New York's Central Park. It's well known in Europe and is apparently modelled on the style of eighteenth-century English parks, which is where it gets its name. I have to admit I've never been to the garden. Even though I've been in Munich for so many years, I've not been anywhere but Neuschwanstein Castle, the major tourist attraction of Munich, because I'm usually busy training. When I have a day off, all I want to do is stay home and sleep; if I can avoid it, I won't go out at all.

My training schedule is generally like this: I get up at seven, start training at eight, and train until ten. After that, I take a shower. At ten-forty, I go to the fitness centre for a forty-minute massage, then train with the coach until one. Then I have lunch before continuing to train from three to five. After that, I take a break and then play tennis from six to seven. At ten, I go to bed.

Training like this every day is difficult. I have a day off on Sunday so that I can regroup. I'm not a young woman any more. Only occasionally do I go out with Jiang Shan. Once in a while we might go to Marienplatz on a Sunday and visit the Christmas Market, maybe getting a Chinese meal somewhere nearby. The main thing that can entice me to go out is the Chinese food there.

Living in Munich changed many of my cultural habits. Chinese medicine says you should drink warm milk, but now I just drink it cold in the morning. I'm also very fond of the beer that people in Munich are so proud of. When Jiang Shan and I have some downtime, we like to have a few.

I like dogs, especially huskies. One day on the subway I saw someone bring his husky onto the train. It was a big dog. Its fur was white, with a bit of grey on the head. The owner sat reading, not holding onto the dog at all as it sat proudly on the floor. When the train reached the station, the doors opened and the big dog suddenly lay on its belly. A group of students boarded the train and walked past the dog. As it turned out, the dog had moved because it was afraid of blocking the way! When the kids had passed by, it sat up proudly again. Throughout the journey, every time the train reached a station, the dog did the same thing. What's more, from start to finish, it sat there obediently, never barking or making noise. Feeling it exceptionally well behaved, I couldn't take my eyes off it.

After spending time in Munich for a few years, I found out that all the dogs there were that well mannered. Jiang Shan, wondering at this, asked me, 'How come the dogs don't bark here?' I often saw people taking their dogs out, and when they reached the entrance to the supermarket, the owner would leave the dog there without even tying it up while they went into the supermarket. The dog would sit and wait without moving a muscle. If the owner shopped for a couple of hours, it would sit obediently for two hours.

When I asked a German friend about it, he said their dogs learned this at obedience school. In German cities, dog regulations are very strictly enforced. If the dog's owner doesn't clean up after it when it does its business on the pavement, the owner is very likely to receive a fine issued by the police. This fine might be several hundred euros. If the dog barks constantly at home, the neighbours can call the police, or several of them can sign a petition to try to force the dog's owners to move. To keep their dogs from barking, owners need to send them to obedience school.

In Germany, having a dog is almost as much trouble as having a child. You have to take it to a pet hospital for check-ups and vaccinations. If you want to take it on holiday, you have to apply for a 'pet passport'. Besides the pet's name, this lists its birthdate, breed, sex and fur colour, as well as its physical condition and a record of its vaccinations. This must be updated for each trip. Other than police and guide dogs, all dogs are taxed, and each household is limited to two. Because a dog might cause harm to a human, it must be insured for as much as a million euros. This insurance is compulsory, and the more dangerous the breed, the higher the premium.

Because I like dogs, and also because I was curious about the 'etiquette training' German dogs undergo, I said to Jiang Shan, 'Let's get a dog!'

Jiang Shan immediately rejected this suggestion. He doesn't like dogs and thinks animals make the house smell and can also cause problems when they shed. Even though I tried both hard and soft persuasion tactics, Jiang Shan wouldn't budge. His last word was, 'Only if you take care of it yourself.'

A dog wouldn't suit my tournament schedule. So for now, I can only content myself with admiring other people's dogs. But we'll see what happens later, when I have more time!

Chapter 26

Bungee Jumping

In January 2010, I went to Auckland for a tournament, and my knee started flaring up again. It was the same feeling I'd experienced after my first surgery. I wanted to put my best foot forward, but found it hard. I was in discomfort and couldn't get myself into any sort of momentum. In short, I didn't find my athletic form at all.

In the first match, my play was very scattered, and I lost. Afterward I was really depressed. I wanted to do something to challenge myself, hoping to stimulate my energy. What could I do? I pondered for several days and finally settled on a New Zealand speciality: bungee jumping.

I'd always wanted to do something that would push my limits, but I'd never found the perfect thing. Now the Auckland Harbour Bridge bungee-jumping platform was right before my eyes; I would jump, then.

The Auckland Harbour Bridge platform, the world's first platform to be built on a harbour bridge, is forty metres high. When seen from afar, it doesn't look very high. I'm actually afraid of heights, but when I looked up at it from under the bridge, it didn't look too terrifying.

So, not feeling too concerned, I went to the safety area beneath the bridge to be weighed and fitted with a helmet, then we queued to walk onto the bridge.

The staircase up to the bridge was narrow and the handrail low. The winds from below were fierce, as if they could knock us off at any time. Unsteadily, we walked for about fifteen minutes, and I began to feel that something wasn't right. I turned to look behind and found that Thomas was gone. There were seven of us in total going to jump, and Thomas, my fitness coach and my trainer had all been behind me, along with a young boy I didn't know. I asked, 'Where's Thomas?'

'He felt dizzy, so he went back,' my trainer replied.

Through the gaps between the metal stairs, we could see the rippling water below. The higher we rose, the more terrified I became and the more tightly I clung to the metal railing, with my hands growing ever colder. I thought, *Who suggested bungee jumping?* Making it to the top of the staircase, there was only me, my trainer and the foreign boy. My trainer, from South Africa, plunged off the bridge without hesitation, dropping very fast. The boy and I looked at each other. His face turned pale and he said, 'I'm not jumping. I'm backing out.'

At that instant, I felt like there were hundreds of claws scratching at my heart. I was very conflicted. I wanted to feel that thrill, yet at the same time, I was shivering with fear. I thought, *What am I doing? Why do I want to do this?*

The platform operators had a camera set up, aimed right at me, so I took a couple of steps forward. The platform wasn't very big, but those few steps were so hard. I felt my legs cramp. I told the supervisor behind me, 'No matter what, don't push me.'

He said, 'I won't push you. You've got to take the step yourself.'

So I inched out onto the platform, step by step, then took a step back. I was scared out of my wits. I stood alone on the platform, waiting for about ten minutes. Finally, I took hold of myself and prepared to jump. The foreign boy yelled, 'Maybe there are sharks down there!'

I replied, 'If there's a shark, I'll catch hold of it and bring it back up here to you!'

The instant before I jumped, I felt that death wasn't such a terrifying thing. It was nothing compared with the period of waiting. I chanted silently to myself, 'For better tennis scores,' then with a shout, I leapt into the air.

For the first three seconds that I dropped, I was completely gripped by fear. It was the most helpless I'd ever felt. Everything around me flew past. There was nothing I could hold onto. Only after I began to rebound back up did I stop feeling afraid. So that's what bungee jumping was all about. It was like flying.

When I started to drop again, I felt weightless and extremely uncomfortable, that same falling sensation that you feel on a rollercoaster. When I'd bounced for the second time and they started to pull me back up, I felt the greatest relief of my life. Nothing much to it, really! If I could dare to do something as thrilling as bungee jumping, then what was playing a bit of tennis?

But standing on top of that bridge looking down, I'd thought I might die. When I told myself to jump, that sort of hopeless fear reached a crescendo. But when I really jumped, I realised that actually, it was no big deal, and the unpleasant results of my earlier match also lost their weight. It was just tennis. If I didn't play well, was it really that terrible?

The boy on the platform backed out and missed the opportunity to experience that feeling. He'll regret it. It was such a special opportunity.

Afterward, Jiang Shan said, 'As soon as I heard the scream, I knew it was you jumping. Why did you have to shout? Just jump!'

I said perfunctorily, 'I shouted to express my feelings.' Jiang Shan hadn't gone bungee jumping that day because only seven people were allowed on the platform. And he said forty metres wasn't high enough.

After we left New Zealand, I went to play in the Sydney International. I was full of hope that I would return to top form as quickly as possible, but I didn't. In Sydney, I was still not in good form, and I lost in the second round to an Italian player.

During that time, my disgust and self-loathing reached its peak. I forget which philosopher said, 'All human suffering is born of anger at our own helplessness'. Jiang Shan said it was a quote from Wang Xiaobo. Maybe so. I'm not very well versed in literature and philosophy, but I feel it's a good saying that makes a lot of sense.

When I left the stadium in Sydney, I didn't speak to anyone. Frustration and regret were silently fermenting inside of me. I hid from my coach and Jiang Shan, and I went to a place where no one could find me. Tennis players always carry a racket bag with them, and I flung my racket bag hard to the ground and, with all my pent-up emotion, plopped down onto the ground. I pulled my jacket over my head and wept. I was plunged in darkness, and that gave me a sense of security. It was as though I were a child again, finding a cave to hide in, and I felt safe to cry and cry.

Why were things like this?

I'd really put in a lot of effort, but then at the crucial moment I couldn't win the match. If you lose because the opponent is stronger and you're always the one being gobbled up, then so be it. But I knew very clearly that the sole reason I was losing was because I couldn't control my emotions. I had the ability to be a champion, but not the mentality. This was my Achilles heel.

I hid inside my jacket and let the tears fall like rain. It was ridiculous to let these idle thoughts keep me from playing at my best level. And then there was this damn leg!

The knee that had so recently undergone surgery wasn't strong enough. No matter how much I wanted it to recuperate, it often sent signals of discomfort. This awkward feeling didn't really interfere with daily life, but during the match it was a constant distraction. Imagine that when you desperately need to jump, run or exert yourself, your body sends sharp signals telling you it wants to give up. As a professional athlete, could there be any feeling more terrible than that? Your own body is betraying you.

As I sat, fear crept inside me. It had been quite a while. Would my leg ever really improve? How much had it really recovered? Would I still be able to continue playing? After working so hard to come back to tennis and working so hard in rehab, I still couldn't perform at one hundred per cent during matches. What was going to happen to me? I was frustrated, helpless and hopeless, a multitude of confusing thoughts and emotions revolving, eating at my heart. These feelings had been pent up inside me for a long time. Today's loss had been the trigger, but they would have broken out eventually. The whole world had forsaken me. I couldn't control anything! I couldn't defeat anyone! I couldn't even overcome the shadow in my own heart. Thinking of this, another wave of weeping washed over me.

When I'd been crying for twenty or thirty minutes, someone pulled back my jacket. By this time, my eyes were red and swollen, and the sudden bright light made me a little unresponsive. Jiang Shan's helpless face appeared before me. I just wanted to run away.

At moments like this, even though Jiang Shan comes looking for me, I'm not willing to acknowledge him. I just want to escape from the whole world. It's best that no one sees me at all. I want to find a hole to crawl into, where no one will ever see me again.

Jiang Shan didn't immediately try to console me. He sat beside me for a while, watching me cry. When I finished my emotional purge and calmed down, he started talking to me about that day's match.

I told Jiang Shan very directly that I didn't want to play any more, that I couldn't do it. I'd spent so much, poured so much into it, and for what? The three operations and the rehab that followed – what had been the point? I couldn't see any results. I didn't know what I should do. I was in especially low spirits that day, and had been hopeless on the court. I didn't have the desire to win, but only wanted to finish quickly and leave. I'd suddenly lost faith in tennis, and didn't see the point of it all.

Jiang Shan seldom encouraged me, and that day, even though I'd cried hysterically in front of him, he was unmoved by my tears. He said coolly, 'It's okay to be frustrated. That shows that you believe you can play better, so you're right to feel frustrated. But you should keep playing. Losing is normal. Everyone knows you just had knee surgery. Whether you win or lose this match doesn't really matter. But you can't just give up. Our team has fought with you. And why did you go through another operation and rehab? Wasn't it just so you could play tennis again? In sport, there are always winners and losers. As long as you play hard, there's no reason to be frustrated. Consider carefully why you failed. Why are you frustrated? It's because you know you didn't give it your all. You think you should win, but it makes more sense to admit that others did well today, well enough to win. But don't think that just because you work hard, you'll necessarily defeat them. That's the ideal situation. Admit that your opponent was better than you, and then you can think about what problems you need to fix in your own game in order to continue the fight. You're an adult, not a child. Don't give up so easily.'

Listening to him, I had mixed feelings. I had to admit that he was right, but I also blamed him. He always seemed to be pushing me forward. Although I knew that I needed this sort of driving force, I still wasn't ready to acknowledge the truth of what he said.

The frustration gradually dissipated. Several months later, I experienced a rebound in my athletic form. People are funny creatures. I gradually learned that when I hit rock bottom, I bounce back in a way that propels me higher than ever before. It's like bungee jumping. When you fall to the bottom, that's the point from which you can bounce back. My mental state is always up and down, wandering between defeat and victory. When I came to understand this about myself, I became more rational in the face of failure.

Chapter 27

Pain

To others, 2010 might seem like the year I was basking in the lime-light, but in fact, the most indelible impression that year left on me was pain.

On the court in Melbourne, my knee was swollen again. After defeating Ira Yanukovich followed by Isabelle Zaoui and Daniela Han-tuchova in the Australian Open, everyone around me could see that I was having problems with my leg.

Injury is as devastating as a mountain toppling. This time, my knee was in very bad shape. After I got into the fourth round, I had to rest for a whole day after each match because the knee couldn't take more than two consecutive days of exercise.

I'd taken a cortisone shot to reduce the inflammation before, but this time it didn't seem to work. I went to seek help from an Austral-ian doctor, and he recommended a very expensive injection, costing about five hundred euros per shot. I got a prescription. The next day, I took the medication with me to the stadium and asked the tourna-ment doctor to administer the injection. The doctor I was familiar with happened to be off-duty, so another doctor said she could help. This doctor knew nothing of my prior injuries. She took one careless look at my leg and said, 'This isn't oedema.' She didn't drain the fluid or do any other treatment. She just administered the injection directly into my knee.

It hurt unbelievably. I couldn't help but scream. To the best of my memory, that was my most profound experience of pain. I've always said that I'm less sensitive to pain than most. After so many tempestuous years on the court, I generally don't take minor aches and pains seriously. But the moment the doctor withdrew the needle from my knee, I cried out in pain. Afterward, I said to my South African trainer, 'Next time, even if I'm dying, I won't see that doctor.'

After the injection, the swelling in my leg didn't go down. My next match was with a Danish rookie, the fourth-seeded Caroline Wozniacki. I took my place on the court with my swollen knee, and I actually won. The victory was almost as unbelievable as the injection had been.

The next morning I told my trainer that I wanted to go and find the tournament doctor I'd originally seen. That doctor was good friends with my surgeon, Eric, and he understood my situation quite well.

With my trainer's help, I found the right doctor. When he heard about the previous day's situation, he checked my knee and observed, 'She didn't even drain the fluid for you.'

I said, 'That's what I thought too, but I couldn't say anything. After all, she's the doctor. She's the professional.'

Later, the tournament doctor drained two and a half syringes of fluid from my knee. When he was draining it, he inserted the needle into my knee and slowly pulled the drum of the syringe back, sucking the fluid in. It hurt, but not at all like the previous day's procedure. The doctor watched the ultrasound monitor as he kept adjusting the needle's position. In this way, little by little, all the fluid was removed.

My trainer accompanied me when I had my knee drained. He's very bold – he had been the one who went bungee jumping with me in Auckland, plunging off the platform without hesitation. But that day, his face blanched. After we came back to the hotel, he told Jiang Shan, 'I've been a trainer for a long time, but that was the first time I've seen such a thing. When I saw the doctor draining all that fluid out, it gave me the creeps.'

After he finished, the doctor gave me a cortisone shot. He warned me, 'You've had two cortisone shots in two weeks. No matter how swollen your knee becomes, you can't get another shot.'

I said, 'Okay, no problem.' After the cortisone shot, I felt much better.

The next day, I played Venus Williams. I lost the first set. The second got off to a slow start, but I broke her second serve, sending the game into a tie-break. I won the tie-break, 7–4.

The score in the final set was very tight, but I finally beat her. This was the first time in my career that I made it to the semifinals in a Grand Slam tournament.

Coincidentally, my opponent in the semifinals was the number-one-ranked Serena Williams. The Williams sisters were born to dominate tennis. When they appear in a tournament together, other players seem to be overshadowed. My match with Serena was more difficult. We played to a tie-break in the first two sets before I finally lost. But when the match was over, my knee felt okay. It wasn't as painful as I thought it would be.

It's worth mentioning that after two weeks of play in the Australian Open I received 3500 points, taking me into the world's top ten. I thought, *I'm a top ten player. It doesn't feel quite as good as I expected!*

This puzzled me. Sometimes my thoughts would take an illogical turn, moving in strange directions. Even now, I still don't understand why I was so down in January, nor can I explain how I bounced back in the Australian Open. I've always been a passive person, rarely taking the initiative. I like to go with the flow, just letting things happen as they will. If no one had been there to encourage me and spur me on, maybe I would have just wandered through life aimlessly, and that's why my mood is often unstable, experiencing these ups and downs. I wish I could be more balanced, like other people, but I just can't. Sometimes I'm quite nervous. I think it has to do with my personality. In one way, I'm very competitive, but at the same time, I'm very easily contented.

After the Australian Open, I started on a long, depressing dormant period again. Maybe it wasn't actually that long, but you know how it is. Hard times seem to drag on forever, and those moments of victory are all too fleeting. I even began to wonder whether choosing to play tennis was a mistake, because I found that the joy of victory wasn't enough to offset the stress of failure. Playing in a professional league was like licking honey off a blade. You stand to gain very little, and there's a lot to lose. But we never seem to tire of trying again and again.

Why was this so? I knew the problem lay within myself. I was satisfied with reaching the Australian Open semifinals, and after I faced the Williams sisters, I lost that hunger for victory.

Victory is not won casually, especially when the game is being played by the world's elite players. Superb technique, a cool head and good health are all important conditions for winning, but not the only conditions. If you want to win, you have to viscerally crave it. You have to want it very, very, very much. Your desire for victory has to be as strong as the desire a dying man wandering in the desert has for water. Only then do you have a hope – but it's just a hope – of winning.

I continued in my half-dead state until 13 June. It was only when I was playing on the grass court at the Birmingham DFS Classic that my hunger for victory returned.

Birmingham really is one of my luckiest spots. In 2006, I defeated Jelena Jankovic here and won my first WTA doubles title. In 2009, I was the runner-up in women's singles, and in 2010, I defeated Maria Sharapova there. This time I won the championship, becoming the first Chinese player to win a title on grass. This gave me some confidence. Unfortunately, it was at this time that my partnership with Thomas came to an end.

From 2004, when I came out of retirement, until now, my results had steadily improved. In 2010, my rank went from fifteen up to eleven in the space of a year. Just as Thomas said, I was drawing nearer to my goal.

But now he said to me sadly, 'I have nothing left to teach you.' We were both silent.

We'd worked together for a long time, and Thomas felt he'd reached the limit of what he could offer me. He thought that I needed a new approach. I also felt that I'd absorbed all I could from him. Perhaps now it was time to try a new direction.

We formally dissolved our partnership after the Asian Games in 2010, and Thomas became Maria Sharapova's coach. I'm very grateful for all the help he gave me during his tenure with me. I wish him the best of luck in all that he does.

Chapter 28

Battling at the Australian Open

After Thomas left, he was temporarily replaced by Jiang Shan, who became busier than ever. He was already responsible for many aspects of our daily life, and now he also had to shoulder the responsibility of a coach. He grew even more silent.

The first tournament Jiang Shan arranged for me was the Sydney International in 2011. By this stage I was well accustomed to the tour lifestyle. Usually, when the pre-tournament ceremonies were finished, the players would eat, rest a while then get ready to play.

But I didn't want to go eat. I lay on the sofa, exhausted. This was a hard time for our little team, and I didn't have any candidates lined up to serve as my new coach. My knee was aching, and I couldn't see the point in continuing with the tournament. The thought of quitting flashed through my mind numerous times, jumping out at me again. I felt very tired.

It wasn't because the training was tough that day. It was my mental stress acting up. The path I'd travelled was beginning to feel gruelling. I wanted to rest.

For a long time, this mingling of anxiety and frustration caused me great stress and anguish. When I achieved something, I was momentarily bolstered. When I went into a slump, the spectre of retirement would rear its ugly head in my mind, lingering there insistently.

I said to Jiang Shan, 'I don't want to play any more. I really don't. Every opponent is so strong. I'm tired. I can't keep going.'

He was very tired too. I could see that just from the gauntness of his face. As usual, he replied, 'No matter what you do, I support you. But I hope you won't regret your choice later. At any rate, we're already here. Why not give it a try?'

At that point, I felt too despondent to even respond to him, so I simply proceeded to prepare for the match.

Perhaps somebody up there didn't want me to say goodbye to tennis so early. Perhaps my opponent was facing the onset of her own injuries. I won that first match quite effortlessly, playing so easily that even I was a little shaken up. How could this be? What had happened?

That was the real turning point in my luck that season. My health was good, my leg settled in, I kept playing each round and everything went smoothly. I gained confidence as I played, and when I defeated Kim Clijsters in the finals to take the title in Sydney, I suddenly remembered how upset I'd been before the tournament. But now, it was as if nothing could get me down. I couldn't help thinking, *It's not so difficult after all!*

Jiang Shan offered this evaluation: 'You're too vulnerable to outside influence. Joys and sorrows come easily, and they go easily. As long as your physical condition is okay and the team environment is stable, you can play at a very high level.'

I thought he might be right.

My win in Sydney was my first premier tournament championship. It was also the first time a Chinese player had won a championship at a high-level tournament. For a moment, I was quite excited.

The smooth win in Sydney allowed me to enter the 2011 Australian Open in a good mood. My spirits were as clear as the Melbourne sky as

I hit the ground running. At this time of the year, when the northern hemisphere is covered in snow and the cold winds howl, Melbourne and the rest of the southern hemisphere enjoy a long, hot summer. The sun is strong and the sky is blue, and Rod Laver Arena is a special place during the tournament.

The one drawback is that sometimes the temperatures soar above thirty degrees Celsius, or even over forty. This can be a major obstacle to competition. Some players hate the heat, the way the high temperatures make them sweaty and unable to think. From time to time, a spectator suffering from heatstroke will be carried out. Playing in such conditions may not sound very enjoyable, but I like it. The summer heat of the Australian Open reminds me of my childhood, and I think of those Warrior-brand shoes, hitting the grey sand in the heat of the day, with the mercury thermometers on the streetside hawker stalls suddenly bursting as the temperature exceeds forty degrees. I'm Wuhanese. We aren't afraid of anything, especially not a bit of weather.

As well as the weather, Australian audiences' courtside manners also make me happy. While watching a sporting event, some basic manners are a given. For example, try not to use a flash when athletes are in the middle of competing. Try not to move around or be too noisy. Put mobile phones and other devices on silent mode. Things like that. For some sports, such as snooker, tennis or other 'noble endeavours', there are more stringent requirements. Most audiences are aware of these and consciously follow them.

At the 2011 Australian Open, my first match was held on centre court, Rod Laver Arena. Before each match, there are five minutes' worth of pre-match activities. While the players warm up, the commentator introduces them both. During that five minutes, you hear lots of voices from the stands, but once the umpire says 'Time', the scene immediately grows silent. You almost feel that the spectators have deliberately slowed their breathing. You could hear a pin drop. During the one hundred years or so since its inception, the Australian Open has garnered the respect of audiences who understand the game and its rules, and they're vigilant about the orderliness of the venue. When athletes play, no one makes a noise. Everyone contains his or her excitement, watching the game quietly so as not to disturb the players on the court. Australia is a nation of immigrants, with people from all over the world. The fact that so many diverse peoples can come together because of tennis and observe all the rules easily is very touching to me.

In this year's Australian Open, I played my way coolly into the semifinals without facing any real hindrance. As usual, the media was interested in things other than my progress. The question of my 'breakup' with Thomas was frequently raised, but it was no longer an obstacle to my progress. It was just as Thomas had hoped. I'd 'grown up'.

In the semifinals, I faced Caroline Wozniacki, the tournament's top seed. Her defence was outstanding, and the media had dubbed her 'a defensive wall'. Off the court, we were quite good friends.

We played three sets that day. She was very strong, and very tough. But I was no longer a frazzled little girl. I eventually turned the match, going 3–6, 7–5, 6–3 to punch my ticket to the finals.

After the match, an Australian television reporter asked me, 'Today's your wedding anniversary, right?' This question really stumped me. I couldn't remember the exact date of our wedding, but I had a vague notion it was on the twenty-ninth of January. I told the reporter, 'I think it's two days from now.'

When I compared notes with Jiang Shan, I realised that I'd been mistaken. But as long as our relationship was good and we knew where we stood with each other, then formalities such as anniversaries didn't matter. I hoped the Australian people felt the same way.

The reporter also asked what had given me the incentive to turn the game around. Without hesitation, I said, 'Prize money.' Everyone laughed. But in fact this was the truth. Tennis was my job, and I got paid to do it. If I was frank about that, was there any need to be embarrassed? Doesn't everyone work for the sake of earning money?

From the first round of the Australian Open, my press conferences were held in the biggest press room, perhaps because I'd broken into the top ten at the close of 2010. When I got into the finals, the foreign media was very excited. After all, it was the first time a Chinese player had made it into the singles finals at a Grand Slam tournament. Everyone felt uplifted – in the pond of international tennis, a new breed of fish had finally emerged.

I felt my heartbeat quickening. It was eager for victory.

Centre court at Melbourne Park has two locker rooms. I usually go to the smaller one because there are fewer people there and it's a little quieter. Going to the same place every year, I began to feel like the locker room was an old friend. There are two staff members responsible for opening and closing the lockers. One, with blonde hair, is Linda, a middle-aged woman who has always been warm and cheerful. Every time I see her she greets me with particular warmth, and I'm very fond of her. She's like an old friend, always there waiting for me. She'd seen on TV that I won the championship in Sydney. When I got to Melbourne, she told me proudly, 'I saved a good locker for you.'

It only really hit me that I'd made it to the finals when I walked out onto the court. My opponent in the finals was my old friend Kim Clijsters. We chatted for a while in the passageway before the match. She was a great player, and had been playing very well that season.

Clijster's thirst for victory was certainly no less than my own. Seven years earlier, she'd played her way into the Australian Open finals, but she'd never come away with the cup. If she won this one, it would be her first Grand Slam title apart from the US Open, which she'd won in 2005, 2009 and 2010.

I knew that I had an uphill battle facing me, but I didn't expect it to be as difficult as it was. We played for more than two hours. I took the first set, but Clijster's firepower was just too potent. She launched a bold defensive attack and came back to win the second set.

When the final set began, the thing I feared most happened. I got impatient and lost confidence, and she eventually succeeded in turning the tide. She won the match. I was runner-up.

Standing on the podium after the match, there were many things I wanted to say to Jiang Shan. I've always been a person who doesn't know how to speak well in public. I always feel awkward saying things like, 'Thank you to my country and our leaders'. Only when I talk to Jiang Shan do I feel natural and relaxed. When the MC handed me the microphone, I asked everyone, 'Do you see that guy wearing the yellow T-shirt? He's my husband. I always like to tease him.'

The audience's attention turned to Jiang Shan, and the cameras all focused on him.

I slowly said all that was on my mind. 'It doesn't matter whether you are fat or skinny, handsome or ugly, I'll always follow you and always love you.'

When I went back to the locker room, Linda and the other staff came over to me. That day happened to be Linda's birthday, and she invited me to have a drink with them. Linda said to me, 'We're all very proud of you. Even though you lost, you're still great.'

After playing in the Australian Open, I planned to go home. The next day, Jiang Shan and I rushed to get our visas taken care of for our next stop after China. It's much faster to get a visa processed in Australia than in China, and you don't need additional documents other than your passports.

I'd just passed one passport over when the staff member recognised me. 'Hey! I know who you are. I'll call you around two o'clock and you can come pick up your passport then.'

We stopped on our way back to the hotel at a luxury jewellery store.

A shop assistant there recognised me too. She said she'd been very touched by what I said, and sat in front of the television crying when she heard it. She wished Jiang Shan and me much happiness.

Maybe relationships resonate with all humans.

A British friend told me that her culture prefers a failed hero. Maybe British people think such heroes have to face more frustration, or that they have to stand a dual test of both body and mind, which is infinitely more challenging. So in British culture, many of the great works tell tragic stories about their heroes. My friend said that this was different from my culture. Chinese people always like a winner. I think she just said this to comfort me.

There's not one tennis player who doesn't care about winning or losing. The meaning of our existence is to keep perfecting our skills and to pursue victory amid our constant trials. Although I didn't win the title at the Australian Open, it was still the first time an Asian person had got as high as runner-up in Grand Slam history. The MC said I was a 'hero of the Chinese people'. I thought that was too much. I'm not a hero, nor do I really represent China. I'm just a Chinese athlete who works hard to do my job.

Many friends comforted me, saying things like, 'Runner-up is very good', or 'You've already made history'. I was very happy to have made runner-up, but also more inspired than ever to finally win a championship. When I buried myself alone in the cabin seat on the plane home from Australia, I covered my face with my hat, knowing that the emotions surging in me weren't pleasure over what I'd achieved, but desire for a Grand Slam championship.

Just one step shy! Fighting through two weeks and six matches to reach the finals was no small feat, whether I was champion or runner-up.

My childhood was devoted to tennis, and this wasn't all my own choice. I played tennis simply because it was what my father wanted me to do. In my teenage years, I played because it was what my coach and everyone on the team needed me to do. I wanted to fight for the honour of my hometown, then for the honour of my country. When I retired, I rethought my life and I decided to be a free person. I no longer wanted to do things just for the benefit of others, nor to be swayed by the opinions of those around me. I'd already dedicated myself to this many years earlier. Now, all I wanted was to do as I pleased.

And what I really wanted to do for myself right now was win a Grand Slam trophy.

Chapter 29

Changing Coaches

Jiang Shan was still acting as my coach. With one's husband as coach, there are bound to be some unavoidable problems. More than once, Jiang Shan and I had to struggle to adapt to our changing roles. He was anxious every day, thinking, *When am I 'husband', and when am I 'coach'?* Jiang Shan was handling two identities, and it was difficult to change from one to the other. When he criticised me, I couldn't help but react in anger. 'You're my husband! Stop yelling at me!'

It's normal for husband and wife to have some friction in daily life. To us, tennis was just another part of life, so our feelings on the court could easily be carried over into our daily life. The coaching responsibility was hurting our relationship, and we began to argue a lot.

Also, Thomas and Jiang Shan had very different coaching styles. As was often the case, a little while after the brief glory of the Australian Open, I fell into a post-climax funk. In February, my results at the Dubai Tennis Championships and Qatar Ladies Open in Doha were not impressive, and I was eliminated early. My mental state began to slump.

I became angry and irritable, and I put much of the blame on Jiang Shan, saying he'd neglected his duties. I needed a coach who could encourage me to face the matches with a positive attitude, and I needed someone with authority and recognition to offer positive guidance.

In April, I took part in the Tennis Grand Prix in Stuttgart, Germany, and was eliminated in the second round. I realised that I couldn't escape the facts. I sat down and talked to Jiang Shan about it.

I said, 'We need to make a change.'

'Yes, I think so too. What do you think we should do?'

'I think I need to find another coach.'

'No problem.'

A weight was lifted off my shoulders, and I felt instantly relaxed. He felt exactly the same way.

My physiotherapist, Alex, recommended a Danish coach, Michael Mortensen. Coach Mortensen had played tennis in his younger days and had also acted as coach for Caroline Wozniacki and other top players. If I wanted to go further, Mortensen seemed like the best person to help me.

The arrival of Coach Mortensen lifted my spirits. After Thomas's training, I was very open to a foreign coach. To make an inappropriate analogy, everyone has read *Journey to the West*, right? The Monkey King followed the first master carefully and himself mastered the skills of the seventy-two transformations and the somersault cloud. He was full of respect and affection for his first teacher, and was very happy when Guan Yin appointed Tang-seng to be his new master – not only because Tang-seng had rescued him from Mt Wuxing, but because 'master' was a word with warm associations in the monkey's mind. So before Coach Mortensen arrived, I had high expectations and I hoped he could work no less magic than Thomas had. I hoped he would ease my nerves and allow my little team to breathe again. We'd all sleep easier, free from anxiety.

What I didn't anticipate was that Jiang Shan would leave the team, and leave me.

We'd planned to go to Madrid to take part in a tournament. I'd already arrived at the airport in Munich, two tickets to Madrid in hand. Our departure time was drawing near, and Jiang Shan still hadn't shown up.

He'd gone AWOL. I was crushed. I couldn't get a hold of him at all. He'd recently lost his mobile phone, and we hadn't had time to buy a new one. In my panic, I even called the hotel we'd stayed in the night before and asked them to see if anyone was in the room Jiang Shan had occupied. The front desk staff said the guest had already checked out, and he hadn't said where he was going.

We'd been through conflict plenty of times before, and Jiang Shan often said, 'I'm leaving.'

I always said, 'Then leave.'

Because we'd had minor disputes before, I never took it to heart. I never imagined he would really fly home on his own – if that was what he'd done. I was terribly upset, constantly wondering, *Where is he? Did he go back to China? Is he in Wuhan? Or is he somewhere else? Is he safe? Has he eaten?*

I couldn't concentrate on the upcoming match at all. Standing there alone in the crowded airport, I felt cold. I didn't know what to do. A corner of my world had collapsed. I couldn't calm down. Then I suddenly remembered that Jiang Shan had a good friend who was in the States at the moment. Would he have gone to the US to visit his friend? I immediately turned on my computer and emailed this friend.

Our friend hadn't heard from Jiang Shan, but she could clearly sense that I was losing my grip on things, and so to comfort me, she sent me a link to a book. She said for me to settle down a bit and read this book online, and when she went back to Wuhan soon, she'd get in touch with Jiang Shan's other friends and then contact me.

I sat there alone waiting to board the flight. It was a familiar feeling, reminding me of the time more than a decade earlier that I'd been alone in the Los Angeles airport, locked in a dark room, missing my flight, and spending the night watching the planes. Here I was again, facing everything alone.

In order to calm my restless mood, I tried desperately to find something to divert my attention. I opened the link my friend had sent and started reading the book. It was called *Meeting the Unknown Self*, by the Taiwanese writer Zhang Defen. I didn't expect much.

After reading the first chapter, I actually felt myself calming down. But as soon as I stopped reading, my mind was immediately thrust back into my distressing reality. I retreated into the book.

When I reached Madrid, my fitness coach was waiting for me at the hotel, planning to introduce me to my new coach that evening. But when he saw me lugging my baggage in all alone, he was very surprised and asked where Jiang Shan was. Not knowing what to say, I answered curtly, 'He went home.'

My fitness coach didn't believe me. 'Don't joke around.'

Not wanting to dwell on the matter too much, I just said, 'Really, he's gone.'

That evening I met Coach Mortensen. He was gentle and had a kindly face. We talked about training methods and plans for the future. I felt positive about the conversation and decided to hire him to help me train for a period of time.

For two weeks, Jiang Shan didn't contact me. I kept calling his number in China, but got no answer. My anxiety meant I had difficulty sleeping. My only consolation was that book. The first night, I read half of it, and during that fortnight I kept reading it over and over.

It really is a wonderful book. The author shares her view thus: 'The root of all human suffering comes from a lack of clarity about the self, causing us to cling blindly to the pursuit of illusory things. When death comes, all these illusory things are swept away, while the true self remains unchanged, even by death. "I should not suffer" – this sort of thinking will make us suffer even more. It's a distortion of facts and is inherently self-contradictory. The truth is, you need to say "yes!" to suffering before you can go beyond it.'

After reading this the first time, I didn't understand its deeper meaning. I went back and re-read it several times. In another section, the author described an older person asking her who she was. The author gave her name, and the older person said, 'No, that's not right.'

I started to ask myself, *Who am I? I know my name is Li Na. I know I can play tennis. But other than that? If you take away my name and tennis, what's left?*

I couldn't find an answer.

This book explores the relationship between 'me' and the 'real me'. The author writes that in interpersonal communication, everyone has his or her own frequency. If you click with someone, it's because you're on the same frequency. It's being on the same frequency that draws you to one another. This really rang true for me. At the same time, my heart ached. I knew who was on my frequency, and I'd lost him.

That two-week period was a very strange time. I was both concentrating on training with Coach Mortensen and looking everywhere for news of Jiang Shan. The second week in Spain, I was able to find out where he was. A friend in Wuhan had located him and immediately let me know that he really had gone home. I breathed a sigh of relief. Knowing where he was put my mind at ease.

Several days later, Jiang Shan emailed me asking for my phone number, and I replied. I guess my concentration was affected by my mood, because I made a mistake in one of the digits when I sent him my number. He sent me another email and said he'd called, but a foreigner had answered, speaking in a stream of German. What was going on? This time I very carefully noted down my number, double-checking it before I sent it to him.

Jiang Shan and I started discussing the situation by phone and email.

I thought he was unhappy, but he denied it. He told me that he wanted to leave at the appropriate time so that the new coach could get to work. If he'd really come with me to Madrid, he might have been in the new coach's way. He'd told me that he wouldn't go to Spain, and he was serious. It was only that I hadn't been willing to take him at his word.

Later when Jiang Shan explained this matter to a friend, he said that men do things that women don't understand. Men can leave because of love, but women can't. It was because he loved me that he left. He was afraid that if he didn't leave, things would be more difficult for me. I had a coach there, and I had everything. There was nothing for him to worry about.

But in fact I was very down in his absence. I went online to chat with friends, but even the best of friends couldn't take Jiang Shan's place. I was completely unable to face the huge void inside. I could lose the support of anyone else, but he was irreplaceable.

Before the French Open, I took part in two tournaments. Every time I made a mistake or faulted, I would think of what that book said: 'Accept the situations you cannot change, and surrender.'

Before, when problems arose, I would find people or circumstances to blame. It was very hard to admit that the problem was me. As I read this book, I started to see that all of my mistakes were due to the fact that I didn't want to accept what had already happened. I was making life difficult for myself. So from that point on, when I made a mistake during a match, I accepted it, and I surrendered to it. I couldn't change what was in the past, so what could I do? I could only accept, telling myself that it was done, and that I should move forward and let it go.

I thought the book was brilliant and recommended it to many friends. It helped me see many things clearly. That book was my first contact with Zhang Defen. She writes that there are some things you have to recognise and understand for them to lose that strong, mysterious control over you. When a person is willing, not resisting knowledge and understanding of the self, he or she can find relief.

I gradually began to face my real self and, as the book said, I found relief. I didn't cry or complain any more, but just opened myself up. After a few days of honest communication, Jiang Shan and I came to understand each other. After playing in Madrid and Rome, I had about a week free to go back to Munich and prepare for the French Open. Jiang Shan flew to Germany from China to meet me. Not wanting to show any weakness, I purposely teased him. 'Look, you weren't here and I made it into the semifinals at both tournaments.'

Jiang Shan retorted, 'If I'd been there, you would've won.'

He's always refused to admit defeat. That's what I love about him.

With my little team on the sidelines to watch the first match of my French Open campaign, we had a pre-game pep-up. My trainer first helped me go through some warm-up exercises, then he and I shook hands. He said, 'Believe in yourself! You can do it!'

Then Jiang Shan bumped my fist with his and said something like, 'Let's play! All right!'

I entered the stadium at Roland Garros with confidence. I knew that behind me was a team full of love, waiting with anticipation in their eyes. Whether I won or lost, their loyalty and friendship never wavered.

Chapter 30

Complications

I'd naively thought that as long as I played well, I could be a happy winner. It didn't take long for circumstances to make a mockery of such a simplistic idea. Fame brought many things with it, not all of them as simple or pleasant as I'd imagined.

Jiang Shan once described me as a hedgehog. I start out small and very soft, and when I'm hurt, I don't know how to fight back. The only thing I know how to do is quickly raise all my quills. I initially refused to admit the truth of this description, feeling quite angry. But later I admitted to myself that maybe, just maybe . . . I really was a hedgehog. A sad, stupid hedgehog.

Because I was afraid of being hurt, I kept my spines up whenever I encountered anyone new. I'm a sensitive person, extremely concerned with what others think of me. Every time the media criticised me, this sensitivity intensified, and the hedgehog nature never really left me. I was extremely afraid. I dealt with my fears by saying, 'Ha! You see! I have quills!'

You can imagine the results.

Of course, the media isn't put off by quills. But at times other small animals – rabbits, kittens and things like that – appear in the media.

They complain, 'What are you doing with those spines? You stabbed me! You aren't a very good member of our little zoo!'

I was very frustrated. I wasn't sure when to put the quills down, nor even how to do so. I had no idea how to deal with the media. I didn't know how to be friends with journalists, which would have helped me understand how to express my own opinions. All of those around me were either athletes or coaches. Between us, there was no distortion, amplification, mistreatment or unwarranted implications. Our world was much simpler than the one outside.

Circumstances being this way, I was very dependent on my team and the friends around me. In front of them, I could completely let my guard down. My happiest times were those spent with my friends. But in 2011, a comment from a friend I'd known since childhood made me realise that even friendships I had valued highly could be very fragile.

That friend asked me to take advantage of my connections to help him secure a project. I was in a difficult spot. I'm not that sort of person, and I wasn't comfortable asking for favours for friends. After I told him this, my friend said, 'How can you be like that?'

I was angry. 'I've always been like this. A favour has to be repaid. I certainly don't want to owe anyone. And anyway, I've never been good at talking to head honchos, so what makes you think I can go to a company boss now and say, "Hey, give me this project to do"? And anyway, why would the boss give me a project?'

My friend – or, by now, my former friend – said, 'Li Na, you've changed.'

But I hadn't changed. I'd always been like this.

Later my friend came to see me again, saying he was opening a restaurant. He was soliciting people to invest and wanted me to allow him to use my name. I told him I didn't want to take part in that kind of thing. I was an athlete now, and I didn't want to go into business. I didn't understand it, and I didn't know how to go about it.

Again he said, 'How can you be like this?'

The one thing I really couldn't understand is why he felt it a natural thing that I had to help him. If I didn't help him, was I doing him some wrong?

We'd known each other for many years and had remained friends through thick and thin. But in the end, there was this sort of awkwardness between us. I'm ashamed to say it, but I was nearly thirty before I understood the fragility of a relationship, and that friendship could be so vulnerable in the face of one's own interests.

Much later, I finally grappled with the issue. Maybe that friend had been away from home, all alone, where the lifestyle and the environment were different, and his perception of things had changed. Maybe he was in a tight spot, and so he spoke rashly.

In my view, friendship should not be exploited. I'm not always in touch with my best friends. Even though we each have our own lives and are spread all over the world, when we meet, there's still that closeness. Not being calculating about how much you give or receive – this is what friendship is.

I'm not someone who really understands how to manage affection. If someone's good to me, I will go all out to be doubly good to them. But once someone hurts me, I put up those hedgehog quills to protect myself. The result is that I have very few friends, and we don't need to be in touch every day. But when we're feeling blue, we think of each other first. Also, most of my friends are people I've known since childhood: I grew up playing tennis with them, or I went to primary school with them. I'm not good at expressing my feelings, and I have a fear of loneliness and can easily feel inferior. Only people who know me well understand me and have an opportunity to come into my inner world. In relationships, I'm almost always the passive one, so I really cherish my friends. They don't treat me differently based on my successes or failures, and they are considerate of my lifestyle. Friendships with those you've grown up with are purer. I always enjoy going home at the end of a tournament so I can be with my friends, eating, chatting, drinking, singing and catching up on all that's been going on.

After experiencing major ups and downs professionally, I was beginning to grow up. How many close friends can a person have in one lifetime? With everything I have now, I'm very happy, and I don't expect everyone to understand me. That would be unrealistic. I know that I'm an introvert, even a shy person, and I can't expect everyone to go to great lengths to understand me. It's impossible to please everyone, but at least I can be worthy in my own mind.

Over time, I've gradually learned to be less burdened by public opinion. The media has its code of conduct, and no doubt reporters and editors have their own challenges to face in life. Who in this world has things easy? It's not hard to misunderstand others. I try not to care too much when this happens and no longer feel compelled to offer pointless explanations. Real friends don't need explanations.

For example, I used to care very much about comments made online. Now I don't focus on these, because I can't let bad reviews affect my mindset. I know that no matter what I do, there will be both positive and negative comments. This is normal, and everyone has a right to express his or her own views. My greatest responsibility is to avoid any distractions and concentrate on my game, and to live my life well.

I also used to be concerned about unfavourable media reports, but now I don't bother. I just want my results to be worth the effort I put into playing. I'm a solid, hard-working and increasingly sophisticated tennis player. As for everything else, I don't really care.

During the first half of 2011, I came to see many things more clearly.

When people hit troubled waters, they grow up quite quickly. Some people say I was very fortunate to win the French Open, that it was by luck that I won. I just smile. It doesn't matter what they think. No matter what anyone says, I'm the one who won that championship, and I was indeed fortunate.

Some people also say that now I must have a lot of money, and they want to tell me how to donate, how I should give back to the community and so forth. I donate to an orphanage. I've done so for a long time, and I will continue to do so. I don't only send money to the children but also go to visit and care for them because I know that love is more important than money. I do this not because someone said I should do it, but because I want the children to have a better life, and I hope they'll have a bright future.

Although tennis has been called a 'noble sport', my job is actually quite similar to a blue-collar job. I do hard physical labour and I've accumulated lots of injuries.

I'm worthy of myself. Now my motto in everything I do is simply, 'First, do nothing to hurt yourself, and second, do nothing against your conscience'. I feel that this is enough. I'm not perfect, but I'm a good person, and a brave person. I don't need recognition on this point. I just need to be able to face my own conscience.

After the French Open, the media described my win as 'China's victory'. This is too big a hat for me to wear. I can't carry a nation and certainly can't represent a whole country. I only represent myself, doing well the things I want to do. When others put those labels on me, it's only to express their own ideas. It actually means nothing to me.

I can't represent anyone else, nor do I want to. I only want to represent myself.

Chapter 31

Stay Hungry. Stay Foolish

After winning the French Open, I went through another downward spiral.

At the US Open, I was eliminated in the first round. I constantly heard voices from the outside, questioning my failure. My anxious, helpless attitude followed me like a shadow. No matter where I went, I kept seeing the same headline: 'Li Na is Depressed'. This time, it was true.

After the French Open, my confidence was soaring. I even felt I could take a second Grand Slam title. But my mental state had inevitably taken a downward plunge, and I'd gone through another round of self-doubt. Why did I train so hard every day only to be so easily shaken when a tournament came? This was a sobering time for my team and me. We realised the situation had to change.

After the US Open, my time with Coach Mortensen came to an end. Even though we'd only been working together for five months, it had been a wonderful experience. Mortensen was an optimistic person, able to see the positive side in any situation. It was as though there was never anything bad in his world. During our partnership, Mortensen treated me with an almost parental concern. He never spoke harshly to me, always calmly explaining our tactics. I never saw him upset.

Perhaps because I grew up in a much more repressive environment, when Mortensen gave me the space to perform, I didn't quite know what to do – especially after the French Open, which led to the end of our time together.

He was a very good man, and he let me have my way. He found the positive side of everything I did, but he never categorically pointed out my weaknesses and mistakes. Pure encouragement can't help me cope with the incessant stress during a match – I need a teacher who offers me technical guidance.

Growing up in such a critical and competitive environment, I need someone who can push me. All those who've really helped me improve have this sort of character. My former coach, Thomas, had this ability. He encouraged me, guiding me all the way. When I needed a push, he mercilessly urged me to forge ahead. When I committed an error, he had no qualms about pointing out the problem. But Mortensen was too good to me. He once said, 'I don't like telling you what you should do. I want you to do it well yourself, not just wait for me to tell you what you should do.' He felt that our relationship on the court was that of friends pushing forward together, not him pushing me forward. The thing he said to me most often was, 'You need to give yourself the opportunity to make mistakes.' He felt I was the sort of player who was too easily upset after committing an error, and he said, 'You need to open your mind, give yourself room to make mistakes. No one is perfect. Everyone will make mistakes sometimes.'

But the scoreboard might not give me a second chance.

I was very sorry to end our partnership. Michael Mortensen was an excellent coach, but our styles didn't match. It was a little like a couple breaking up. The partner might be good, or even great, but if there's no fit, there can be no mutual understanding. In the end, we parted amicably.

This 'firing my coach' incident caused a bit of media uproar. I had to continually explain myself. It wasn't such a serious matter, but just a normal transition in my profession. In fact, in sports circles, this was a very common occurrence. Finding the right coach is no easier than finding the right life partner. While training together, you discover some problems, and this sort of split is very normal. Caroline Wozniacki was coached by her father, but after losing Wimbledon and then the US Open, her agent encouraged her to replace her coach. Does this mean she fired her father? Of course not! Coaches come and go, but a father is forever. Their father-daughter relationship wouldn't be affected by this. Work and life are separate things.

After Mortensen left, Jiang Shan once again took on the role of coach. When we were on the court, Jiang Shan went back to being that stern teacher, continually dictating things to me. I wanted to adapt, but no matter what he said to me, I struggled to calm down and take his recommendations to heart. He wanted me to do as he requested, but I just couldn't.

After the US Open, I went home to play in the China Open. Two days before the tournament, I got very sick, so I submitted an application to the organising committee, hoping to delay my arrival to the tournament by a day, allowing me that crucial extra time to recover. But the WTA office staff said they didn't have the authority, and that the China Open tickets had all sold out, so I would have to play the first round.

I would play, then.

Just imagine entering a competition in that state, with minimal expectations. All I wanted was for the match to end quickly so that I could return to the locker room and calm my churning stomach. I was like a bit actor taking the stage. I had no desire for victory, and it was humiliating. I knew my heart was only craving one thing – just let this match end quickly.

Again, it was a first-round exit.

It's common for WTA players, after winning a Grand Slam, to hit a rut. It happens almost without exception. But I was still full of anxiety and repeatedly berated myself, *You have to do it! Soon! Now! Get yourself out of this rut!*

But it was to no avail. I was still wandering at the bottom of a pit. I could even be defeated by a minor player in a qualifier.

The next tournament was in Istanbul at the end of the year. My mind was a blank. I not only didn't know how to play, but I'd also forgotten why I should carry on playing. Jiang Shan confronted me. 'Your attitude has changed.'

I knew this, but I kept refusing to admit it. Before I won a Grand Slam, others would suggest things to me in training, and I knew it was for my own good. I listened carefully to their suggestions, and my own expectations were very high. Thomas once praised me, saying, 'Other players will try to execute eighty per cent of what a coach requires, or even ninety, but Li Na is a very strict, disciplined player. She can do one hundred per cent.' But after winning the French Open, I became a little complacent. I'd attained a childhood dream, something that had once seemed so distant, and I'd discovered the cause of my bad attitude. I'd unwittingly thought too highly of myself, and my attitude changed accordingly.

Prior to the 2010 Australian Open, I struggled against the current. Before my leg was even fully recovered, I could win every match. At that time, I kept being accused of 'attitude problems' but I still believed in myself, knowing that outsiders might not really understand much about the specifics of my situation. It's impossible to always remain enthusiastic, and a sort of ebb and tide of attitude is normal. Struggling in that sort of environment, I could focus instead on pushing myself to the limit.

But after I won the French Open, I was too lenient on myself. Once I started taking it easy, endless regression followed, swallowing up all my past efforts. Ultimately, tolerance turns into laziness. I lost my hunger for victory.

At the same time, I became sceptical about Coach Mortensen's advice. When we were training, my own thoughts kept asserting themselves.

I've been doing that all along, and didn't I win a Grand Slam title like that? What makes you think I'm not good enough?

Jiang Shan was also a professional athlete, a former National Games champion. I knew I should trust him, but I couldn't. This also contributed to my slow response on the court. When my opponent attacked, I couldn't fight back decisively, but put considerable effort into a sort of internal debate, which was clearly reflected in my game. Even my shots had become timid, full of self-doubt and ambiguity.

Jiang Shan and I were on the same page when it came to the reasons behind this. A Grand Slam victory is the supreme goal of all professional tennis players. But for eighty or ninety per cent of them, there's a period of confusion after a Grand Slam title, because it takes some time to adapt to the identity of a Grand Slam champion. I needed time to adapt to this new identity, the ideals and goals attached to it, and I had to rearrange my whole life, from the choice of coach to my most basic expectations and desires.

In the course of one year, I'd been crowned French Open champion, become a representative of women's tennis in Asia and signed a business contract worth more than one billion yuan. Glory and the high-dollar contract put me under a huge amount of pressure. I couldn't stay calm and just relax and accept it all.

Novak Djokovic has unparalleled skills, but after taking his first Grand Slam title in 2008, he still needed a long period of time to adjust. A great player, Roger Federer, after winning Wimbledon for the first time, took six months to fully adapt to his new identity. And after so many years, Andy Roddick has only managed to win one Grand Slam. Marat Safin took a Grand Slam in 2000, and it was another five years before he took his second.

This is completely normal. When you achieve a long-held goal, it's actually the loneliest time in your life. It's a time when fear and anxiety arise because, with the target reached, you wonder what you should do next.

All of those players were between twenty and twenty-two years of age when they won those Grand Slams. I was twenty-nine when I won my first Grand Slam, which meant I'd been struggling for twenty years. No one could give me advice, because no one had lived my life and no one could really understand the sort of life I'd experienced. I had no one to share the experience with. I really envied the Williams sisters or the brother and sister pair of Marat Safin and Dinara Safina. They must have been able to share their feelings and help each other overcome the loneliness as quickly as possible. But I was like a lone traveller, struggling to find my way through the fog alone. I could hear all the curses and insults around me clearly enough, but no one could tell me what I should do.

Every person has a caged beast in their heart. It's aggressive, irritable, violent, scarred and brutal beyond comparison. It was my habit to open the cage during a match and let the beast out to work for me. When I was mentally vulnerable, the beast would turn on me instead. It ridiculed me and humiliated me, making me constantly weep and blame others for my own mistakes.

I could only try to soothe my emotions. Jiang Shan helped, and his company made me feel a little better. While I was relentlessly punishing myself for my mistakes, he would keep me company in silence, and when I wanted to rest or to train, he came along too.

'I think things are very tough for her. All I can do is keep her company and give her a little encouragement at the right moment,' he told reporters. He understood the fear deep in my heart.

Some people fear their parents will abandon them, or that their talent will shrivel up, or that they'll go senile with age. I'm more afraid that I'll blame myself in the future for not giving my all while I still had strength to do so. I don't want to look back with regret and blame my younger self.

Sometimes I train very hard, pushing myself to the furthest limits. But other times I can't help but think, *I've already won a Grand*

Slam. Why keep training so hard? If my play at this particular moment is good, I'm able to quickly neutralise the negativity inside me. When things aren't going well, two voices will sound in my head at the same time, as if I were fighting with myself.

I know there will come a day when I can no longer play tennis. I've always been a little afraid of this. Especially as I went through each operation, I kept thinking, *If the rehab isn't successful and I can no longer play tennis, what am I going to do?*

One 'me' is very happy, thinking, *Finally, you don't have to train any more and you can do things you've always wanted to do!* But the other side of me is very sad. After all, this is what I've done all of my life, and I've played up to this level. The whole thing's very contradictory.

I once told a friend that in the future, my dream is to be a housewife. Wherever Jiang Shan goes, I'll follow. This is my ideal – or my dream – lifestyle. But I also know that if I throw myself completely into being a housewife, I'll be out of touch with society. I don't want to see myself falling behind the times. All these years, Jiang Shan has been following me. When I retire, I'll go wherever he goes, whether it's Wuhan or elsewhere. If he goes to Beijing, I'll follow him there.

When the day comes, Jiang Shan and I will sit down and discuss our plans for the future. He doesn't like children much – he thinks they're too noisy – but I'm still keen to have a child. Before I embarked on my tennis career, we had no idea about the different teaching methods in other countries, but now we've had the chance to go overseas and see the way children are raised in other places. I was really shocked by the differences. If I do have a child in the future, I'll certainly raise him or her personally. A child's first teachers are their parents, and I want to be involved from the very beginning.

I don't want my child to go through the Chinese education system; being a child in China is too difficult. There are too many people to compete with, and resources are limited. The competition children face is getting even fiercer, and as a result of this, children compare themselves constantly and develop distorted views. I especially dislike these types of children, and Jiang Shan feels the same. He thinks that the lack of confidence in many Chinese people stems from education in the home and at school. To go a step further, the problems start at home, because the parents are always teaching children that they must do this or that, arranging everything for them. And parents always employ a preachy tone, constantly nagging the child: 'You wash up!' 'You go to bed!' 'You go and study!' Everything the child does is under the constraining hand of adults. The child doesn't learn for himself what's right or wrong. He doesn't trust himself. This is a problem all Chinese people have. And unless parents take on a more 'natural' style of parenting it will continue.

Why are foreigners more confident than Chinese people? Because they're allowed to grow up on their own. Jiang Shan and I have lived overseas for many years, and we've seen first-hand how foreigners teach their children. They don't restrain their child's initiative. The child believes that, as long as it's not illegal or seriously wrong, he can try anything. For example, if he plays tennis today, or reads books, or plays basketball or whatever, he gains confidence by choosing an activity for himself. Chinese children are always taught to first think, 'Can I do it?' Then, when they grow up, they continue to employ this sort of thinking when they run into problems. 'Can I do this? Am I capable?' The sort of person these approaches produce is completely different. The same two people may have gone through college, postgraduate studies, and even through doctoral studies together and may possess similar knowledge, but because they've been raised differently, their future development will be completely different.

This attitude of responsibility toward oneself should be taught by the parents, not the schools. The school only teaches knowledge. Our earliest textbooks in primary school taught us 'Love the people, love the nation'. Yet it's only in university that we're taught not to spit carelessly on the street. This is the completely wrong order. I'm a product of the Chinese style of education, which has led me to hesitate before making any decisions, to lack confidence, to not dare to speak up and to constantly calculate what the result of my action will be. What I hate most is my lack of self-confidence when I'm playing tennis. Athletes like me might be even more troubled by this issue of confidence, because from childhood we frequently face wins and losses. The coaches like to undermine players' confidence by comparing them, establishing the coach in a position of authority. But this sort of comparison is unscientific. Everyone is different, and there's no way to make a comparison.

Perhaps one of the reasons Jiang Shan and I don't display many tennis trophies at home, nor much of anything related to tennis, is because of our views on this subject. When we have children, I don't want them to have a sense of superiority because 'my mother is so-and-so' or 'my father is so-and-so'. I won't make a point of telling my children, 'I used to be a tennis player.'

We both think that after our children turn eighteen, they should be allowed to make their own choices, including where to live. We won't interfere with their lives. We've seen the TV series *Heaven*, with Wang Zhiwen, in which there's a saying that we both agree with: 'Raising children is not for the sake of your old age.' If we have a child, it's definitely because we like children and want to voluntarily fulfil our obligations to them, not so that they'll support us when we're old. We don't want to be a burden to our children. It's strange to admit, but whenever I think of the future, I think of our baby and my mood improves.

After I crashed out in the first round of the US Open that year, my friend Dinara Safina sent me a message. It read, 'I've been through the same thing. Many people said I couldn't do it, but you have to believe yourself to be a champion.'

Dinara clearly understood what I was going through. Some people don't know anything, but that doesn't stop them from judging others. They have no experience of pursuing a dream, so their advice or criticism counts for nothing. But Dinara was different. She'd been the world's number one female player before and, like me, she'd fought through matches with the same pain of injury. She could empathise with my disappointment and suffering, and her encouragement gave me a lot of strength. There's a Chinese saying: 'A few pleasant words can bring warmth in winter, and harsh words can make you freeze in June.' This is true. When I read her text message, I felt warmth surge in my heart. No matter when or where, I'll always remember her as my friend.

After the death of Steve Jobs, a lot of people took a phrase from a speech he gave at Stanford University as a motto: 'Stay hungry. Stay foolish.' But very few people know how difficult – and important – it is to 'stay hungry' and 'stay foolish'.

After winning the French Open, I took part in many tournaments, and the results were all first-rounder tours. It was only when everything bottomed out that I regained my confidence. The situation couldn't get much worse, could it? At the beginning of 2012, my results gradually started to improve.

The 2012 Australian Open was held in late January, during the Chinese New Year. My mother had told me that her greatest wish was for me to spend the Spring Festival at home, but ultimately I couldn't. For a tennis player, nearly every Chinese New Year will be spent under the sun in Melbourne.

Armed with the hope of returning to peak condition, I travelled to Australia. I always think of this country as my lucky place, and this luck lasted until the last night of the Year of the Rabbit on the Chinese lunar calendar. I was in the quarterfinals and wasted four match points. Kim Clijsters won the match. My disappointment was at its height as I left Australia.

Lovely fans back home were urging me to forget my disappointment and hurry home for the holiday. I sent a message to them on my microblog on the first day of the Year of the Dragon, saying, 'This year's Australian Open is over. Hope to see you there next year for a better showing on the Melbourne court. See you next year! Happy New Year!' And after that, I made the world of microblogging and the media disappear from my mind.

On the sixth day of the New Year, Jiang Shan and I started preparing for the Confederation Cup in Shenzhen. Despite my loss at the Australian Open, Jiang Shan had scored a win of his own: he was named 'Best Husband/Boyfriend' of the year on the Australian Open's official website, defeating golf superstar Rory McIlroy and NBA star Sasha Vujacic to take the title. According to the website, he won the award because of his tolerance. It read, 'Jiang Shan is not only Li Na's happy husband, but also her coach on the sidelines. He is often the object of his Grand Slam wife's glares as she vents her frustration.'

This made us both laugh. Anyway, it was the start of a new season. It was time to cheer up.

Chapter 32

My World, I Call the Shots

All of the people who'd entered professional tennis around the same time I did were retiring, one by one. Many thought my own career was coming to its final stages, and suddenly it seemed that everyone was mentioning the word 'retirement'. In many reports, I was bluntly referred to as an 'older' player, and every now and then some busybody would write a 'Li Na retiring' story. Sometimes the reporters even asked very directly: 'Li Na, have you thought about when you'll retire?'

Hearing such questions so frequently was quite annoying. My physiotherapist, Alex, said to me, 'Next time you answer a "how old are you?" question, tell them age is just adding one more mark on a piece of paper.'

Some people look like teenagers, but are in fact already in their twenties. Others look like they're in their thirties when they're still in their twenties. To me right now, age is just a scale, and I feel that my body and the wisdom I've accumulated haven't yet reached their peak. Some friends told me that, compared to American and European players, Chinese players develop somewhat later, and so on the court, we might flourish later too. A twenty-nine-year-old tennis player is not considered young, but my tennis career is different from that of most players, and I had the experience of having retired for two years while I studied. In terms of physical wear and tear, I have a distinct advantage over other players of the same age, and my career might be able to stretch longer in correspondence with the missed time. Alex thinks I can maintain my current state for at least two or three more years. Only two or three more years? I don't believe that. I think I can go even longer.

According to Chinese belief, a woman loses her youth at thirty, but I feel I'm still in good shape. As long as I keep up this sort of training over the long term, maintaining my competitive condition, I'm confident I can continue. Of course, there'll finally come a time when I can no longer go on, but I don't believe that time is imminent. Everyone's growth and ageing process is unique. Agassi was thirty-six before he retired, and at thirty-five he got into the finals at the US Open. At age forty-two, Kimiko Date-Krumm is still part of the tennis scene in Japan. Able men who are tied down to routine posts have high aspirations. Age doesn't have to become a roadblock for me either.

What I really need is a change in my mindset. Whether it's financial considerations or a matter of honour, I need to learn how to live at this new level, to manage a new lifestyle and to adapt to a new game, improving and expanding my own abilities.

This mentality thing is very elusive. It's said that 'conquering a country is easy; ruling it is difficult', because it requires a completely different mindset. Conquering is about working hard without worrying what comes next, pushing aside all thoughts and just pressing forward. But once you advance to the next arena, if you find it tough to manage, you're filled with dread. A duel between two highly skilled players is largely about harnessing the mind. An experienced player can quickly determine whether an opponent is mentally steady; while you wander about doubtfully and nervously, your game will immediately suffer. This mental aspect of sport has nothing to do with physical fitness.

Everyone goes about things differently, and we each come from different backgrounds. If we find ourselves in a privileged position, we can forge ahead easily and get things done. But privilege is no guarantee of happiness. Only when I immerse myself completely in tennis itself do I feel really happy.

In my eyes, tennis grows increasingly more appealing. There are so many events each year. Perhaps today you play this opponent and then three days later, you play her again. Almost every week, your experience will be different. Whether I win or lose, I gain something new in every match. Watching my opponents grow and change, I gain a greater understanding of my own body. Winning is not the only reason to play the game. No matter what others say, I comfort myself, thinking, *I've felt the things I've felt, but no one else has.* Only you can know your own experience.

As 2012 wore on, I gradually began to feel more proactive. I knew I was doing something I loved. I also knew that I had the right to determine my own life. If I liked what I was doing, I could continue, and if I lost interest, I could stop at any time and pursue something else. It's my world, and I call the shots.

I made another discovery too: I was gradually coming to terms with life. Though I'm still alone on the court, facing everything on my own, I've discovered the other side of loneliness. Tennis is a combination of many things, a beautiful complexity. It's a perfect mix of strength and strategy all rolled into one, testing the athlete's ability on many fronts. Some people say, 'Tennis is very simple.' They haven't fully appreciated the sport's mystique and depth. Its beauty entices me to keep going, exploring and learning.

In tennis, everyone sees the umpire in the chair, the players on the court. But in fact, the players are umpire, coach and athlete rolled into one. When there's a possibility of a missed call, you have to play the role of referee, protesting with the umpire. In a single tennis match, a player has to make a decision between 800 and 1200 times, which no other sport can compare with. In competition today, all of the big matches use Hawk-Eye cameras to verify line calls, and where there's a disagreement, the player can raise a challenge. Because the linesmen and umpires sometimes sit for two or three hours at a time, they can suffer from fatigue and make errors. When a player asks to see the Hawk-Eye replay, he or she doesn't agree with the call made by the umpire and is effectively challenging the authority of the umpire on the court. The introduction of Hawk-Eye in 2005 was huge in tennis – on a par with the introduction of the tie-break system a couple of decades earlier – and wasn't only welcomed by the players; it also ensures that the umpires meet higher standards, making them more focused.

But when you play, you're also an athlete. Not only are you facing off with the opponent across the court and the spectators around you, but most importantly, you're facing off with yourself. Through tennis, I've battled myself daily. Sometimes my opponent is especially strong, sometimes the audience likes to heckle me, sometimes I can't calm my own mind, and sometimes there are problems within my team. Almost no single day passes by smoothly.

The demands on tennis players to display appropriate etiquette are quite high. Umpires learn swear words in many languages, and if they hear you cursing, they'll issue a warning. With the second warning, there's a fine. If you shout at the umpire, you need to have a pocketful of cash, because there's sure to be a fine. You're prohibited from intentionally losing to an opponent, and there are special means for limiting this sort of behaviour. If the tournament doctor says beforehand that you can't play but you still choose to play, you have to accept a fine if you lose the match, because this is counted as playing half-heartedly. Tennis has its own mode of operation, and it has many rules to bind the athlete. All these regulations are ways of saying,

'We do not appreciate or tolerate this kind of behaviour.'

I remember very clearly playing a match in Tokyo in 2010. I said something in Wuhan dialect after I missed a shot, and the umpire thought I used the Mandarin swear word *cao* and he issued me a warning. I was confused. In tennis, you can only rest for twenty seconds between points. I thought, *Is he warning me for a delay violation?*

After the match, the more I thought about it, the more I felt something wasn't right. I went to the office to ask the umpire what had happened and was told, 'You were swearing.'

I immediately declared, 'I didn't swear.' The umpire didn't believe it. Fortunately, it was easy to prove my innocence. I asked him to review the video. Later I learned that if I hadn't questioned the decision, I might have been fined US$1500. That was close!

Chapter 33

The New Coach

Time passed very quickly after the Australian Open in early 2012. This book, which is like a comb through the strands of the first thirty years of my life, was published in Chinese. After its publication, I sighed in relief, as if I'd finally been accountable to myself. But it also felt to me as though the first three decades of my life that had flowed away would quietly stay put now. They wouldn't disappear without a trace.

The process of writing a book had helped me know myself better. I could say with confidence that I knew who I was, and I knew what I was doing. I knew I liked myself and the things I was doing. I even knew that some of the things I was working so hard to forget had actually never left me. But now I am able to look at life from a different perspective and try to accept these things completely. I've happily discovered that although I can't forget, I can at least let go.

After the book was published, I went to several events organised by the publisher. When I went to Beijing University and met the students there, I had a cold and was feeling miserable, but the enthusiasm of the students touched me. I remember one student who said that when he sat for the college entrance exam in 2011, my victory in the French Open spurred him on, helping him to score really well on the exam and get into Beijing University. I knew this was partly said in jest, but it was still very encouraging. This world is badly in need of positive energy, so if my life and what I'm doing can contribute a little to our planet's supply of positive energy, I'll be very happy, and very honoured.

After Beijing University, we went to my hometown, Wuhan, and held several events there. Returning to Wuhan made me feel at home, with both the host and the audience speaking my hometown dialect, the language closest to my heart.

At Huazhong University, I saw my old dean, Li Peigen, affectionately known as Uncle Gen. He'd originally been scheduled to catch a flight that day, but he rearranged his travel schedule so he could meet up with me, and I was very embarrassed to have inconvenienced him like that. While we were chatting, he mentioned that when he played table tennis he hated to lose, so was only willing to play against people whose skills were below him. I wondered why he was telling me this, but he changed the subject and said, 'Well, it's a mental problem – I'm not very educated.'

I almost choked on my laughter. I knew what he was getting at. Recently, the media had been creating a lot of hype with reports saying, 'Li Na lacks mental strength. She's not well educated'. This was the dean's way of using a little humour to support and comfort me. It was greatly appreciated.

Huazhong University celebrated its sixtieth anniversary in 2012, and the dean invited me and Jiang Shan to be part of the celebration. I actually wanted to go along, as I've always had special feelings for Huazhong. In my mind it's a pure place, full of many good memories. Unfortunately, the anniversary celebration was at the beginning of October, clashing with the China Open, so I definitely couldn't make it. I said, 'I would very much like to come, but there's a tournament then, so I don't think I can make it.'

The dean enquired carefully about the start and finish dates of the tournament. I told him, and he immediately said, 'I hope you don't come.'

I knew what he meant. He hoped I would go far in the competition. I was touched by this.

Later, I was chatting with a friend who'd been part of the conversation and she said, 'Your dean really looks out for you.'

I said proudly, 'Of course, he's our Uncle Gen.'

He wasn't just our dean – he was also like a wise but slightly naughty patriarch, and his students were more like his children. He might tell us off now and again, but he didn't let others criticise us. Idle tongues liked to say things about me like: 'How could she be from Huazhong?' or 'You mean she studied at Huazhong?' This made the dean quite angry, and one day he stood at his podium and said, 'If you hear anyone say this kind of thing about our Huazhong graduates, from now on you can tell them directly, "Shut up! Li Na did study here." '

My friend said, 'A dean who looks out for his students is a good dean.'

After Wuhan, I returned to Beijing, with the 2012 London Olympics just around the corner. Honestly, I was looking forward to the Olympics this time. Because I'd grown up in a national sporting environment, snaring an Olympic medal and winning glory for my country were things I believed in very strongly, almost as if they were embedded in my DNA. But before the Olympics, something happened that made me very uncomfortable. It was the 'double defeat' incident.

At the Olympics, in addition to competing in singles events, the team assigned me to play doubles with a teenage partner, Zhang Shuai. The team had only mentioned this as a possibility to Jiang Shan once in March, saying I might play doubles with Zhang Shuai in the Olympics. At the time, Jiang Shan had said, 'Li Na hasn't played doubles in a long time, and I don't think she can play very well.'

In fact, it had been five years since I last played doubles at the 2007 Australian Open. It had been much too long. And given that the 2012 London Olympics was very likely the last time I would compete in the

Olympic Games, I really hoped it would go well. I therefore wanted to concentrate on having a good singles campaign, free from distraction and interference.

Many people in the national team told me, 'You'll have to play doubles.'

I'd been left completely in the dark and could only say, 'No, I don't know anything about that.'

We didn't hear anything more about it until it was in the form of a final decision, an order. No one had talked to me about it, and I was the last to know. I felt very honoured to be taking part in the London Olympics, but I never thought it would be so complicated. I'm not a person who likes to be secretive about my actions. After all, I'm not a thirteen-year-old girl who needs a guardian to manage me. I was thirty, and the matter of my playing doubles should have been laid on the table and discussed openly. The way it was handled was very disconcerting.

But by this stage the team list had been published, so what could I say? I could only obey. A week before the Olympics, my team and I arrived in London. Wimbledon was the Olympic venue, and it was rather far from the Olympic Village, so to facilitate training, I didn't stay in the Olympic Village, but rented a house next to the stadium.

I was fortunate enough to be a torchbearer in the Olympic torch relay, and my part occurred two days before the opening ceremony, on 25 July at Haringey, a place north of London. Before the official start, all of the torchbearers would first gather together. We'd all been assigned a number, so I found the numbers before and after me, then went over to greet them and chat casually for a while. It was a young mother before me, and when the moment came I took the torch from her and passed it on to the next torchbearer, waved to the crowd very normally, and then it was over. Honestly, I wasn't nervous at all, but when I looked up and saw the roadside filled with enthusiastic crowds, I became quite excited. This was very different from China. In Britain people's enthusiasm for the Olympics only really built up during the actual events. Even though the torch relay was very close to Wimbledon, there was hardly any publicity for the Olympics around. On this day, seeing the crowd swell with enthusiasm, I could finally feel the Olympic atmosphere.

On 28 July, in the first round of singles competition, my opponent was Slovakia's Daniela Hantuchova. I'd played her many times, and our record against each other was fairly even, with her holding a slight advantage. Our most recent clash had been the previous year at Eastbourne, where she defeated me on the grass court. This first match was very difficult for me, and even though I won the second set, I lost the match. The long-awaited Olympic Games had turned into 'a one-round tour'. I didn't say anything, but I was sad.

The next day, Zhang Shuai and I played together in the first round of doubles competition, facing Argentina's team of Gisela Dulko and Paola Suarez. The pair was dubbed the 'doubles specialists', on account of their great rapport with each other. Moreover, they'd been training together for the Olympics for more than half a year. This was the first time Zhang Shuai and I had played together, but this time, fortunately, the scales tipped in our favour. Even though there was a rain delay, we took the match in straight sets. It really cheered me up.

But in the second-round match a couple of days later, we lost to a pair of Czech players. Given our lack of experience together, we were destined not to advance very far in the competition, but it still got me down. I'd held such high expectations for the Olympics, and to meet this abrupt end made me very sad. What got to me even more was the fact that many so-called experts began to say things like, 'Li Na didn't try hard at the Olympics as she doesn't attach any importance to the Olympic Games.' Representing one's country in the Olympics is a real honour, and on a personal level, it's a unique experience that can foster many fond memories. And anyway, how could I not want to win a match? This is the fundamental mindset of an athlete. I would like to ask those who said such things if they've ever been an athlete. Do they understand the competitive mindset an athlete takes to the court? If you're not playing to win, why would you train day after day? In sport, there are winners and losers. How can I guarantee I'll always win? This time I was defeated. It's fair to say that I didn't adjust well to the situation, but where would anyone get the idea that I didn't try? I really don't get it.

Just when I was really down and feeling utterly disheartened, I started to work with my new coach, Carlos Rodriguez. He was formerly the Chinese player Hai Ning's coach, and he's outstanding.

It was a month or two earlier, at Wimbledon, when I'd started planning to find a new coach. I had sent an email to my agent at IMG in the hope that he could help, and my agent contacted Carlos. During the Olympics, Carlos and I exchanged emails. Because he still had a few matters to deal with, we decided that from 16 August, just over a week before the beginning of the US Open, we would begin our coaching partnership. At that time, I was playing in the Western and Southern Open. Carlos came just in time to help me play that tournament, allowing us to get to know one another as we prepared for the US Open.

The Western and Southern Open is a tournament with a long history and tradition. Every year in mid-August it's held in Cincinnati, Ohio, and is sometimes called the Cincinnati Open. It's a hard-court tournament and has developed into one of the more important international tennis events, just one level below the four Grand Slams and WTA premier mandatory tournaments. Because of when it's scheduled, everyone plays it as a warm-up for the US Open.

The final day of the Western and Southern Open was 20 August 2012. On that day, the men's singles finals were first, followed by the women's singles finals. When the men's finals finished, I was eating lunch at the stadium restaurant. There's a balcony there, and the champion traditionally holds the cup on that balcony while the fans snap photos from below. While I was eating, I saw the recently crowned men's singles champion, Roger Federer, holding his trophy on the balcony, posing for a photo. He was so handsome and looked very impressive. A sudden longing sprang up in me, and I thought, *If I could just win the next match like him, that would be great.*

My opponent in the finals was the new German star Angelique Kerber, the tournament's number seven seed. We'd played each other five times before, and I'd won four of them. Despite this small advantage, I got off to a rough start, quickly losing the first set. Behind a set, I was a little frustrated, so I called Carlos to the court. When he arrived, he first asked how I was feeling, and I told him. He said he thought I could try a certain approach. When I returned to the battle, I gave it a shot, and the outcome was good. Ultimately, I won the next two sets and the match and got my wish to hold the championship trophy and be photographed on the balcony like Federer had been. This was my first title of the season, and the media said, 'Li Na finally breaks through, fifteen months after winning the French Open.'

In mentioning calling the coach to the court, perhaps I should explain that in tournaments such as Cincinnati, unlike the four Grand Slams, you can call your coach to the court for advice once during each set. As the so-called 'father figure' standing by, the coach can sometimes see things more clearly than the player. But the four Grand Slams are different, with the coach not allowed on the court to interrupt the rhythm of play, the strategic decisions rest solely with the player. It's truly 'playing alone'. A professional tennis player must get used to reading her own game if she's to take hold of the match. This is something I'm presently trying very hard to change. I must be assertive. I haven't asked my coach to the court since that match.

The day I won, Jiang Shan, Carlos, my physiotherapist Alex and I planned to celebrate together that evening at Paramount Park. It's a famous amusement park, and all of the players who took part in the Cincinnati tournament were offered free admission. By the time every-thing was finished after the awards ceremony and the interviews, it was almost eight o'clock. Last entry for the amusement park was at eight. We quickly ran to the priority queue at the entrance. The staff member there asked me, 'Did you win the tournament?'

I said, 'Yes.'

He said, 'Then go on in.'

And just like that, we got in before the gates closed.

The amusement park had a suspended rollercoaster, leaving passen-gers dangling rather than sitting in a car. It looked quite scary. Carlos took one look, waved his hand and said, 'You can ask me to do any-thing else and I'll do it. Just don't ask me to ride that.'

After the match I was feeling a little dizzy, so I opted out as well. In high spirits, Jiang Shan and Alex joined the queue and ended up seated in the front row. I stood below to take pictures.

When Alex is in work mode, his typical German rigorousness will come to the foreground, but most of the time he's a happy, funny, talka-tive guy, up for anything. He has a Pekingese dog, and every Christmas he buys it a set of clothes as a gift. He's always keen to try new foods, too. I like to snack, and always have a variety of things to munch on. Alex even bravely tried the unusually sour preserved plum I once of-fered him. Jiang Shan and Carlos never touch this sort of thing.

Carlos seemed to be my lucky star, bringing me the Western and Southern Open title. In fact, every coach has brought a change for me, whether technical or tactical, or in terms of mindset. If you want to know the difference between Carlos and my former coaches, I think it was that he was very keen to chat with me. He wanted to get to know my inner thoughts so he could begin a more targeted training. Since he started coaching me, we spend most of our time together just chatting, whether about technique or other things. After every match, we find a chance to chat. *What happened in this match? What did you do well, and what did you do poorly? What were you thinking before the match? Now when you think of the next match, how do you see your opponent?* Things like that.

Sometimes we talk about stuff completely unrelated to the match, like my childhood, my past and the deepest and most obscure wounds I've suffered over the years. Carlos wants to dig out anything that might be affecting me so that I can confront and resolve it. He can go into great detail, not allowing me to escape from my innermost thoughts. He's attuned to very subtle things that most people would overlook, and he'll keep digging, like peeling layer after layer off an onion until all my thoughts, including the most minute fluctuations, are exposed to the sun. He makes sure nothing is vague, probing until there's clarity. I feel I've become transparent before him.

Self-analysis is a very painful thing for me because there are many things that I know subconsciously, but I don't want to face. Carlos told me, 'You must admit these things, and you must let yourself understand them deeply. That's the only way to settle them.'

Digging is a painful process, but since I've begun placing these thoughts before me, I've found there's actually no need to flinch. It's best to resolve things, to face up to them. Running away isn't my style.

As for the issue of my temperament on the court, Carlos has spoken to me about it many times. He believes that it's the result of how my coach treated me in my youth. If I didn't play well, she would roar, losing her temper. This made a deep impression on me, to the point where I now unconsciously imitate her. With this in mind, he brought up a very bold proposal. He wanted me to go talk with Coach Yu. Imagine: a thirty-year-old Li Na going to Coach Yu to talk about fifteen-year-old Li Na's psychological state! At first, I was very unwilling, because this was what I desperately wanted to forget; I had no interest in going back to meet my past. Those things were ancient wounds and I had no desire to reopen them. But Carlos told me, 'They didn't heal. If you continue to evade them, they'll never heal.' He added, 'You have to do this for me, but more importantly, you have to do this for yourself. You need to talk to your old coach and tell her what you were thinking back then, because if you don't tell her, she'll never know, and you will never get past this.'

After thinking about it overnight, I decided to approach Coach Yu.

Coach Yu's impact on my personality and thinking was enormous. When I was fifteen, I was still just a child, and my coach was like a god. As an old saying in China goes: 'A teacher for a day is a father for a life-time'. In my eyes she was a parent, but a very stern, strict parent. During the nine years that she coached me, I never heard a word of praise. Ever since, I've been trying hard to build confidence and acceptance of myself. I thought I'd succeeded, but when I encounter adversity and slip under the pressure of competition, my true form is totally exposed. Her effect on me had been even greater than I'd imagined.

On the way to meet Coach Yu, I was extremely ill at ease, nervous and jumpy as a rabbit. I ran through my mind a variety of scenarios, but in the end none of them eventuated. When we met, it was very calm, entirely the way a dialogue between two adult women should be. We talked for about fifteen minutes. I said, 'Coach Yu, I want to tell you now how it felt when you treated me, the fifteen-year-old Li Na, the way you did.'

She said, 'Okay.'

I said, 'I was really damaged by your coaching, and the damage is even greater than I first realised. I thought I could forget it, but when things aren't going well, this negativity immediately comes to mind.'

When I finished speaking, she talked to me about her life at the time.

I listened carefully, quietly hearing her out, and I came to understand the difficulties she'd faced, and I felt that there was a soft heart deep inside that tough exterior. At last, the ice inside started to melt. We two women reached across space and time to shake hands and make up.

When I left, I felt relaxed. Looking at the sky, it was the first time I noticed that the summer sky in Wuhan is very blue.

The greatest result of this dialogue was that, when tough times came along, the short-tempered Li Na didn't make an appearance or at least didn't come out so easily. I didn't expect a brief fifteen-minute chat to have such a magical effect.

A few days before I met Coach Yu, I'd read a story on Weibo about Nelson Mandela's time in prison. While he was in jail, his captors abused him, and later, when Mandela became president of South Africa, he invited his jailer to the presidential palace. Bowing to the warden, he said, 'If I can't leave behind my grief and resentment, then I'm still imprisoned.'

I can't compare myself to such a great man, but the point I'm making is that there's a common human wisdom. Resentment and evasion aren't a recipe for healing. Only when we really put something behind us can we finally start on the road to self-redemption. Failure, misery, frustration and challenges can help you become more resilient, if you see them as an aid to growth. They can empower you, and that gives them a positive value in life. I'm very grateful to Carlos for suggesting I talk to Coach Yu, and am glad that he's my coach.

When we began working together, Carlos repeatedly watched videos of my matches. He realised that I have a strong forehand and an accurate backhand, but that my serve was inconsistent and I needed a breakthrough and a change. He said, 'You can add a little side- and topspin to change things up.' At first I was hesitant. But he said that my talent and feel for the ball were superb, and that I still had great potential for development. He believed I could make my way to the world's top three, and could win another Grand Slam. He believed I could do it.

It felt amazing to actually hear a coach saying this to a thirty-year-old woman and I was pleasantly surprised that there was actually a coach willing to help a woman my age change. A different coach may well have said things like, 'This woman is already thirty. Her technique is mature and she's set in her ways.'

To be honest, change requires a great deal of courage for a thirty-year-old woman. She might even lose some of her strong points in changing. Not everyone has the capacity to bear what's going to happen and the possible consequences.

When Carlos said I 'could enter the world's top three', he looked so calm and there was such sincerity in his eyes. He portrayed such a wonderful prospect, which inspired longing inside me, a longing to push my limits, and an eagerness to create new miracles, to aim higher and become stronger. I felt possessed and believed those words as strongly as he did.

As time went on, his training proved to be effective. In any partnership, the most basic thing is trust. With trust, change can happen. Carlos said two things that made a real impression on me. The first was in Cincinnati. One morning during the tournament he said, 'In tennis, playing well on the court is not enough to make you a winner, because you never know what state your opponent will be in when she shows up on the court. So you have to know what you need to do for yourself, and take care of your own level of play.'

I'd never heard anyone say something like that, but when I thought about it later, I realised it was true. In the past, what everyone said to me was, 'If you play well, you'll surely win.' So I felt that there was no room for losing, and that I had to always win. But now, my coach was telling me that even if I played well, my opponent might play better and I could still lose. This was completely normal. I was so relieved.

The second thing Carlos said was, 'You're a champion. You must behave like a champion everywhere, not only on the court.' He added, 'No one will make you bear some great social responsibility, but you're a champion, a public figure, and you're obliged to bear it.

At first I didn't really understand. I said, 'I don't have to take it on. I'm just a tennis player.'

He said, 'You're wrong. You're a tennis player, and at the same time you're a public figure, so there are some things you have to bear. It's not just a matter of whether or not you want to take it on.'

On reflection, I found I agreed with him. When I won the French Open, I believed that if I just played well, that was enough. But I needed to act like a champion in everything I did. If I only thought of myself as a tennis player and believed that playing well on the court was sufficient, the implication could be that I would neglect everything else, which might negatively influence children who watched me play. Perhaps I'd only been looking at things from my own perspective. My coach was looking at it from a higher plane.

Before winter, we developed a plan. Carlos said, 'Tactics, nutrition, fitness, attitude. As long as you take care of these four things, the rest will fall into place. But if you're lacking in one of these four areas, you never know where you'll end up.'

Jiang Shan and I spent two weeks in Germany then returned to Wuhan together toward the end of the year to settle some things. After that, I went alone to Beijing to train with Carlos. It was quite intense. The training methods were different from what I was used to, and after two or three days of it, I was completely worn out. When I chatted with Carlos it felt like he was an approachable friend, but as soon as it came to training, there was no letting up.

I called Jiang Shan and told him my training regimen. At first, he didn't believe it. I said, 'I'm serious. Hurry to Beijing, old man. I might die if you don't get here soon.' He immediately bought a plane ticket and flew over to watch me train. When training in winter, you have to warm up thoroughly before you practise, so I usually started with fitness training. When I was halfway through, Jiang Shan said, 'Are you going to play now?'

I said, 'No, we're only halfway through.'

He said, 'Are you kidding?'

I replied, 'I'm serious.'

Jiang Shan is not a guy who's overprotective of his wife, but even he had his doubts, wondering if the training was too intense.

One day Carlos was feeding me the ball, and I ran after it for an hour. Jiang Shan complained, 'I'm tired of picking up balls, and you still haven't finished.'

I said, 'What are you griping about? I'm playing and don't whinge. You just pick up the balls like a good boy.'

Actually, I had faith in Carlos's training, and I called Jiang Shan to Beijing for company and not to check on the training, as some media outlets suggested at the time. I was in Beijing, and Jiang Shan was in Wuhan. I worked all day until I was dead tired and then went back to the hotel room alone every night without anyone to talk to. It was pathetic. With him there, even if he was just playing video games and ignoring me, I still felt more at ease.

A good coach is usually also a good friend, and Carlos helped me not only change my technique, but also adjust my mindset. He helped me be more mature and less impetuous. These changes, even aside from tennis, were very helpful for my future life. When we first started working together, we needed to understand and adapt to one another, so at the time, we signed up for a trial period, taking us through the end of 2012. When the time came we didn't say anything like, 'Our contract is up. Do we want to renew it?' The day after we arrived in Beijing, Carlos said, 'We can talk about our contract in the morning.'

The next day, after we discussed my last match, we naturally went on to consider our plans for competition in 2013. We were on the same wavelength, and since our partnership had been so positive, I found it natural to assume we would continue. Actually, there's an idea I harbour in my own mind. If possible, I hope that Carlos will coach me until my retirement.

Chapter 34

I Like Myself Very Much

Thinking back on 2012, the happiest memory is not the matches I won or the championships I took, but the fact that I finally went on a holiday.

To most people, taking a holiday is nothing special, but to me it was an unimaginable luxury. Since my comeback, my life was like clockwork, every day proceeding in accordance with a precise timetable of training and tournaments. From Monday through Saturday, unless I was too injured to get out of bed, I didn't let up. When Sunday finally arrived, my only day of rest, I was usually so tired that I just wanted to stay home. But finally I was able to plan a holiday, and my expectations were high.

A week before our departure, I was shooting an ad in Beijing for a sponsor. Because of my training and competition schedule, I have to limit the time dedicated to advertisers each year, so shooting an ad for me means working from basically eight in the morning until eight at night, sometimes for a week, to get it done quickly. After the first day of shooting I was especially tired and felt like I was barely surviving. My agent said, 'Never mind. Just think of your holiday in five days.'

Aiyoh. As soon as I heard the word 'holiday' I was immediately revived, full of energy. On the last day of shooting, when we were packing up, despite my weariness, I was so excited. The next day I would be on my holiday.

What really had me excited was the fact that I was travelling with my girlfriends, without Jiang Shan. That's not to say I didn't want to be with him, but I believed that being apart for a short while, doing our own things or hanging out with our own friends, wouldn't hurt our relationship – it would actually make us cherish our time together even more. One of my older female friends said that, besides a life partner, a woman should have a few special lifelong girlfriends who are like sisters, friends who can't be replaced by a husband or children. It's essential for a woman's mental and physical health. I think this is true.

But perhaps not everyone thinks so. My friends and I had planned to go to Korea, but there was a slight problem with my visa. Jiang Shan immediately said, 'What do you want to go to Korea for? It's no fun. Why don't you come to Sanya with me?' His glee at my misfortune was visibly apparent. But in the end, my visa problem was settled. The look of disappointment on a particular person's face made me laugh.

During that week in Korea, I felt more relaxed than I ever had. Each of my travelling companions was someone I'd been close to for a long time; they were all friends I knew well and from whom nothing need be hidden. Every day, I woke without an alarm, then joined my friends for coffee, shopping and chatting. We had nothing planned and just followed our whims. Competitions, training – I put them all out of my head. When I went to bed at night, I didn't need to think about preparing for the next day, and when I woke up in the morning, I didn't need to worry about the time. My only regret was that the week was much too short! Before the holiday, I'd been counting down the days on my fingers, and after I arrived, I thought I had a week of free time to do whatever I wanted. At the end of the holiday, however, time had flown by so quickly. There were still many things that I hadn't had time to do.

After my holiday, I flew to Germany from Korea and continued winter training. The first day, I was too exhausted for words, and I thought, *Why do I want to continue?* When this question appeared in my mind, it startled me. Maybe it was because I'd enjoyed myself too much in Korea. Never mind though. Since I was already here, I would practise.

I knew that the reason I stayed on the court was the same reason I'd practised and competed in tournaments day after day. It was because I liked it. Sometimes, I might tell myself I continued to play simply to safeguard a more comfortable life in the future. But when I thought carefully, I could see that wasn't all there was to it. I'm very satisfied with my own life and the state of my mind now. I'm playing because I enjoy it. And that's good.

At the end of the year, I took part in the WTA Tour Championships in Istanbul, the last tournament of the year, in which only the world's top eight participate. At this time of year, everyone's ranking is basically static, unlike the beginning of the year when everyone is on tenterhooks, so we all enjoy the event and the atmosphere is quite relaxed. Although we still play our hearts out on the court, once the spectacle is over, we often ask, 'Where are you off on holiday? What are you going to do?' At the tournament party, we wear casual clothes, and take photos together and ask each other, 'What are your plans for next year?' When we leave, everyone says things like, 'Enjoy your holiday', or 'Have a good rest', or 'See you next year'.

In the 2012 season, I was victorious in forty-eight matches, lost seventeen, took one championship and was runner-up three times. I didn't shine in the four Opens like I had in 2011, but was more stable in my performance overall, unlike the ups and downs I'd faced the previous year. In fact, I was fairly satisfied with my own performance. More importantly, I felt more in control, keeping myself on course and less prone to being swayed by arbitrary factors.

But I know many people don't feel this way. Seeing my 'satisfaction', they might even accuse me of a lack of motivation. Everyone was much too impressed by my 2011 French Open championship, and they have high hopes for me. Moreover, in China, we're very results oriented. If you get good results, everyone thinks you're good in every way. If your results are average, all your hard work goes unnoticed. For an athlete, this isn't quite fair. There can be only one champion. Everyone else is also working hard, and they may be no less a champion.

In January 2013, I took part in the WTA Shenzhen Open, a new tournament. As professional players, if you get a chance to play on home soil, it's always a happy occasion – it saves on travel time, and spectators will cheer for you in your mother tongue, making you feel more at home. Eventually, I hit my stride and picked up the championship. Even though this wasn't one of the more important tournaments, I was very pleased. It was an affirmation of my offseason training and it boded well for the future. To Chinese people, an auspicious beginning is important.

The Shenzhen Open venue isn't in Shenzhen itself but on the outskirts of town. Even so, there were a lot of people there. This showed the development of tennis in my home country, and that there's a love for the sport now. I was very pleased to see this.

There's an especially funny picture on my phone, taken during the tournament in Shenzhen, of Jiang Shan and Carlos. The match wasn't quite over, but all of the fans thought that I'd already won so they rushed forward, blocking the court entrance. Jiang Shan and Carlos had planned to come onto the court post match, but because of the rush they couldn't get through. Left with no other choice, they jumped from the stands onto the court to meet me, and when they jumped, they both landed in a pretty funny sitting position on the ground.

During the second match, the organisers asked Carlos, 'Do you want the same seat as yesterday?'

He said, 'No, no. Let's change to another. That one scares me.'

When the Shenzhen Open finished, I flew to Sydney for the WTA Sydney International. On Friday, 11 January, I lost to Agnieszka Radwanska in the quarterfinals. It was the ninth match I'd played in ten days, with a flight from China to Australia on one of the days. It was hot in Sydney, and the temperature difference between China and Australia was huge. Coupling this with the time difference, I needed a little time to adjust. After the match, I was as exhausted as I'd ever been.

The following Monday was the beginning of the Australian Open, and I was a little concerned about my physical condition. On Saturday, Carlos gave me the day off and told me to relax and get some rest. After resting, I still felt very tired, but Carlos told me, 'Never mind. When Monday comes, you'll perk up. You need to believe in yourself.'

My physiotherapist Alex gave me a remedial massage, encouraging me to let go, but it really hurt. After two days of massages, I was bruised all over.

On Monday, I was a little tired after the first match. Fortunately, in the opening rounds of the Australian Open, there's an off day between matches. But when I was off, I couldn't relax – I had to train. Carlos said to me on the off day, 'Relax, the match isn't until tomorrow. Today, just warm up a little.'

On the day of the second match, he said, 'Never mind, the match isn't until later. For now, just do some warm-ups.' He kept reminding me, 'You won't lose your tennis skills. Just keep yourself fit and focused, and you won't have any problems.'

Carlos always has a way to unburden me and calm me down. With him helping me focus, Alex helping me relax and Jiang Shan training with me, I couldn't have had it any better. We all work together on the same wavelength.

With my relatively good opening to the year, including playing well in Sydney and the tireless encouragement from my coach and team, my confidence began to gradually build, and my mindset was improving. Maybe this was why I played my way into the semifinals.

My opponent in the semifinals was Maria Sharapova. Years ago, when I'd just started playing in Grand Slams, we'd faced each other in Melbourne Park. From the moment I entered the court I was nervous, and my hands were still trembling when I got back to the locker room after losing the match. In the 2011 French Open I'd had a showdown with her at the Roland Garros Stadium, and I knew well what a daunting opponent she was.

To be honest, I was particularly tense before that 2013 Australian Open match. Even during the warm-up, I couldn't quell my inner turmoil. Carlos noticed how nervous I was and asked, 'How do you feel today?'

I told him honestly, 'I'm very nervous.'

He said, 'Why?'

I kept quiet.

He asked, 'Is it because your former coach is now training her?'

I nodded and said, 'I really, really want to win.'

He said, 'Don't think so much. The match happens on the court, and it's all up to you. There's no point overthinking it right now. Try to relax. Just focus on what you need to do, and don't worry about the result.' Carlos gave me a note with the words 'Believe in yourself' on it. When I got my first match point, he gestured for me to keep cool. When I dropped the match point, he motioned strongly to indicate 'Let's go!' When I finally won the match, I turned to look at him and saw him calmly applauding. I turned to shake hands with Sharapova and the umpire, waved to the fans, then turned and saw that Carlos had picked up his bag and left.

When I finished my shower and did the press conference, nearly two hours had passed. Still caught up in the joy of victory, I rushed to see Carlos. I hadn't imagined that he would just look up and say softly,

'Well done, girl.' I thought he'd say more, but he didn't. It was like any other win, with the two of us simply analysing where my strengths and weaknesses had been.

I felt like a student who'd done well in my exams, rushing excitedly with my report card to my parents, eagerly awaiting their praise and then hearing them say, 'Not bad.' But when I thought about it, I realised this was the right approach. When I was playing, my team was very close and, whether consciously or unconsciously, I would try to read their expressions. If they'd seemed too happy or too depressed, I would certainly have noticed, and it might have affected me. If Carlos kept his face a mask, then no matter what happened I wouldn't know what he was thinking and I wouldn't be affected. By nature, Carlos isn't such a serious guy, and jokes around a bit. But at courtside he is completely even-tempered – because he has to be.

On 26 January at the Rod Laver Arena, I again stood in the finals at the Australian Open. I've been told that eight Chinese television stations broadcasted the match, and many people watched it online. It was also widely reported in the Chinese news, which made me very happy.

My opponent in the finals was the defending champion, Victoria Azarenka, so it was destined to be an uphill battle. As soon as the match started, I held on to my positive state of mind and the positive energy I'd channelled before the match, labouring for forty-five minutes amid Azarenka's high-decibel screams to win the first set 6–4. As we battled through the first five games of the second set, I had a slight advantage. As I was running for a baseline shot, I felt a sharp pain in my left leg, and I couldn't respond quickly enough. I fell heavily to the ground. I'd sprained my ankle.

I gestured for a medical time-out. The tournament doctor immediately came and helped me check my left foot, bandaging it up tight. I went back to the court and the spectators gave me an enthusiastic round of applause. But the balance of fortune no longer seemed to tip in my favour. I lost the second set 4–6. When the third set started, I felt all right, but when I gained a small advantage of 2–1, there was another delay in the proceedings. This time it was due to the Australia Day ceremony.

Practically every year, Australia's national day coincides with the Australian Open. I remember once the men's semifinals were on Australia Day, and this year it was the women's final. This is considered one of the special features of the Australian Open, a sort of tradition. If you happen to be playing when it's time for the ceremony, play is halted and you wait for the fireworks to finish before resuming. I guess the site where the fireworks are set off is near the stadium because I could hear the noise, although I couldn't see them because the stadium's centre court is partially covered, with only a small patch of sky visible.

This interruption lasted about ten or fifteen minutes, then play was resumed. We went right back into the heat of battle. Suddenly, I felt myself losing balance, and before I had time to figure out what was happening, I came crashing down. I heard a *boom*, which must have been my head hitting the ground. I think my hat flew off, and for a couple of seconds, my mind was a blank, and everything before my eyes was dark. I couldn't see anything, nor could I remember anything. Afterward, I saw that the tournament doctor had rushed to the court to help me.

Oh, I fell, and my head hit the ground. I felt the back of my head anxiously to see if it was bleeding. Good, no blood. The doctor asked me several questions, like, 'Do you know where you are?' and 'Do you know what happened?' She also held up a finger in front of me and moved it here and there. She was afraid I had a concussion or had lost consciousness. But how could it be that serious? I felt a little odd, like I was a child again, at the children's hospital answering the doctor's questions. I don't know if I was more amused by the doctor or by my current circumstances. I didn't look at her fingers, but looked into her eyes and laughed. She immediately knew my brain hadn't suffered too serious an injury.

Later, reporters asked me, 'Did you think of withdrawing from the match?'

Withdrawing? No, not at all. It wasn't a light fall, and I'd bumped my head, but I didn't for one moment consider withdrawing. This was my battlefield, and as long as I could get up, I would keep playing.

I returned to the court once again. The audience responded with even more enthusiastic and enduring applause, cheering me on. The umpire had to remind the spectators to restrain their cheers so as not to affect the flow of the game. Thank you, everyone. I really appreciated your support. The fans on the scene that day, including not only my own compatriots but also Australian spectators and people from all over the world, showed me real love and support. That carried me a long way.

I ultimately lost the third set. Once again, I had to settle for runner-up at the Australian Open.

In three days, it would be my seventh anniversary with Jiang Shan. My secret plan had been that if I won the trophy, I'd give it to Jiang Shan as an anniversary gift. Everyone talks about the 'seven-year itch' so I thought that if I could give him the big prize, I'd head any 'itchiness' off early. But now, that wasn't possible.

Next to me, Azarenka was covering her face with her towel as she sobbed. The battlefield is cruel, and no matter who you are, it's hard to get to that highest spot. Tonight, it was her. I sincerely wished her all the best.

When all the lights on the court were off, I pulled my cap down over my face so no one could see my tears. Darkness was my best cover.

I said to myself, *I know you wanted to win. I know you feel bad about this. But how many people advance to the finals? Runner-up is also a result of your own hard work. This past year and a half, you've been through so much, you've achieved this sort of result, and it's not too bad. You're heading in a good direction. There's no need to feel distressed.*

You should be happy that you've come out of the woods, and you should be proud of yourself.

This sort of self-comfort was effective. When the awards ceremony began, I felt much calmer and was able to control my tears and emotions. I congratulated Azarenka, thanked my sponsors and team, and also thanked the audience for all of their support. I said, 'I know I'm not young, but I'm really looking forward to next year.'

This was what I really felt. If my physical condition allows me to continue to play, then the Australian Open is the event I most want to take part in. It's always been my favourite of the four Grand Slams. The staff at the Australian Open don't change, with the same people in charge of the same tasks every year. For example, the guy who books cars has been there every year, like my friend Linda in the locker room. Moreover, the staff all seem to be aware of your preferences, and they know how your past year has been. You can chat with them about mundane things, which makes you feel like you're not so much at a tournament, but coming home, meeting old friends. It's a lovely feeling. And the fans here like me, too. If there are no locals playing, they take me as one of their own. They hold Chinese flags and have learned a few phrases in Mandarin to cheer me on. This feels great. I love the Australian Open. If I can, I'll be back.

In the locker room after the award ceremony, Jiang Shan, my team and a few other people were waiting for me. They all said encouraging words, and hoped I would be proud of myself. I knew what they were thinking, and I knew why, but when the hustle and bustle let up and I had a moment in solitude, that deep pain of regret once more crept into my bones and got hold of me all over again. I was so sad I was moved to tears. I often say there are many possibilities in the world, but there's no such thing as 'what if'.

In the blink of an eye, it was February and the Chinese New Year was approaching. In 2013, Chinese New Year, Valentine's Day and my birthday all fell in the same month. One day I said to Jiang Shan on a whim, 'Chinese New Year gift, please.'

He looked at me and said, 'You're not a child. What kind of New Year's gift do you expect?'

When Valentine's Day was drawing near, I said, 'Valentine's Day gift, please.'

He didn't even look at me as he said, 'We aren't young lovers. What sort of Valentine's Day gift do you expect?'

When my birthday was just around the corner, I said the same thing. I thought to myself, *Let's see what smart answer he can come up with this time.*

Without looking up from his video game, the old man said, 'You have a birthday every year. What's special about this one?'

Ah . . . ! Is there no justice?

When my hints for a present had fallen on deaf ears, I decided to find out how solid Jiang Shan's resolve was in refusing me. I'd decided not to give up, but after he said, 'you have a birthday every year', I was speechless. I couldn't win. I thought, *You might be vicious, but I'll wait.*

Sure enough, I got my revenge. After two weeks in Germany, we flew to Beijing on 23 February. On the plane, there was lots of duty-free stuff for sale. Bored, Jiang Shan was flipping through the shopping guide. He said, 'My birthday's coming up. You should buy me a few presents.'

I thought, *My birthday's on the twenty-sixth and you appear to have not bought me anything, and now you're saying it's almost time for your birthday and you want a gift?* I used my briskest tone and said, 'I'm not buying anything. Your birthday comes every year. Why bother with this one?'

The tables were turned. As soon as I said this, a stunned expression crossed his face. I was so pleased that I had to restrain myself from shaking the whole plane with my laughter.

Once when I was chatting with a friend about Jiang Shan's refusal to give presents, she said, 'Have you thought of another possibility? Maybe you should give him a present first, then he'll be so embarrassed that he'll remember to get you a gift the next time.'

This definitely wouldn't work. Jiang Shan would never feel embarrassed. I know him too well. He's just not someone who gives gifts. He's always been a very down-to-earth person, not the romantic type. He doesn't surprise me on my birthday, but will give up his own career to help me pursue my dream. He doesn't give me gifts on Valentine's Day, but will silently cook nourishing tonics for me during my long periods of rehab. He doesn't whisper sweet nothings in my ear, but will tear up if I fall during my matches. What I'm saying is that no matter what, I'll follow him for life. As long as he doesn't leave me, I'll be with him until the day I die.

Although I didn't get a gift from Jiang Shan on my birthday, I got many small presents from other friends. One gave me an English version of the picture book, *I Like Me!* There's a cute pig in a dress on the cover. Knowing what she meant by it, I smiled and said, 'Don't worry, I like myself very much now.'

It's true. I'm now thirty-one years old and my life is no longer aimless, my dreams no longer out of reach. I'm satisfied with myself and my life. If you ask me my birthday wish, it's this: I wish I could get into the world's top three, or take another Grand Slam; I wish for good health for my mother and all of my family, which is the most anyone can ask for; and as for my own life, there's nothing else I particularly want to achieve. I just want to earnestly live for each moment, and enjoy every day.

Chapter 35

Next Stop, Life!

I've been asked, 'Do you think you are a lucky person?' I have my health and can pursue my dreams. I have a happy family who has supported me. I have many fans who love and support me. And I have the most sincere friends beside me. I must say, yes, I'm indeed lucky.

I used to live in fear, day and night. I feared opponents, tournaments, the thick black lines of newspaper sports headlines and many other things. Sometimes before walking onto the court, I would head out of the locker room and down the corridor, in fear the whole time, until the match was over. You can't let your opponent see your anxiety. The real strength of your opponent comes when she exposes that anxiety and goes in for the kill. You have to pretend to be calm. The best thing to do is to keep a poker face, as if you are completely indifferent. Even when you're so nervous you can hardly bear it, you can't let your opponent see this.

Unquestionably, 2011 was a very special year, during which I enjoyed a brilliant accomplishment. But I also fell very low. At the very instant I realised my dream, I also lost my ambition. In life, it was a terrible year. My career soared when I wasn't yet ready to face the battle and when my mindset wasn't mature enough to bear it, bringing tremendous change. Going from being a virtual unknown to being a hot topic, from being showered in fame to approaching the brink of collapse, was very tough. The celebrity tennis brought led me to deviate from the path I wanted to take. I had to face many things I'd never faced before – endless interviews, meeting swarms of VIPs and being forced to put on hypocritical smiles – some of which was beyond the scope of my imagination.

The last half of 2011 was the most difficult six months of my life. Yes, difficult. Because those days couldn't be described as 'living'. I think I was depressed. I feared going to crowded places and was also unwilling to face myself. When I walked into the stadium, there was no fight, no desire to win. My only thought was to lose quickly, leave the court and find someplace where I could hide. Every morning when I opened my eyes, I didn't know how to carry on that day, how to face everything. I even asked myself why I'd wanted to win the French Open. If I hadn't taken the title, maybe my life would have been better.

Fortunately, I came out stronger. Time is magical and wonderful. It can change so many things. No matter what, in years to come, when I think back on 2011, it will be as a year worth feeling proud of.

The feelings I have toward tennis are very contradictory. It took fifteen years for me to learn to love the sport. But life is full of contradictions: I don't like flowers because their life is too short, but I really admire the beauty of plum blossoms in winter. Obviously, I know that some people say things just to flatter you, but I still take them at face value. When I know I've made a mistake, I like to blame others or find an excuse. I clearly know it was my own fault, but I also look for a reason to stall. I'm so miserable I want to die, but I pretend to be strong and bear up under it. When I lose a match the thing I hear and read most are things like 'Li Na lost because she lost her cool'. These reports used to make me angry – how could those who hadn't been through it dare to say such things?

Is it wrong to fight on the court I love? Is it wrong to lose? But now I look at these reports and I realise that this isn't what I learned at university. When I studied sports journalism, we learned that the news must be true. How many journalists adhere to that? What I read now is often just reporters expressing their opinions. Sometimes a word of encouragement might make a person change, but a hurtful word can have equally strong consequences. Being exposed to criticism made me strong, and my capacity for holding up is much greater than I ever imagined.

It seems like there are two Li Nas inside me. The powerful Li Na will always suppress the weak one. Whenever the weak Li Na thinks of something beyond the match, the powerful one tells her to stop thinking so much and concentrate on swinging her racket. Restraining yourself, putting yourself in a straitjacket – that's not something others can do for me. It's all up to me.

The me that everyone sees on the court appears straightforward and confident, energetic, careless, reckless, individualistic, and brave enough to say whatever I feel. But that's on the tennis court. Off the court, when only Jiang Shan is with me, I'm able to reveal the happy, simple, real me.

One of my best friends says that I'm too strong, putting things on my shoulders that aren't my responsibility and allowing myself to feel the pressure. If I don't find a way to vent, I doubt myself and become very unhappy. I think what she says makes a lot of sense.

But I'm over thirty years old now. I no longer need to use camouflage to make myself look strong. I've gradually come to terms with the world, and I have reached an agreement with it. I've come to see those things and people I used to dislike from a different perspective. It's not hypocrisy, but simply because I've finally became mature enough to accommodate what I don't like.

I can articulate what's on my mind and look for answers. I no longer need be afraid that overthinking things will interfere with my game. I don't need to suppress my feelings. In one match after another, I've become gradually happier, more confident and more daring as I fight right up to the last second – and then I'm free to go sing happily at a karaoke session with my friends. I know who I am, and I know what I want. Every day, I grow a little more mature.

I want to thank those in the media who have spurred me to grow. Now their attitude toward me has eased up a lot, and they no longer take my words out of context but listen carefully to what I say. After so many years, we've finally started to reach an understanding, and more Chinese reporters are focusing solely on tennis. This is a change that makes me proud. Some reporters asked if they could visit Jiang Shan's and my house in Munich to film a program, but we refused politely. I wanted to keep our small refuge in Munich simple and pure. In Germany, I'm just an athlete who is constantly trying to attain the highest honours. I'm not a champion, nor am I an idol. I can put aside my burdens and move forward freely.

Tennis has made progress by leaps and bounds in China in the recent past. I remember the 2008 World Extras Tournament when I was part of the national team, playing against the French team in Beijing. When I first entered the court, I couldn't help but say, 'Oh! There are so many fans here today!' The spectators courtside were clapping in a very orderly way, though, which made me a little suspicious, so I took a closer look. Nearly all of the audience was French. It wasn't even like we were playing on our own home court.

Fast-forward to February 2012 when I played in a three-day tournament in Shenzhen. The sidelines were filled with Chinese tennis fans, and the tournament was almost sold out. The spectators were friendly and disciplined, not making unprovoked rude noises at the foreign players. Everybody seemed to be beginning to learn how to behave decently during international competitions. I felt this was a huge improvement and showed that tennis was becoming a part of people's lives. This is even more rewarding than producing a world or Grand Slam champion. If I wish for anything, it's that tennis will flourish in China. I'm eager to see more young Chinese people stand out and step onto the world arena.

When I tour overseas, many tennis fans support me and encourage me online. Even though I can't reply to everyone, I hope you all know how much I appreciate your understanding and support. Thank you for your tolerance and love. I haven't studied much, so I can't use flowery words to express the friendship I feel for you. But thank you for all you've done for me, and for your support and companionship.

Finally, I want to thank my husband, Jiang Shan. I've expressed my gratitude to him throughout this book, but the respect and attachment I feel toward him continue to grow. He's the best thing God has given me, and it's thanks to him that I've learned that love is a kind of perseverance, a kind of faith that won't change with time.

I met Jiang Shan when I was twelve, and I fell in love with him when I was sixteen. We've been together for fifteen years now, during which we've had glorious times together, retired together, studied together, come out of retirement together, worked together and lived together. He was by my side the first time I underwent surgery in Germany, the two of us alone, fending for ourselves in a foreign country. At that point we didn't know what kind of rehab I would go through or if I could return to a competitive state, but he was there to encourage me all the way, to accompany and support me. We grew up together, and there are no secrets between us. Sometimes it's like we've already grown old together, and we're still together. I know he is the love of my life. Thank you, my love. And thank God I met you.

I still have a long way to go. I don't know where I want to go, or how far I can go, but I say to myself, *However far the mind wants to journey, that's how long the road will be. Regardless of the next stop – whether it's Paris, Melbourne, Madrid or somewhere else – my destination has a name that will not change. It's called 'Life'.*

Credits